# Family Treasures VOL II Cookbook

## More Recipes from the Heart

COOKBOOKS AVAILABLE FROM:

Freeman & Mabel Yoder

Rt #1 Box 472 CR 800

Freedom, IN 47431

phone # 1-812-828-9660

Carlisle Printing
WALNUT CREEK

2673 TR 421
Sugarcreek, OH 44681

# Contents

*Please Note: Perma-Flo and clear jel are thickeners similar to cornstarch and can be bought at Amish bulk food stores.*

---

**ABBREVIATIONS**

| | |
|---|---|
| cup = c. | teaspoon = tsp. |
| pint = pt. | tablespoon = Tbsp. |
| quart = qt. | envelope = env. |
| gallon = gal. | dozen = doz. |
| ounce = oz. | package = pkg. |
| pound = lb. | |

*O Lord, through this food grant unto us bodily health and spiritual power. Bless these hearts united in Thy praise, and may we eventually sit together at the marriage supper of Thy dear Son, in whose Name we ask it. Amen.*

The Lord is my Light and my Salvation; whom shall I fear? The Lord is the strength of my life; of whom shall I be afraid? Ps. 27:1

AMY Y.

# *Introduction*

Our family wishes to extend a welcome once more to a second helping of Family Treasures Cookbook Vol. II . . . More Recipes from the Heart (over 550 homestyle recipes).

Our lives often center around our kitchens, so with this thought in mind we once more opened our treasure chests of recipes to bring you joy as you cook. Many of these recipes are special and have been handed down through the generations. There are new and unusual ones too; also tried and true favorites that take only minutes to prepare.

We want to thank all of our extended families for sharing your recipes, thoughts and inspirations. Thank you also to each one who contributed to the publication of this cookbook in any way.

A special thank you to Mrs. Lester (Verna) Bontrager for painting the roses on the cover.

Last but not least, a special thank you to our daughters, Charlene and Amy, for the special artwork found on the dividers.

I hope you will enjoy using this cookbook. May your hearts be drawn closer to God as you read the many inspirational notes, sayings, scriptures, poems and songs found throughout this book. May God richly bless you all.

> *Happy Cooking!*
> Sincerely,
> Freeman & Mabel Yoder & family,
>     Charlene, Amy, Lonnie, LuAnn, Jason,
>     Mervin & JayLee

# Appetizers, Beverages & Dips

Lord, hold my hand,
Guide my feet,
Bridle my tongue,
And keep me sweet.

Words
Actions
Temper
Companions
Heart

I AM THE WAY, THE TRUTH AND THE LIFE: NO MAN
COMETH UNTO THE FATHER BUT BY ME.
JOHN 14:6

# Recipe Book

Take some friendliness and mix it
With a little bit of cheer;
Blend a touch of morning sunshine
With a pleasant atmosphere.

Sprinkle just a pinch of kindness
In amongst the deeds to do;
Mellow freely with compassion
And with tenderness endue.

With some sympathy be generous,
Spare its candor not a mite,
Season well with such expression
As befits a dawning bright.

Garnish freely with the beauty
That is deep within the heart,
Spread around and up and over
For the purpose 'twould impart.

It's the recipe for friendship . . .
Use it often, use it long,
Careful in its preparation
That results be never wrong.

# Cheese Ball

2 - 8 oz. pkg. cream cheese
(softened)
2 tsp. Worcestershire sauce
4 oz. shredded cheddar cheese

1 tsp. lemon juice
1 Tbsp. chopped onion
1 Tbsp. parsley flakes
1 c. chopped nuts

Mix first 6 ingredients together when at room temperature. Chill, then roll in nuts.

*Mrs. Wilmer (Marilyn) Schmucker*

# Christmas Cheese Ball

8 oz. cream cheese (softened)
8 oz. shredded cheddar cheese
2 green onions (chopped)
1 jar (2 oz.) diced pimentos
(drained)

$^1/_4$ tsp. salt
$^1/_2$ c. real shaved bacon
$^1/_4$ tsp. hickory smoke
2 tsp. Worcestershire sauce

In a mixing bowl, beat cream cheese until fluffy. Beat in the rest of the ingredients. Press into a small bowl; smooth top. Cover and refrigerate. Remove from refrigerator 15 minutes before unmolding. Serve with crackers.

*Mrs. Freeman (Mabel) Yoder*

# Pepper Poppers

8 oz. cream cheese
1 c. shredded cheddar
cheese
1 c. mozzarella cheese
6 bacon strips (cooked &
crumbled)

$^1/_4$ tsp. salt
$^1/_4$ tsp. chili powder
$^1/_4$ tsp. garlic powder
1 lb. fresh jalapeños (halved
lengthwise & seeded)
$^1/_2$ c. dry bread crumbs

In mixing bowl combine cheeses, bacon and seasoning; mix well. Spoon about 2 Tbsp. into each pepper half. Roll in bread crumbs. Place in a greased 15" x 10" pan. Bake uncovered at 300° for 20 minutes for spicy flavor, 30 minutes for medium flavor, 40 minutes for mild flavor. Serve with sour cream, onion dip or Ranch salad dressing.

*Mrs. Dan (Esther) Miller*

# Monster Cheese

2¹/₂ gal. sour milk
2 heaping tsp. soda
¹/₂ c. butter

2 c. sweet cream
1¹/₂ Tbsp. salt

Let sour milk set until thick like junket (very sour). Then put into a large kettle and scald until it is too hot to hold your hand in (approx. 150°). Then pour the curds into cheesecloth. Let hang until curds are dry (overnight or about 12 hours). Crumble curds and mix soda and butter into them. Let set for 2 hours, then put in a double boiler. Add 1 cup sweet cream and melt. When melted, add other cup of cream and salt. Mix well and pour into buttered mold or Tupperware container. Let set until completely cold and slice. You may add some cheese powder when adding cream the last time or just leave it white. The amount of cream will vary, according to how dry the curds are. Sometimes you may not need the full 2 cups cream.

*Mrs. Leland (Orpha) Yoder*

# Pineapple Pecan Cheese Ball

2 - 8 oz. pkg. cream cheese
(softened to room temp.)
8 oz. can crushed pineapple
(well drained)
¹/₂ c. chopped green pepper

¹/₂ c. chopped green onion
1 tsp. lemon pepper
1 tsp. seasoned salt
2 c. chopped pecans (divided)

In a mixing bowl, whip cream cheese until smooth. Gently stir in pineapple, green pepper, onion, seasonings and ¹/₂ c. chopped pecans. Turn out onto a sheet of plastic wrap and shape into a ball. Refrigerate several hours or overnight. Before serving, roll cheese ball into remaining nuts. Serve with crackers. Yield: 12–14 servings. *Delicious!*

*Mrs. David (JoAnn) Mast*

---

*One of the greatest faults is to be unaware of our own.*

# Tortilla Pinwheels

1 1/2 c. sour cream
1 can refried beans
1 pkg. taco seasoning

1 pt. salsa
tortillas

Mix ingredients together. Divide evenly over tortillas. Roll up tortillas. Slice 3/4" thick. Lay pinwheels flat on serving plate. Garnish with parsley.

*Mrs. Wayne (Marilyn) Yoder*

# Velveeta Cheese

2 1/2 gal. milk
2 tsp. soda
1/2 c. butter

3 Tbsp. cheddar cheese powder
1/2 c. cream
1 Tbsp. salt

Let milk sour until thick. When thickened, scald until too hot to touch. Let set several hours, then drain through a cheesecloth or strainer. Crumble curds to make fine crumbs; add soda and mix well. Let set for 2 hours. Place in a double boiler and add butter. Melt butter with curds then add cream and salt. Cook and stir until smooth, then add cheese powder. Pour into buttered container and let set until completely cooled. Slice.

*Mrs. Samuel (Wilma) Miller*

# Creamy Orange Drink

12 oz. frozen orange juice
2 c. water
2 c. milk

1/2 c. sugar
1 Tbsp. vanilla
24 ice cubes (crushed)

Mix together and serve.

*Mrs. Harley (Martha) Raber*

# Cranberry Tea

1 - 64 oz. bottle cranberry juice
1 - 6 oz. container frozen
    orange juice concentrate
1 - 6 oz. container frozen
    lemonade concentrate
3 c. sugar
6 whole cloves
6 whole allspice
1 cinnamon stick

Mix all ingredients together and heat. To serve, mix one part cranberry tea to 2 parts hot water. Measure, then add twice as much water. May be served hot or cold.

*Mrs. Freeman (Mabel) Yoder*

# Friendship Tea Mix

1 c. instant tea (peppermint
    or spearmint)
2 c. Tang or orange flavored
    drink mix
3 c. sugar
$^1/_2$ c. red hots
1 tsp. cloves, *optional*
1 tsp. cinnamon

Mix all together. Store in airtight container. To serve: Mix 2–3 tsp. with 1 c. hot water. Stir till red hots dissolve and strain.

*Mrs. Noah (Verena) Schwartz*

# Mr. Misty

6 oz. strawberry Jell-O
    (or other flavor)
$1^1/_2$ c. sugar
1 qt. boiling water
46 oz. pineapple juice
1 qt. cold water
1 - 2-liter 7-Up or Sprite

Dissolve Jell-O and sugar in 1 qt. boiling water. Add pineapple juice and 1 qt. cold water. Freeze mixture. Add 7-Up or Sprite. Serve slushy. *A refreshing drink.*

*Mrs. Ray (Irene) Mullett*

# Picnic Fruit Punch

2 qt. cranberry juice
3 c. pineapple juice
3 c. orange juice

$^1/_4$ c. lemon juice
1 liter ginger ale (chilled)
1 med. navel orange (sliced)

Combine juices in large container. Refrigerate. Just before serving, stir in ginger ale and orange slices. *A tangy, not so sweet, refreshing drink!*

Mrs. Floyd (Darlene) Yoder

# Punch

3 qt. pineapple juice
12 oz. frozen lemonade
   concentrate
2 - 12 oz. cans frozen orange
   juice concentrate

2 c. sugar
4 qt. ginger ale
2 qt. water
3 limes
1 orange

Mix all together and chill. Serve in a large glass bowl. Float lime and orange slices on top. *Cool and refreshing!*

Charlene Yoder (Daughter)

# Ruby Red Punch

5 pkg. cherry Kool-Aid
5 pkg. strawberry Kool-Aid
5 - 12 oz. cans frozen orange
   juice concentrate
4 - 12 oz. cans frozen
   lemonade concentrate

10 cups sugar
4 gal. water
1 - 2-liter 7-Up
several drops red food coloring

Mix all together and stir well. Serve over ice.

Mom (Rosa) Bontrager

---

*Failure is not defeat unless you stop trying.*

# Coffee Punch

1 c. water
3 c. sugar
$1/4$ c. instant coffee
1 gal. milk

$1/2$ gal. vanilla ice cream (softened)
$1/2$ gal. chocolate ice cream
 (softened)

Bring water to a boil; add sugar and coffee; simmer until dissolved. Cool. Combine coffee mixture and milk. Just before serving, gently stir in softened ice cream. Serve immediately. Yield: 7 quarts.

*Mrs. Daniel (LeAnn) Yoder*

# Hot Chocolate Drink Mix

1 box (8 qt.) dry milk
8 oz. coffee creamer
1 tsp. salt
1 c. instant vanilla pudding

$1/2$ c. cocoa
1 lb. instant chocolate mix
 (Nestlé Quik)
2 c. powdered sugar

Mix thoroughly in a large bowl. Store in an airtight container. To serve: Mix 4 rounded tsp. to 1 c. boiling water.

*Amy Yoder (Daughter)*

# Minty Chocolate Mix

2 c. chocolate malted
 milk powder (divided)
$1^1/2$ c. dinner mints

$3^1/2$ c. nonfat dry milk powder
$1^1/2$ c. instant hot cocoa mix

In a blender or food processor, combine 1 c. malted milk and mints; process until smooth. Pour into a large bowl and add remaining ingredients; mix well. Store in an airtight container. To serve: Mix $1/4$ c. mix to 1 c. boiling water. Stir well. This drink combines 2 great flavors—chocolate and mint.

*Mrs. Freeman (Mabel) Yoder*

# White Mocha Chocolate Mix

10 oz. box Swiss white mocha
   chocolate drink mix
2 c. dry milk
1$^1/_2$ c. nondairy creamer
1 c. sugar
3 Tbsp. instant coffee

1 c. malted chocolate milk
$^3/_4$ c. Nestlé Quik
$^1/_2$ tsp. salt
1 c. instant vanilla pudding
$^1/_2$ c. powdered sugar

Mix all together in a large bowl. Store in an airtight container. To serve mix 4 rounded teaspoonfuls to 1 cup boiling water.

*Mrs. Freeman (Mabel) Yoder*

## Root Beer

2 c. sugar
2 Tbsp. root beer extract

$^1/_2$ tsp. dry yeast

Mix together and add enough water to make 1 gal. Put in gal. glass jar. Set in sun 1 day. Cool and serve.

*Mrs. Marvin (Katie) Miller*

## Fruit Slush

12 oz. frozen orange juice
20 oz. crushed pineapple
1 qt. canned peaches

6 bananas (sliced)
1 c. sugar (more or less to taste)

Mix orange juice with 1 can water. Take juice from peaches and pine-apple and add enough water to make 3 cups. Mix all ingredients together and freeze.

*Mrs. John (Susie) Kuhns*

---

*A lie can travel across the country and back again
while the truth is lacing up its boots.*

---

# Slush

| | |
|---|---|
| 1 c. sugar | 1 - 48 oz. can pineapple juice |
| 1 large box Jell-O (any flavor) | 1 qt. cold water |
| 2 qt. boiling water | Sprite |

Freeze, but stir often so it remains slushy. Put in glasses (about 3/4 full) then add Sprite until they are filled.

*Mrs. Darrell (Erma) Yoder*

# Apple Dip

| | |
|---|---|
| 8 oz. cream cheese | 1/4 c. brown sugar |
| 1/2 c. sour cream | 1 1/2 Tbsp. maple syrup |
| 1/4 c. white sugar | |

Cream first 4 ingredients together. Add maple syrup and stir or whip until nice and smooth. Chill and serve with apples or any other fresh fruit. *Very good!*

*Mrs. Daniel (Arlene) Beechy*

# Fruit Dip

| | |
|---|---|
| 8 oz. cream cheese | 1 c. brown sugar |

Mix together. Serve with your favorite fresh fruit. *Especially good with apples.*

*Mrs. Levi (Carolyn) Schrock, Mrs. John (Lora) Bontrager*

---

*Happiness is as a butterfly, which when pursued, is always beyond our grasp, but which, if you will sit down quietly, may light upon you.*

# Hamburger Dip

1 lb. hamburger
1 onion
garlic powder
salt & pepper

1 can refried beans
1 can nacho cheese soup
1 lb. Velveeta cheese

Brown hamburger with chopped onion. Add garlic powder, salt and pepper. Mix in refried beans and cheese soup. Add Velveeta cheese and cook on low heat until melted. Serve with tortilla or Doritos chips.

*Mrs. James (Sara Marie) Yoder*

# Pizza Dip

2 - 8 oz. pkg. cream cheese
  (softened)
12 oz. bottle chili sauce
1 - 6 oz. pkg. Canadian bacon
  (chopped)
1 small onion (chopped)

$1/2$ c. finely chopped green pepper
1 c. finely shredded mozzarella
  cheese
1 c. finely shredded cheddar cheese
10 strips bacon (cooked &
  crumbled fine), *optional*

Spread cream cheese on a 12" pizza pan. Spread with chili sauce. Sprinkle with Canadian bacon, onions, green peppers, cheeses and crumbled bacon. Serve with corn chips, Doritos and tortilla chips.

*LuAnn Yoder (Daughter)*

# Salsa Dip

1 lb. Velveeta cheese

1 cup chunky salsa

Heat salsa, then cut up cheese and stir in salsa until melted. Serve hot with tortilla chips or assorted vegetables (cut up). Yield: 3 cups.

*Mrs. Toby (Vera) Yoder*

---

*God often digs wells of joy with spades of sorrow.*

# Taco Pizza Dip

2 - 8 oz. cream cheese
  (softened)
1 small container onion
  chip dip
1 lb. hamburger
$^1/_2$ pkg. taco seasoning

chopped green peppers
mushrooms
black olives
plain or taco-flavored shredded
  cheese

Mix cream cheese and onion dip. Spread into a 9" x 13" pan. Brown hamburger and drain; add taco seasoning. Spread over cream cheese layer. Top with chopped green peppers, mushrooms, black olives, plain or taco-flavored shredded cheese. Bake at 350° until cheese is melted. Serve with any snacks—pretzels, chips, Doritos, etc.

*Mrs. Daryl (Marsha) Miller*

## Easter Jelly Beans

RED is for the blood He gave,
GREEN is for the grass He made.
YELLOW for His sun so bright.
ORANGE is for the edge of night.
BLACK is for the sins we made,
WHITE is for the grace He gave;
PURPLE for His hours of sorrow,
PINK is for our new tomorrow.

*A bag of jelly beans,*
*Colorful and sweet;*
*Is a prayer! Is a promise!*
*Is a special treat!*

# Breads & Rolls

*Seven days without prayer*
*makes one weak.*

*In the tears of His saints*
*God sees a rainbow.*

GOD IS GONE UP WITH A SHOUT, THE LORD WITH THE
SOUND OF A TRUMPET. SING PRAISES TO GOD, SING PRAISES:
SING PRAISES UNTO OUR KING, SING PRAISES.
PSALM 47:5–6

IN EVERYTHING GIVE THANKS: FOR THIS IS THE WILL
OF GOD IN CHRIST JESUS CONCERNING YOU.
I THESSALONIANS 5:18

# Teach Me, Lord

Teach me, Lord, to wait down on my knees
Till in your own good time you will answer my pleas,
Teach me not to rely on what others do
But to wait in prayer for an answer from you.

They that wait upon the Lord shall renew their strength,
They shall mount up with wings as eagles,
They shall run and not be weary,
They shall walk and not faint.
Teach me, Lord, teach me, Lord, to wait. Isaiah 40:31.

Teach me, Lord, to wait while hearts are aflame,
Let me humble my pride and call on your name;
Keep my faith renewed, my eyes on Thee,
Let me be on this earth what you want me to be.

# Apple Bread

| | |
|---|---|
| ¹/₂ c. shortening | 1 tsp. baking powder |
| ²/₃ c. sugar | 1 tsp. salt |
| 2 eggs | 1 c. finely chopped nuts |
| 2 c. sifted flour | 1 c. finely chopped apples |
| 1 tsp. baking soda | |

Cream shortening and sugar. Beat in eggs, one at a time. Add sifted dry ingredients to creamed mixture, with apples and nuts. Do not beat. Pour into greased 8" x 4" x 3" loaf pan. Bake at 350° for 1 hour.

*Mrs. Lonnie (Norma) Bontrager*

# Batter Bread

| | |
|---|---|
| 1 Tbsp. yeast | ¹/₄ c. sugar |
| ¹/₂ c. warm water | 2 tsp. salt |
| 1 c. warm milk (110°–115°) | 3 eggs |
| ¹/₂ c. butter or margarine (softened) | 5¹/₂–6 c. flour |

In a large bowl combine yeast and warm water. Add milk, butter or margarine (softened), sugar and salt; stir well. Then add eggs and 3 c. flour; beat until smooth. Stir in enough remaining flour to form a soft dough (do not knead). Cover and let rise until double. Stir the dough down. Spoon into a greased and floured 10" tube pan or divide into 2 bread pans. Cover and let rise until doubled (about 1 hour). Bake at 375°–400° for 25–30 minutes until golden brown. *This bread is good to start in the afternoon and have fresh warm bread for supper. Delicious!*

*Mrs. Freeman (Mabel) Yoder*

---

*A woman's character can be judged by her faithfulness in little things.*

# Bread

| | |
|---|---|
| 4 c. warm water | 4 tsp. salt |
| 2 Tbsp. yeast (level) | 1 egg (beaten) |
| $1/3$ c. vegetable oil | 4 c. whole wheat flour |
| $1/2$ c. sugar | 8–10 c. white flour (approx.) |

Put water and yeast in a large bowl. Let set for 5 minutes. Then add oil, sugar, salt, egg, 2 c. whole wheat flour and 4 c. white flour. Stir well with a big spoon. Add remaining whole wheat flour and knead with hands. Gradually add more white flour to form a soft dough. Knead about 20 minutes. Cover and let rise until double; punch down. Let rise again, then divide into 4 loaves. Let rise until double. Bake at 325° for 10 minutes. Increase to 350° and bake for 20–25 minutes longer or until golden brown. This bread keeps a long time without getting rancid or moldy. *This is our favorite!*

*Charlene Yoder (Daughter)*

# Buttermilk Chocolate Bread

| | |
|---|---|
| $1/2$ c. butter (softened) | 1 tsp. salt |
| 1 c. sugar | $1/2$ tsp. baking powder |
| 2 eggs | $1/2$ tsp. soda |
| $1^1/2$ c. flour | 1 c. buttermilk |
| $1/2$ c. cocoa | $1/3$ c. chopped pecans |

**CHOCOLATE SPREAD:**

| | |
|---|---|
| $1/2$ c. butter (no substitute) | 3 Tbsp. chocolate syrup |
| 2 Tbsp. honey | |

Cream butter and sugar. Add eggs and beat well. Combine the flour, cocoa, salt, soda and baking powder. Add to creamed mixture alternately with buttermilk. Fold in pecans. Pour into a greased 9" x 5" x 3" loaf pan. Bake at 350° for 55–60 minutes or until toothpick comes out clean. Cool for 10 minutes in pan. Remove to wire rack. Serve with chocolate spread.

*Mrs. Freeman (Mabel) Yoder*

# Cheddar Cheese Bread

2 c. warm water (120°–130°)
2 Tbsp. yeast
5¹/₂ c. flour (divided)
2 Tbsp. sugar
1³/₄ tsp. salt

¹/₄ tsp. pepper
2 Tbsp. butter or margarine (melted)
1 c. shredded cheddar cheese
¹/₂ c. onions (chopped fine)

In a large bowl, combine water and yeast. Let set 5 minutes. Then add 2¹/₂ c. flour, sugar, salt and pepper. Beat until moistened. Add butter, remaining flour, cheese and onions. Beat until smooth. May need to knead several minutes. Shape into a ball. Place in a greased 2-qt. casserole (round) baking dish. Let rise until double. Bake at 350° for 40–45 minutes or until golden brown. Sprinkle with additional cheddar cheese. Bake until cheese is melted. Remove from pan to cool. This is good with any pasta or pizza dishes.

*Mrs. Freeman (Mabel) Yoder*

# Cheddar & Garlic Bread

4 c. warm water
2 Tbsp. yeast

¹/₃ c. sugar

Combine and let set for 10 minutes. In a large bowl combine the following:

¹/₃ c. sugar
2 tsp. salt

³/₄ c. oil

Combine the two mixtures and add the following according to directions below:

10 c. all-purpose white flour (divided)

2 tsp. garlic powder
1 c. cheddar cheese powder

Add 5 c. of flour, garlic powder and cheddar cheese powder; blend well. Add the other 5 c. of flour, one at a time, and blend well. If dough seems too sticky add 1 more cup flour. Cover dough with lid and let rise 10 minutes; knead down. Repeat 3 times every 10 minutes. Let rise until lid bulges. Bake at 200° for 10 minutes, then at 325° for 20 minutes.

*Mrs. Perry (Lena) Lehman*

# French Bread

2 c. boiling water
3 Tbsp. sugar
2 tsp. salt
2 Tbsp. shortening

$^1/_2$ c. warm water
2 pkg. dry yeast
$6^1/_2$ c. flour (approx.) (divided)

Pour boiling water over sugar, salt and shortening; stir and cool. Dissolve yeast in warm water. Add to shortening mixture. Add $2^1/_2$ c. of flour and beat until smooth. Add 4 more c. flour. Knead well. Punch down 4–5 times every 5 minutes. Divide dough in half and roll out to $^1/_2$" thickness. Roll up tightly, like a jellyroll. Seal ends. Place on cookie sheets and slash tops $^1/_4$" deep. Let rise until double, brush with a mixture of **1 egg** and **2 Tbsp. milk (beaten)**. Bake at 400° for 10 minutes. Reduce to 350° and bake for another 20 minutes.

*Mrs. Samuel (Viola) Miller*

# Garlic Parmesan Bread Sticks

1 Tbsp. dry yeast
$1^1/_2$ c. warm water
2 Tbsp. sugar
$^3/_4$ c. butter or oleo (melted) (divided)
$^1/_2$ tsp. salt

$4^1/_2$ c. flour
garlic salt
grated Parmesan cheese
Marinara or spaghetti sauce (warmed)

In a mixing bowl, dissolve yeast in water; add sugar. Let set for 5 minutes. Add $^1/_2$ c. of butter, salt and 2 c. flour; beat until smooth. Stir in enough remaining flour to form a soft dough. Let rise until doubled, about 45 minutes. Punch dough down and turn onto a lightly floured surface. Roll into a 24" x 10" rectangle. Cut dough in half lengthwise, then into 5" x 1" strips. Twist each strip and place 1" apart on greased baking sheets. Brush strips with remaining butter; sprinkle with garlic salt and Parmesan cheese. Cover and let rise in a warm place until doubled (about 20 minutes). Bake at 350° for 20-30 minutes or until light brown. Serve with warm sauce. *Very good!*

*Mrs. Leland (Orpha) Yoder*

# Hillbilly Bread

| | |
|---|---|
| 4¹/₂ c. hot water | 2 Tbsp. honey |
| ²/₃ c. brown sugar | 2 c. whole wheat flour |
| ¹/₂ c. oil | 10 c. bread flour |
| 4 tsp. salt | 4 Tbsp. instant yeast |

Heat water to hot and add sugar, oil, salt and honey; let cool to luke-warm. Add 2 c. whole wheat flour and yeast. Then add rest of flour. Let rise until 2" above bowl. Knead down and shape into 4 loaves. Bake at 375° for 30 minutes.

*Mrs. David (Mary Lou) Whetstone, Mrs. Gerald (Darla) Yoder*

# Honey Wheat Bread

| | |
|---|---|
| *3 c. very warm water | 1 egg (beaten) |
| ¹/₃ c. vegetable oil | 2 Tbsp. yeast |
| ¹/₃ c. honey | *2 c. whole wheat flour |
| 2 Tbsp. brown sugar | about 9 c. white bread flour |
| 1 Tbsp. salt | |

Stir first 6 ingredients together in large bowl. Add wheat flour, then sprinkle yeast on top of wheat flour before stirring in. Then add the white flour. Mix and knead well, about 10 minutes. Let rest 15 minutes, knead, grease bowl and let rise about an hour. Punch down and let rise 1 more hour. Divide into 3 loaves and let rise until double in size. Bake at 350° for 30 minutes. *Sara Marie uses 4 cups warm water and 4 cups whole wheat flour and less white flour.

*Mrs. Harley (JoAnna) Miller, Mrs. James (Sara Marie) Yoder*

---

*Refusing to ask for help when you need it is refusing someone the chance to be helpful.*

---

# Italian Cheese Bread

| | |
|---|---|
| 1 Tbsp. yeast | 2¹/₂ c. flour |
| 1 c. warm water | 1 tsp. salt |
| 1 tsp. sugar | 1 Tbsp. oil |

TOPPING:

| | |
|---|---|
| ¹/₄ c. Italian dressing | ¹/₂ c. mozzarella cheese |
| ¹/₄ tsp. salt | ¹/₄ tsp. dried oregano |
| ¹/₄ tsp. garlic powder | ¹/₄ tsp. dried thyme |
| 1 Tbsp. Parmesan cheese | dash of pepper |

Mix together and add flour as needed to make a soft dough. Turn onto floured surface; knead 1–2 minutes or until smooth and elastic. Place in greased bowl, turning once to grease top. Cover; let rise for 20 minutes in a warm place. Punch dough down and place on greased 12" pizza pan. Brush with Italian dressing. Combine seasoning and sprinkle over top. Sprinkle with cheeses. Bake at 450° for 15 minutes.

*Mrs. Ervin (Edna) Bontrager*

# Mock Zucchini Bread

| | |
|---|---|
| 2 c. sugar | 3 c. flour |
| 1 c. vegetable oil | 2 tsp. soda |
| 3 eggs | 1 tsp. salt |
| 2 tsp. vanilla | 1¹/₂ tsp. cinnamon |
| 1 c. shredded pineapple | 1 c. chopped nuts, *optional* |
| (well drained) | 1 c. raisins or chocolate chips |
| 2 c. unpeeled shredded zucchini | |

Mix first 4 ingredients well then add pineapple and zucchini. Mix flour, soda, salt and cinnamon together and add; mix well. Then add chopped nuts and raisins or chocolate chips. Bake in greased pans at 350° for 1 hour. Yield: 2 loaves.

*Mrs. Wilbur (Esther) Yoder*

*Why value the present hour less than the future hour?*

# Pizza Bread Stix

| | |
|---|---|
| $1/2$ c. milk | 2 eggs |
| $1/2$ c. butter | 4 c. flour |
| $1/2$ c. sugar | 3 Tbsp. salsa |
| $1/2$ tsp. salt | Parmesan cheese |
| 1 pkg. yeast | oregano or pizza seasoning |
| $1/2$ c. warm water | |

Scald milk and add butter, sugar and salt. Dissolve yeast in warm water. Add to milk mixture. Add beaten eggs and flour; mix until well blended. Cover and let rise 45 minutes. Take half of dough and roll out to 10" x 14" on floured surface. Cut in half lengthwise. On one half spread salsa, sprinkle with Parmesan cheese and oregano or pizza seasoning. Top with other half of rolled out dough. Cut into $1/2$" strips width wise. Place on greased cookie sheets. Repeat with the other half of dough. Let rise for 30 minutes. Bake at 350° for 15 minutes. Very good when served with cheese sauce.

*Mrs. Glen (Ruby) Yoder*

# Pizza Sticks

| | |
|---|---|
| 2 pkg. yeast | 5 c. flour (may use some whole |
| 2 c. lukewarm water | wheat flour) |
| $1/2$ c. sugar | butter |
| 1 egg | pizza seasoning |
| 3 Tbsp. oil | Parmesan cheese |
| 1 tsp. salt | |

Dissolve yeast in lukewarm water and sugar; let set 5 minutes. Beat egg, oil and salt together. Stir into yeast mixture. Gradually add flour to make a soft dough. Knead well. Place in greased bowl and cover. Let rise until doubled. Punch down and roll out on floured surface. Spread with butter and sprinkle with pizza seasoning and Parmesan cheese. Roll again lightly to press down seasoning. Cut into 6" long sticks with pizza cutter or knife. Place on greased baking sheet. Let rise until doubled. Bake at 350° for 8–10 minutes or until just a bit brown. Serve with pizza sauce or spaghetti sauce.

*Mrs. Orla (Ruby) Raber*

# Poppy Seed Bread

| | |
|---|---|
| 2¹/₄ c. sugar | 3 eggs |
| 3 c. flour | 1¹/₈ c. cooking oil |
| 1¹/₂ tsp. salt | 2 Tbsp. poppy seeds |
| 1¹/₂ tsp. baking powder | 2 tsp. vanilla-butternut flavoring |
| 1¹/₂ c. milk | 1 tsp. vanilla |

**ORANGE GLAZE:**

| | |
|---|---|
| ³/₄ c. sugar | ¹/₄ c. water |
| ¹/₂ c. frozen orange juice | 1¹/₂ tsp. vanilla butternut flavoring |

Sift together dry ingredients. Beat eggs into milk; add to flour mixture. Mix together, adding oil, seeds and flavoring; beat well. Pour into 2 greased loaf pans. Bake at 350° for approximately 30 minutes. For Glaze: Mix ingredients and melt over low heat. Pour over warm loaves before they are removed from pans. *One of Mom's specialties! Very good!*

*Mrs. Ervin (Anna Mary) Miller*

# Pull-Apart Bacon Bread

| | |
|---|---|
| 12 bacon strips (diced) | 2 Tbsp. olive oil (divided) |
| 1 - 16 oz. loaf frozen bread dough (thawed) or use your favorite bread dough | 1 c. shredded mozzarella cheese |
| | 1 env. (1 oz.) Ranch salad dressing mix |

In a skillet cook bacon until partially cooked; drain. Roll out dough to ¹/₂" thickness, brush with 1 Tbsp. olive oil. Cut into 1" pieces and place in a large bowl. Add the bacon, cheese, dressing mix and remaining oil; toss to coat. Arrange pieces in a 9" x 5" oval on a greased baking sheet, layering as needed. Cover and let rise in a warm place until doubled (30 minutes). Bake at 350° for 15 minutes. Cover with foil and bake for 5–10 minutes longer or until golden.

*Mrs. David (JoAnn) Mast*

---

*Take time to laugh; it is the music of the soul.*

# Pull-Apart Cinnamon Bread

1 pkg. yeast (dissolved in
 ¹/₄ c. lukewarm water)
1 c. scalded milk
1¹/₃ c. sugar
¹/₃ c. butter (melted)
¹/₂ tsp. salt

3 eggs (well beaten)
4 c. flour
melted butter
1 c. sugar
¹/₂ c. nuts
3 tsp. cinnamon

Soak yeast in warm water. Add sugar, butter and salt to scalded milk.
Cool to lukewarm then add yeast, eggs and flour; beat thoroughly. Cover
and let rise until doubled, pinch off pieces of dough, the size of a walnut; dip in melted butter. Mix sugar, nuts and cinnamon together and
roll buttered dough in mixture. Pile balls loosely in ungreased angel
food cake pan. Let rise for 30 minutes. Bake at 400° for 10 minutes,
then at 350° for 30 minutes. Turn pan upside down immediately when
done baking. Serve warm.

*Mrs. Eli (Martha) Mullet*

# Starter for Friendship Bread

## 10-day bread

¹/₂ Tbsp. yeast
1 c. warm water

1 c. flour
2 Tbsp. sugar

Mix yeast and warm water together, then add flour and sugar. Pour into
1-gal. Ziploc bag. Keep in a cool place. Do not refrigerate. *Friendship
Bread recipe on following page.*

*Mrs. Freeman (Mabel) Yoder*

---

*It's a great deal better to do all the things you should do,
than spend the rest of your life wishing you had.*

---

# Amish Friendship Bread or Cake

Day 1: Do nothing.

Day 2–5: Squeeze the bag 2 times a day.

Day 6: Add **1 c. flour, 1 c. sugar** and **1 c. milk** to the mixture in the bag. Squeeze, mixing well.

Day 7–9: Squeeze and let air out of bag 2 times a day.

Day 10: Pour and squeeze contents into a large bowl. Add **1 c. flour, 1 c. sugar** and **1 c. milk**. Stir and pour 4 - 1-c. starters into 4 - 1-gal. Ziploc bags. Give one bag to each of your friends along with a copy of this recipe. Keep one for yourself. You should have 1 cup starter left; if not, use 1 more cup from a reserved bag. Add **1 c. oil**, **$^1/_2$ c. milk**, **3 eggs** and **1 tsp. vanilla**. Mix well. Then add **2 c. flour, 1 c. sugar, $1^1/_2$ tsp. baking powder, 1 tsp. salt, 2 tsp. cinnamon, 1 - 3.4 oz. box vanilla instant pudding mix** and **1 c. chopped nuts**. Mix well. Mix a little **sugar** and **cinnamon** to sprinkle on the bottom of pans and to sprinkle on top of batter. If making bread, pour batter into 2 bread pans. Bake at 325° for 1 hour. If making a cake, pour batter into a 9" x 13" pan and bake at 325° for approx. 45 minutes or until toothpick inserted near center comes out clean. *(Starter recipe on previous page.)*

*Mrs. Freeman (Mabel) Yoder*

---

*Every day of our lives we should make it a point to do some small thing we would rather not do. Then we will enter the doing of the larger tasks of life with zest and spirit.*

---

# Apple Rolls

| | |
|---|---|
| 1/3 c. milk (or more) | 4 tsp. baking powder |
| 1/2 tsp. salt | 3 Tbsp. shortening |
| 2 c. flour | 2–3 apples (peeled & chopped) |
| 2 Tbsp. sugar | |

SYRUP:

| | |
|---|---|
| 1 Tbsp. flour | 1 c. boiling water |
| 3/4 c. sugar | 1 Tbsp. butter |
| 3/4 c. brown sugar | 1 tsp. vanilla |
| 1/2 tsp. salt | 1/2–1 tsp. cinnamon |

Mix all together and add enough milk to make a soft, biscuit-like dough. Double recipe for a full 13" x 9" pan. Bake at 350° until almost done. Poke holes around the edges and pour syrup over it and finish baking. For Syrup: Boil ingredients together before pouring over dough.

*Mrs. Lester (Verna) Bontrager*

# Cake Mix Cinnamon Rolls

| | |
|---|---|
| 1 box white or yellow cake mix | 2 pkg. yeast |
| 1 tsp. salt | 2 1/2 c. warm water |
| 5 c. flour | 1/3 c. oil |
| | 3 eggs (beaten) |

Place water in a bowl, add salt; mix yeast with cake mix and add to the water. Add oil and eggs. Add flour; mix well. Let rise until double in size. Roll out half at a time into a rectangle. Spread with butter, cinnamon and brown sugar. Roll up and slice. Place in greased pans. Let rise until doubled. Bake at 350° for 15 minutes. Frost with your favorite roll frosting.

*Mrs. Wayne (Marilyn) Yoder, Mrs. Wilbur (Alta) Beechy*

---

*To the man in us, time is quantity;*
*To the God in us, it is quality.*

---

# Caramel Pecan Rolls

1 Tbsp. yeast
³/₄ c. warm milk
³/₄ c. warm water
¹/₂ c. sugar

3 Tbsp. oil
2 tsp. salt
4–4¹/₂ c. flour

FILLING:
¹/₄ c. butter (softened)
¹/₄ c. sugar
3 tsp. cinnamon

³/₄ c. brown sugar (packed)
¹/₂ c. whipping cream
1 c. chopped pecans

In a mixing bowl dissolve yeast in water and milk. Add sugar, oil, salt and 2 cups flour. Beat well. Stir in enough flour for a soft dough. Knead until smooth and elastic. Cover and let rise until doubled. Roll into a long rectangle ¹/₄" thick. Spread with butter, sugar and cinnamon. Roll up and pinch seam to seal. Cut into 12 slices. Stir cream and brown sugar until sugar is mostly dissolved. Pour into a greased 13" x 9" baking pan. Sprinkle with pecans. Place rolls in pan. Cover and let rise about 1 hour. Bake at 350° for 30–35 minutes. Cool 1 minute, then invert onto a serving platter. No icing needed.

*Mrs. Freeman (Mabel) Yoder*

# Cinnamon Glaze for Rolls

2¹/₂ Tbsp. Perma-Flo
1¹/₂ c. sugar
1 tsp. cinnamon

¹/₂ tsp. salt
2 c. hot water

Stir everything together except Perma-Flo. Mix Perma-Flo with a little water and stir to the remaining ingredients in a saucepan. Boil for several minutes until mixture is thickened and spread over still warm cinnamon rolls. This is a glaze that makes frosting faster and keeps rolls soft for several days.

*Mrs. Omer (Mabel) Schwartz*

# Cinnamon Rolls

2 pkg. yeast
1 c. warm water
2 Tbsp. sugar
2 c. milk
6 Tbsp. butter

1 tsp. salt
3 eggs (beaten)
$^1/_2$ c. sugar
8 c. bread flour
brown sugar & cinnamon

Dissolve yeast and 2 Tbsp. sugar in warm water. Scald milk and melt butter in it. Cool to lukewarm. Mix everything together, along with salt, eggs, and $^1/_2$ c. sugar. Mix and knead in bread flour. Let rise. Punch down, then roll out the dough on greased surface to about $^1/_2$" thick. Spread margarine on the surface of the dough. Put on a thin layer of brown sugar and sprinkle some cinnamon on top. Form into a long, tight roll. Slice into roll-size pieces. Put in greased pans; let rise. Bake at 350° until golden brown. Do not overbake. Frost with favorite icing.

*Mrs. Paul (Rhoda) Yoder*

# Cinnamon Rolls

1 pkg. yeast
3 c. lukewarm water (divided)
$^3/_4$ c. butter
1 c. sugar

2 eggs (beaten)
2 tsp. baking powder
$1^1/_2$ tsp. salt
8–9 c. flour (divided)

Dissolve yeast in 1 c. lukewarm water. Add 2 more cups water with butter. Mix in beaten eggs, sugar and salt. Add 6 cups flour with baking powder. Add remaining flour. Let rise until twice the size. Punch down and let rise again. Roll out and spread with butter, brown sugar and cinnamon. Cut and let rise again. Bake at 400° for 25–30 minutes.

*Mrs. John (Susie) Kuhns*

---

*The man who trusts men will make fewer mistakes*
*than he who distrusts them.*

---

## Cinnamon Yeast Rolls

3 c. lukewarm milk
2 Tbsp. yeast
1/4 c. sugar
3 tsp. salt

6 eggs (beaten)
3/4 c. melted shortening or
    salad oil
9 c. flour (divided)

Soften yeast in milk. Add sugar and 3 c. of flour. Let set until bubbly. Next add salt, eggs, melted shortening or salad oil and remaining flour. Knead. Let rise until double, knead and let rise again. When doubled, roll out to desired thickness and spread with melted butter or oleo. Sprinkle with brown sugar and cinnamon. Roll like jellyrolls, cut into 1" slices. Place in greased pans and let rise until double. Bake at 350° for 15–20 minutes.

*Mrs. Vernon (Nelda) Miller*

## Verna's Cinnamon Rolls

3 Tbsp. yeast
4 1/2 c. warm water
2 tsp. sugar
2 1/4 c. milk

1 1/2 c. butter
3 tsp. salt
6 eggs (beaten)
11 1/4 c. flour

CARAMEL ROLL SAUCE:
3/4 c. Karo
1 1/4 c. butter
pecans or walnuts, *optional*

4 1/2 c. brown sugar
vanilla

Mix first 3 ingredients and let set. Heat milk, butter and salt together. Stir in 3 cups of flour. Beat well; then add beaten eggs. Beat again and add remaining flour—8 1/4 c. Let rise 1 hour. Punch down and let rise again. For Caramel Roll Sauce: Stir all ingredients together and heat until butter is melted. Pour a thin layer into pans, then place rolls on top. Bake at 350° until lightly browned. Dump rolls upside down onto another pan as soon as they're out of the oven. *Very delicious!*

*Mrs. Allen (Elsie) Bontrager*

# English Tea Ring

| | |
|---|---|
| 1 Tbsp. yeast | $^1/_2$ tsp. vanilla |
| $^1/_4$ c. warm water | 3 c. flour (or more) |
| $^1/_2$ c. milk (scalded) | $^1/_4$ c. brown sugar |
| $^1/_4$ c. shortening | 1 tsp. cinnamon |
| 1 tsp. salt | butter |
| $^1/_2$ c. sugar | $^1/_2$ c. chopped nuts or candied |
| 1 egg (beaten) | fruit, *optional* |

Put yeast in warm water. Combine milk, shortening, salt and sugar. Cool to lukewarm. Add beaten egg, vanilla and yeast mixture. Mix in flour and knead to a soft elastic dough. Let rise until double in size. Divide dough into 2 parts. Roll out 1 portion into a rectangle, butter dough and sprinkle with sugar and cinnamon and nuts or fruit. Roll up like rolls. Shape into a ring and transfer to a greased 10" pie plate. With a sharp scissors, snip almost to the center (1" apart). Pull sections apart and twist slightly so the parts lay against one another. Let rise until double. Repeat with other half of dough. You do not have to do this in 2 parts. When doing 1 big ring, a bigger baking sheet must be used. Bake at 375° for 15–20 minutes or until golden. Frost with your favorite frosting. (*Featured on the cover of this cookbook.*)

*Amy Yoder (Daughter)*

# Lollipops

| | |
|---|---|
| your favorite bread dough | 2 c. regular cream (no substitute) |
| 4 c. brown sugar | |

Make your favorite bread dough. Form dough into ping-pong-sized balls. Put into a 9" x 13" greased cake pan. Mix brown sugar and cream together. Pour over bread dough. Bake at 350° for 25–30 minutes.

*Mom (Elsie) Yoder*

---

*Reality may be a rough road, but escape is a precipice.*

# Friendship Cinnamon Rolls

| | |
|---|---|
| 2 c. starter* | butter |
| 2 c. flour | cinnamon |
| 1/2 tsp. salt | sugar |
| 1/2 tsp. soda | 1/2 c. butter (melted) |
| 4 tsp. baking powder | 1 c. brown sugar |
| 1/2 c. oil | 1/2 c. chopped nuts |

Combine starter, flour, soda, salt, baking powder and oil. Knead lightly on floured board until dough is no longer sticky. Roll to 1/4" thick and spread with butter. Sprinkle with sugar and cinnamon. Roll up and cut into slices. Combine melted butter, brown sugar and nuts. Spread on bottom of a 9" x 13" pan. Place rolls, flat side down, on mixture. Bake at 350° for 30 minutes or until golden brown. Invert pan on serving plate immediately. *Starter recipe found in this section of cookbook. Instead of giving starters to friends you can bake a variety of cakes, rolls, or breads to use up the starters.*

*Mrs. Freeman (Mabel) Yoder*

# Monkey Bread

| | |
|---|---|
| 2 tubes Pillsbury biscuits | 1 c. butter |
| 1 c. sugar (divided) | 1/2 c. brown sugar |
| 1/2 tsp. cinnamon | |

Cut each Pillsbury biscuit into four pieces. Mix 1/2 c. sugar and cinnamon together and roll biscuits in mixture. Divide into 2 - 9" cake pans. Now make a syrup of butter, brown sugar and 1/2 c. sugar. Heat this until melted and pour over biscuits. Bake at 350° for approximately 35 minutes. When done, dump out on a plate and cool. *Enjoy!*

*Mrs. Leland (Orpha) Yoder*

*You are none the holier for being praised, and none the worse for being blamed.*

# Blueberry Muffins

4 c. flour
2 Tbsp. baking powder
2 c. sugar
1 Tbsp. soda
4 eggs

16 oz. sour cream
1 c. oil
1 tsp. vanilla
3 c. blueberries

Mix all ingredients well except blueberries; add those last. Fill muffin tins ²/₃ full. Bake at 400° for 20–25 minutes.

*Mrs. Delmar (Pauline) Weaver*

# Oatmeal Muffins

³/₄ c. milk
³/₄ Tbsp. vinegar
³/₄ c. quick oats
1 c. brown sugar
1 egg (beaten)

¹/₂ c. margarine (melted & cooled)
1 c. flour
¹/₂ tsp. soda
1 tsp. baking powder
¹/₂ tsp. salt

Mix milk with vinegar. Soak quick oats in milk mixture for 1 hour. Then add brown sugar, egg and melted margarine. Sift together remaining dry ingredients and add to first mixture. Mix all ingredients well. Bake at 400° until lightly browned.

*Mrs. Devon (Marietta) Troyer*

# Popover Muffins

1 c. flour
¹/₂ tsp. salt
2 large eggs

1 c. milk
1 Tbsp. butter (melted)

Mix all ingredients together and bake in lightly greased muffin pans. Bake at 450° for 15 minutes, then reduce heat to 350° and bake 20 minutes longer until well browned and crusty. Do not open oven while baking as this will deflate them! Remove from oven and puncture sides with a sharp knife to let steam escape. Serve with butter and maple syrup. *Delicious!*

31                    *Mom (Rosa) Bontrager*

# Pumpkin Muffins

1 c. oil
2 c. sugar
4 eggs (beaten)
2 c. pumpkin
2 c. flour

$^1/_2$ tsp. salt
2 tsp. cinnamon
$^1/_4$ tsp. cloves
1 tsp. baking soda
2 tsp. baking powder

**CREAM CHEESE FROSTING:**
3 oz. cream cheese (softened)
1 tsp. vanilla
6 Tbsp. margarine (softened)

1 tsp. milk
$1^3/_4$ c. powdered sugar

Mix oil and sugar; add eggs and pumpkin. Mix well. Mix dry ingredients until moistened. Bake at 350° for 20–25 minutes. You may insert toothpick in center to check as time may vary. For Frosting: Mix until smooth. Frost cooled muffins. Yield: 24 muffins.

*Mrs. Daryl (Marsha) Miller*

# Butter Horns

1 c. warm water
$^1/_2$ c. shortening
$^1/_2$ c. sugar
$^1/_2$ tsp. salt

3 eggs (beaten)
1 Tbsp. yeast
5 c. flour

Knead well; let set in refrigerator overnight. Divide into 2 parts and roll out in 12" circle. Cut into 16 wedges; roll up, starting with wide end. Let rise for 2–3 hours. Bake at 400° for 15 minutes. Brush with butter. Serve while warm.

*Mrs. David (Arlene) Chupp, Mrs. Wilbur (Waneta) Nisley*

---

*To admit error is a sign of strength, not a confession of weakness.*

# Orange Rolls

| | |
|---|---|
| 1 c. warm milk | 1 tsp. salt |
| 1/4 c. shortening | 1 Tbsp. yeast |
| 1/4 c. sugar | 1/4 c. warm orange juice |
| 1 egg (slightly beaten) | 3–4 c. flour |

**FILLING:**

| | |
|---|---|
| 1/2 c. brown sugar | 1/2 c. butter or oleo (softened) |
| 1/2 c. sugar | 2 Tbsp. grated orange peel |

**GLAZE:**

| | |
|---|---|
| 1 1/2 c. powdered sugar | 2 tsp. milk |
| 4 tsp. butter or margarine | 1/2 tsp. lemon extract |
| 5 tsp. orange juice | |

In a large bowl mix milk, shortening, sugar, egg and salt. Soak yeast in warm orange juice, then add to ingredients in bowl. Stir in enough flour to form a soft dough. Knead on a lightly floured surface until smooth and elastic. Let rise until doubled (about 1 hour). Punch down and divide into 2 balls. Roll each ball of dough into a large rectangle. Mix filling ingredients well and spread over each rectangle. Roll up, starting with long end. Cut into rolls 1/2" thick. Place on greased 11" x 7" x 2" baking pans. Cover and let rise until double. Bake at 375° for 20–25 minutes or until lightly browned. Mix glaze ingredients well and spread over warm rolls (I like to double the glaze ingredients). *Deliciously different!*

*Mrs. Freeman (Mabel) Yoder*

# Cloud Biscuits

| | |
|---|---|
| 2 c. flour | 1/2 c. corn oil |
| 4 tsp. baking powder | 1 egg (beaten) |
| 1/2 tsp. salt | 2/3 c. milk |
| 1 Tbsp. sugar | |

Mix first 5 ingredients to resemble crumbs. Combine the egg and milk, then pour all of it into the crumbs. Knead gently. Bake at 375° for 10–12 minutes. Variation: Susie does not put in an egg and sugar for plain baking powder biscuits.

*Mrs. Darrell (Erma) Yoder, Mrs. John (Susie) Kuhns*

# Angel Biscuits

| | |
|---|---|
| 1 Tbsp. yeast | 1 tsp. salt |
| 2 Tbsp. warm water | 3 Tbsp. honey |
| 5 c. flour | 1 c. shortening |
| 3 tsp. baking powder | 2 c. buttermilk |

Dissolve yeast in warm water. Let set. In mixing bowl sift flour with dry ingredients. Cut shortening into flour mixture. Add buttermilk and yeast mixture all at once. Add honey. Stir until flour is dampened. Knead dough onto floured board for 30 seconds. Roll out to $1/2$" thickness; cut with biscuit cutter. No rising is necessary. Bake at 400° for 12–15 minutes. This dough may be refrigerated up to 1 week and used as needed. This recipe may be used for a sugar-free/whole wheat recipe: 3 c. whole wheat flour and 2 c. white flour.

*Mrs. Ervin (Anna Mary) Miller*

# Melt-In-Your-Mouth Biscuits

| | |
|---|---|
| 2 c. sifted flour | 2 Tbsp. sugar |
| 2 tsp. baking powder | $1/2$ c. shortening (Crisco) |
| $1/2$ tsp. cream of tartar | 1 egg (unbeaten) |
| $1/2$ tsp. salt | $2/3$ c. milk |

Sift dry ingredients together and cut in shortening until mixture resembles a coarse meal. Pour milk in slowly. Add egg and stir well. Bake at 450° 10–15 minutes.

*Mrs. Samuel (Norma) Yoder, Mrs. Delmar (Pauline) Weaver*

---

*This isn't a dress rehearsal . . . we get only one chance to be the best we can.*

---

# Cream Sticks

2 Tbsp. yeast
1 c. water
1 c. milk
1 c. shortening

$^2/_3$ c. sugar
2 eggs
1 tsp. salt
6 c. flour

**CREAM FILLING:**
1 c. milk
3 Tbsp. flour
1 c. shortening

1 c. sugar
$^1/_2$ c. margarine

**CARAMEL ICING:**
$^1/_4$ c. butter
$^1/_2$ c. brown sugar

3 Tbsp. milk

Dissolve yeast in warm water. Scald milk and cool. Cream shortening, sugar, eggs and salt. Add scalded milk and yeast mixture. Add flour. Cover and let rise until double. Roll $^1/_2$" thick. Cut in strips 1" x 4". Let rise 10 minutes and deep fat fry. When cool, slit open lengthwise and spread cream filling in. Then frost with Caramel Icing. For Cream Filling: Cook milk and flour; cool. Add shortening, sugar and margarine. Beat well. For Caramel Icing: Boil butter, brown sugar and 3 Tbsp. milk. Cool, then add powdered sugar to make it nice to spread.

*Mrs. Delmar (Pauline) Weaver*

# Dinner Crackers

5 c. whole wheat flour
   (pastry is best)
$1^1/_2$ tsp. salt

$1^1/_4$ c. butter
2 c. whole milk

Mix together all ingredients and knead very well. Add herbs or sesame seeds to taste, if you like. Roll out very thin on cookie sheet. Prick all over with a fork. Cut into squares. Bake at 400° until light brown.

*Mrs. David (Arlene) Chupp*

# Long Johns

¹/₂ c. butter or oleo
²/₃ c. sugar
2 eggs (well beaten)
1 tsp. salt

1 c. milk (scalded)
2 pkg. yeast (soaked in
   1 c. warm water)
6 c. flour

FILLING:
2¹/₂ c. milk (heated & cooled)
8 oz. instant pudding (vanilla)

1 pkg. cream cheese

Put butter or oleo, sugar, eggs and salt into scalded milk. Let cool, then add yeast, then flour. Let rise once. Roll out and cut into strips. Let rise then deep fat fry in oil. For Filling: Combine milk and pudding until thickened. Add cream cheese. When long johns are cooled, put filling in middle, then frost with frosting of your choice.

*Mrs. Wilbur (Waneta) Nisley*

# Flour Tortillas

2 c. flour
¹/₂ c. lukewarm water
¹/₄ c. lard or shortening

2 tsp. baking powder
1 tsp. salt

Combine dry ingredients and lard until very fine. Add water gradually. Form into a ball and knead thoroughly until smooth. Divide into 6–12 balls evenly (depending if you want 8" or 10" tortillas). Roll as thin as possible. Fry on a hot griddle; turn frequently until done (about 1 minute). Put foil between layers to keep warm for immediate use. To store, place wax paper between each one, place in bag and freeze.

*Mrs. Harley (Martha) Raber, Mrs. David (JoAnn) Bontrager*

---

*Speak only well of people and you need never whisper.*

# Cakes & Frostings

*A good traffic rule for the road of life:*
*When you meet temptation, turn to the right.*

BLESSED ARE THEY WHICH DO HUNGER AND THIRST AFTER
RIGHTEOUSNESS: FOR THEY SHALL BE FILLED.
MATTHEW 5:6

# A Prayer

Let me be a little kinder.
Let me be a little blinder
To the faults of those about me.
Let me praise a little more.
Let me be—when I am weary
Just a little bit more cheery!
Let me serve a little better
Those that I am striving for.
When temptation bids me waver,
Let me strive a little harder,
To be all that I should be.
Let me be a little meeker
With the brother who is weaker.
Let me think more of my neighbor
And a little less of me.
Let me be a little sweeter—
Make my life a bit completer,
By doing what I should do
Every minute of the day.
Let me toil without complaining,
Not one humble task disdaining.
Let me face the summons calmly
When death beckons me away.

*Practicing the Golden Rule is not a sacrifice;*
*it is an investment.*

*Add a teaspoon of vinegar to cooked frosting.*
*This will keep it from cracking when cake is cut.*

# Apple Blossom Cake

| | |
|---|---|
| 1 c. vegetable oil | 1 tsp. cinnamon |
| 1 1/2 c. brown sugar | 1 tsp. nutmeg |
| 2 eggs (unbeaten) | 3 c. flour |
| 1 tsp. vanilla | 1 c. nuts |
| 1 1/2 tsp. soda | 3 c. chopped apples |

Cream first 3 ingredients until well mixed, then add the remaining ingredients in the order given. Top with 1/3 c. **brown sugar, 1 tsp. cinnamon** and 1/2 c. **nuts.** Pour into a 9" x 13" pan and bake at 350° for 30–40 minutes.

*Mrs. Ivan (Inez) Yoder*

# 30-Day Friendship Cake Starter

| | |
|---|---|
| 3/4 c. sliced or cut up peaches (undrained) | 1 1/2 c. sugar |
| 3/4 c. crushed pineapple (undrained) | 1 pkg. yeast |
| 1 - 1 3/4 oz. jar maraschino cherries (cut up & drained slightly) | |

Combine all ingredients in a glass bowl or gal. jug. Cover loosely. Stir several times the first day; let set at room temperature. Store at room temperature an additional 13 days, stirring once a day. Do not refrigerate. After the 13th day, starter is ready to use. Drain fruit and use the liquid to start your Friendship cake in the recipe as follows. Discard starter fruit or use to make cake. This cake takes lots of time but is well worth it. Good to start 2 months before Christmas, so you'll have fruit cakes for the holidays. Freezes well. (*Friendship Cake recipe is on following page.*)

*Mrs. Freeman (Mabel) Yoder*

---

*Encouragement means your friend gains courage from being with you.*

---

# 30-Day Amish Friendship Cake

Day 1: Mix 2$\frac{1}{2}$ c. sugar, 1$\frac{1}{2}$ c. starter, 1 - 29 oz. can peaches (undrained). Stir every day (all 30 days). Keep at room temperature in 1-gal. glass jar. Put lid on, leaving half turn. It is normal for fruit to bubble some. Do not refrigerate.

Day 10: Add 2 c. sugar, 1 - 20 oz. can crushed pineapple (undrained); stir well.

Day 20: Add 2 c. sugar, 2 - 10 oz. jars maraschino cherries (undrained); stir well.

Day 30: Drain juice from fruit and divide fruit into 3 parts to make 3 cakes. Divide juice into 1$\frac{1}{2}$ c. portions (you should have 5 portions). Put juice in jars and give to friends, along with a copy of recipe. Use juice within 3–5 days. May freeze cake, but do not freeze juice.

## Cake Recipe

1 Duncan Hines butter
  recipe golden cake mix
$\frac{2}{3}$ c. oil
4 eggs
1 small pkg. instant vanilla
  pudding

$\frac{1}{3}$ of fruit (about 1$\frac{1}{2}$ c.)
1 c. nuts
1 c. coconut

Do not add butter to cake mix. Mix all ingredients together with a wooden spoon (do not use mixer). Bake in greased and floured tube or bundt pan at 300° for 60–70 minutes or until golden brown. Keep in fridge or freeze after baking.

*Mrs. Freeman (Mabel) Yoder*

---

*Because you have an occasional low of despondency, don't despair.*
*The sun has a sinking spell every night, but rises again*
*all right the next morning.*

---

# Black Cherry Angel Food Cake

| | |
|---|---|
| 2 c. egg whites | 1¹/₄ c. sugar |
| ¹/₂ tsp. almond extract | 1¹/₂ c. flour |
| 2 tsp. cream of tartar | ¹/₂ c. sugar |
| 1 tsp. vanilla | ¹/₂ c. black cherry Jell-O |
| ¹/₂ tsp. salt | |

Beat egg whites with almond extract, cream of tartar, vanilla and salt. Add 1¹/₄ c. sugar, 2 Tbsp. at a time, and beat until stiff. In a separate bowl, sift flour, ¹/₂ c. sugar and Jell-O. Add gently to egg whites and mix until no dry mixture shows. Bake at 350° on lower oven rack for approximately 60 minutes. Cool completely. Make 7-Minute Frosting (found in Vol. 1 cookbook), or your favorite recipe and serve with blueberry pie filling. Jell-O flavor may vary. (*Black Cherry Angel Food Cake is featured on the front cover of this cookbook.*)

*Mrs. Freeman (Mabel) Yoder*

# Blueberry Kuchen

| | |
|---|---|
| ¹/₂ c. shortening | 2 c. flour |
| 1 c. sugar | 2 tsp. baking powder |
| ¹/₂ tsp. salt | 1 c. milk |
| 1 egg | 1 tsp. vanilla |

**TOPPING:**

| | |
|---|---|
| 2 c. blueberries | ¹/₄ c. sugar |

**CRUMBS:**

| | |
|---|---|
| 1¹/₂ c. flour | ¹/₂ c. brown sugar |
| pinch of salt | ¹/₂ c. margarine |

Mix shortening, sugar, salt and egg. Mix in flour and baking powder alternately with milk and vanilla. Mix well and spread on greased cookie sheet. Sprinkle blueberries over top and sprinkle sugar over berries. Mix crumb ingredients until crumbly and put on top. Bake at 375° for 25–30 minutes.

*Mrs. Fred (LeEtta) Yoder*

# Blueberry Pudding Cake

2 c. fresh or frozen blueberries
1 tsp. cinnamon
1 tsp. lemon juice
1 c. flour

$^3/4$ c. sugar
1 tsp. baking powder
$^1/2$ c. milk
3 Tbsp. melted oleo

TOPPING:
$^3/4$ c. sugar
1 Tbsp. cornstarch

1 c. boiling water

Toss the blueberries with cinnamon and lemon juice; place in greased 8" square greased baking dish. Combine flour, sugar and baking powder. Stir in milk and oleo. Spoon over berries. Mix sugar and cornstarch; sprinkle over batter. Slowly pour boiling water over all. Bake at 350° for 45–50 minutes. May also used canned blueberries, then use only $^1/3$ c. boiling water.

*Mrs. Lester (LaVerda) Yoder*

# Cake Mix Cakes

1 box chocolate cake mix
3 c. flour
2 c. sugar
3 eggs

3 tsp. soda
3 Tbsp. cocoa
$3^1/2$ c. water
1 c. vegetable oil

Bake at 350° for 30–35 minutes. Makes two soft cakes that taste like cake mix cakes.

*Mrs. Toby (Vera) Yoder*

---

*Since we are made up of bits and pieces of people,*
*may each of us be a chip of love.*

---

# Carrot Cake

4 eggs
2 c. sugar
1 1/4 c. vegetable oil
2 c. flour
2 tsp. cinnamon

1 tsp. baking powder
1 tsp. soda
1/2 tsp. salt
1/4 tsp. nutmeg
2 c. carrots (grated)

FROSTING:
1/2 c. butter or oleo
8 oz. cream cheese
4 c. powdered sugar

1 tsp. vanilla
3–4 Tbsp. milk
1/2 c. walnuts (chopped)

Combine eggs, oil and sugar; mix well. Add all dry ingredients then stir in carrots. Pour into two greased and floured 9" round cake pans. Bake at 350° for 30-40 minutes or until toothpick inserted near center comes out clean. Cool. For frosting: Mix all together then put a generous layer between the cakes, then frost over the top and sides.

*LuAnn Yoder (Daughter)*

# Carrot Pineapple Cake

1 c. salad oil
3 eggs
2 c. sugar
2 1/2 c. flour
1 tsp. soda
1/2 tsp. salt

1 tsp. cinnamon
1 tsp. vanilla
1 c. nuts (chopped)
1 c. grated carrots
1 c. crushed, drained pineapple
1 c. coconut

Place oil, eggs and sugar in a large bowl and beat well. Add flour, soda, salt and cinnamon; beat well. Add vanilla, nuts, carrots, pineapple and coconut. Bake in a greased 9" x 13" pan at 350° for 40–50 minutes.

*Mrs. Allen (Elsie) Bontrager*

*Good example has twice the value of good advice.*

# Cherry Treat

1 pkg. yeast
$^1/_2$ c. scalded milk
$^1/_4$ c. sugar
1 tsp. salt
2 eggs (beaten)

$^1/_4$ c. lukewarm water
$^1/_2$ c. oleo
$2^1/_2$ c. flour (or a little more)
approx. 4 c. cherry pie filling

FROSTING:
1 c. sugar
$^1/_2$ c. flour
1 c. milk
$^1/_2$ c. oleo

$^1/_2$ tsp. almond flavoring
1 tsp. vanilla
$^1/_2$ tsp. salt

Mix all ingredients together like bread dough, except pie filling. Let dough rise, then punch down. Let rise for another 2 hours. Then roll out half of dough and put in bottom of a 9" x 13" cake pan. Spoon pie filling on top. Roll out rest of dough and put on top. Let rise for 1 hour again before baking. Bake at 350° for 35–40 minutes. Frost when it has cooled a bit. For Frosting: Mix flour, sugar and milk in saucepan. Heat slowly until mixture thickens. Cream oleo and add remaining ingredients. Mix all ingredients together and spread on cake. *Very good with ice cream.*

*Mrs. Omer (Mabel) Schwartz*

# Black Magic Cake

2 c. flour
2 c. sugar
$^1/_2$ c. cocoa
2 tsp. baking soda
1 tsp. baking powder
$^1/_2$ tsp. salt

2 eggs
1 tsp. vanilla
$^1/_2$ c. vegetable oil
1 c. sour milk
2 tsp. instant coffee (in 1 c. hot water)

Sift dry ingredients together into a bowl. Add remaining ingredients and mix well. Bake at 350° for 35–40 minutes.

*Mrs. Mervin (Ruth) Yoder*

# Chocolate Cake Roll

¹/₃ c. flour
¹/₃ c. cocoa
2 Tbsp. cornstarch
¹/₂ tsp. soda
¹/₂ tsp. baking powder

¹/₃ tsp. salt
4 eggs (separated)
1 c. sugar (divided)
powdered sugar

**FILLING:**

8 oz. container whipped topping (thawed) or use jelly, pie filling or
pudding

Combine flour, cocoa, cornstarch, soda, baking powder and salt; mix
well. In a separate bowl beat egg yolks and ¹/₄ c. sugar until fluffy. In a
small bowl, using clean beaters, beat egg whites until foamy. Gradually
add ¹/₂ c. sugar, beating until stiff (but not dry) peaks form. Fold ¹/₃ of
egg whites into egg yolk mixture. Alternately fold in remaining whites
and flour mixture. Pour batter into a 15" x 10" jellyroll pan, lined with
waxed paper. Grease and flour lined pan. Smooth batter top. Bake at
350° until toothpick comes out clean (about 15 minutes). Dust a clean
cloth with remaining sugar. Turn cake out onto prepared cloth and remove waxed paper. Starting with long side, tightly roll up cake with
cloth. Cool, seam-side down. Then unroll, spread whipped topping on
cake and reroll. Place seam-side down on a plate. Dust with powdered
sugar before serving.

*Mrs. Leland (Orpha) Yoder*

# Chocolate Frosting

3¹/₂ c. powdered sugar
1 tsp. vanilla
¹/₄ c. shortening or soft butter

3 Tbsp. chocolate syrup
brewed coffee
2–3 Tbsp. milk

In a medium bowl combine first 4 ingredients, then gradually add coffee and milk until spreading consistency. Beat until fluffy. Always stays
nice and soft. Enough for a 9" x 13" cake or a layered 9" cake. May use
more milk instead of brewed coffee.

*Mrs. Freeman (Mabel) Yoder*

# Chocolate Chip Cake

$^1/_2$ c. butter or margarine
(softened)
$1^1/_2$ c. sugar (divided)
2 eggs
1 tsp. vanilla extract
2 c. all-purpose flour

$1^1/_2$ tsp. baking powder
1 tsp. baking soda
8 oz. sour cream
$^3/_4$ c. semisweet chocolate chips
1 tsp. ground cinnamon

In a mixing bowl, cream butter and 1 c. sugar. Add eggs, one a time, beating well after each addition. Stir in vanilla. Combine flour, baking powder and baking soda. Add to creamed mixture alternately with sour cream. Spread half of the batter into a greased 9" square baking pan. Sprinkle with chocolate chips. Combine cinnamon and remaining sugar; sprinkle over chips. Spread with remaining batter. Bake at 350° for 40–45 minutes or until toothpick inserted near the center comes out clean.

*Mrs. Eugene (Ruth) Yoder*

# Chocolate Mint Dream Cake

2 c. flour
$^3/_4$ tsp. salt
$1^1/_2$ c. white sugar
3 tsp. baking powder
$^1/_2$ c. cocoa

$^2/_3$ c. shortening
1 c. milk
1 tsp. vanilla
2 eggs

FILLING:
1 pt. whipped cream
$^1/_3$ c. powdered sugar

$^1/_2$ tsp. peppermint flavoring
3 drops green food coloring

Sift all dry ingredients together. Add shortening, milk and vanilla. Mix, then add 2 eggs; beat well. Bake at 350° for 30–35 minutes. Cut off the top of the cake through the center with a very sharp knife. Spread filling in middle. Save some for top of cake. For Filling: Beat cream until stiff. Add powdered sugar and peppermint flavor. Tint with food coloring.

*Mrs. Orva (Marietta) Yoder*

# Chocolate Pudding Cake

1 c. shortening
2 c. sugar
2 eggs
1 tsp. vanilla
1 c. buttermilk or sour milk

3 c. flour
2 tsp. soda
1 tsp. salt
$^1/_2$ c. cocoa
nuts, *optional*

Cream shortening and sugar together. Add eggs then mix well. Add the rest of ingredients. Pour into a 9" x 13" cake pan. Mix the following and pour over cake batter.

$1^1/_2$ c. sugar
$^3/_4$–1 c. hot water

2 Tbsp. cocoa

Bake at 350° for 50–60 minutes.

*Mrs. Raymond (LeEtta) Yoder*

# Friendship Chocolate Cake

$^2/_3$ c. starter*
1 c. lukewarm milk
$1^1/_4$ c. flour
1 c. sugar
$^1/_2$ tsp. cinnamon
$^1/_2$ tsp. salt

$^1/_2$ c. cocoa
$1^1/_2$ tsp. soda
$^2/_3$ c. shortening
2 eggs
1 tsp. vanilla

Combine first 3 ingredients in a large bowl and let set to bubble in a warm place for 2 hours. Sift sugar, cinnamon, salt, cocoa and soda together; cut in shortening. Add eggs, vanilla and starter mixture and mix well. Pour into a 9" x 13" pan and bake at 350° for 30–40 minutes or until toothpick inserted near center comes out clean. *Starter found in the bread section of this cookbook.

*Mrs. Freeman (Mabel) Yoder*

---

*Be the kind of person your dog thinks you are.*

---

# Salad Dressing Cake

2 c. flour
1 1/2 c. sugar
4 Tbsp. cocoa
2 tsp. soda

1 c. hot water
1 tsp. vanilla
1 c. salad dressing

Combine all dry ingredients and add remaining ingredients. Bake at 350° for 30–40 minutes.

*Mrs. Samuel (Wilma) Miller*

# Our Favorite Chocolate Cake

3 eggs
2 c. sugar
3/4 c. oil
1 1/2 tsp. baking powder
3/4 tsp. salt

2 1/4 c. flour
1 1/2 tsp. soda
1 1/2 tsp. vanilla
1 1/2 c. hot water
3/4 c. cocoa

Beat eggs and sugar together. Add oil then baking powder, salt, soda and flour. Mix the cocoa and hot water together and add to first mixture. Add vanilla. Bake at 350° for 20–25 minutes.

*Mrs. Dan (Esther) Miller*

---

*Speech may sometimes do harm; but so may silence and worse harm at that. No insult ever caused so deep a wound as a tenderness expected and withheld; and no spoken indiscretion was ever so bitterly regretted as the word one did not speak.*

---

# Peanut Butter Chocolate Cake

| | |
|---|---|
| 2 c. flour | 2 eggs |
| 2 c. sugar | 1 c. milk |
| ²/₃ c. baking cocoa | ²/₃ c. vegetable oil |
| 2 tsp. soda | 1 tsp. vanilla |
| 1 tsp. baking powder | 1 c. water |
| ¹/₂ tsp. salt | |

**PEANUT BUTTER FROSTING:**

| | |
|---|---|
| 3 oz. cream cheese (softened) | 2 Tbsp. milk |
| ¹/₄ c. creamy peanut butter | ¹/₂ tsp. vanilla |
| 2 c. powdered sugar | |

In a mixing bowl, combine dry ingredients. Add eggs, milk, oil and vanilla; beat well. Stir in water (batter will be thin). Pour into a greased 9" x 13" pan. Bake at 350° for 35–40 minutes. For Frosting: Beat the cream cheese and peanut butter until smooth. Beat in powdered sugar, milk and vanilla. Spread on cake after it has cooled. *Our favorite!*

*Mrs. David (Rachel) Plank*

# Reeses Cake Squares

| | |
|---|---|
| 1 c. butter | 2 c. sugar |
| 4 Tbsp. cocoa | 1 tsp. baking powder |
| 1 c. water | 2 eggs |
| 2 c. flour | 1 tsp. vanilla |

**FROSTING:**

| | |
|---|---|
| ¹/₂ c. margarine | 1 Tbsp. vanilla |
| 4 Tbsp. cocoa | powdered sugar |
| 6 Tbsp. buttermilk* | |

Bring butter, cocoa, and water to a boil. Pour over dry ingredients. Add eggs and vanilla. Pour into a greased 10" x 15" cookie sheet. Bake at 350° for 20 minutes. When cooled, spread a layer of peanut butter on top. For Frosting: Heat margarine, cocoa and milk; add vanilla and powdered sugar till the right consistency. Spread over peanut butter. *You may substitute 5 Tbsp. milk and 1 Tbsp. vinegar, combined, instead of buttermilk.

*Mrs. Wilbur (Esther) Yoder*

# Coffee Cake

| | |
|---|---|
| 1 box yellow cake mix | 1 c. plus 1 Tbsp. vegetable oil |
| 1 box instant vanilla pudding | 1 c. water |
| 1 box instant butterscotch pudding | 4 eggs |

CRUMBS:
| | |
|---|---|
| 1 c. brown sugar | $^1/_2$ c. crushed pecans |
| 1 Tbsp. cinnamon | |

Put half of batter in a 9" x 13" pan then put half of the crumbs on top. Put the other half of batter on crumb mixture in pan and top with remaining crumbs. Bake at 350° for 30–40 minutes.

*Mrs. Darrell (Erma) Yoder*

# Coffee Cake

| | |
|---|---|
| 1 c. margarine | 1 tsp. vanilla |
| 1 c. sugar | 2 c. flour |
| 3 eggs | 2 tsp. baking powder |
| 2 Tbsp. milk | 2 c. apple pie filling |

Cream margarine and sugar. Add remaining ingredients except pie filling. Spread half of batter into a 9" x 13" pan. Spread pie filling on top of batter, then put remaining batter on top. Sprinkle with powdered sugar and cinnamon before and after baking. Bake at 350° for 30–45 minutes.

*Mrs. Gerald (Darla) Yoder*

---

*Life is easier than you think. All you have to do is accept the impossible, do without the indispensable, and bear the intolerable.*

---

# Coffee Cake with Cream Cheese

1 c. margarine (softened)
2 c. sugar
2 eggs
2 tsp. salt
2 tsp. baking powder

2 tsp. soda
4 c. flour
2 c. sour milk or buttermilk
1 tsp. vanilla extract

CRUMBS:
$^1/_2$ c. brown sugar
$^1/_2$ c. flour

$^1/_4$ c. margarine

FILLING:
3 heaping tsp. flour or
  clear jel
$^1/_2$ c. sugar
1 c. milk
8 oz. cream cheese

$^1/_2$ c. Crisco
$^1/_2$ c. sugar
1 Tbsp. vanilla
2 lb. powdered sugar

Cream margarine and sugar together; add eggs, salt and vanilla. Gradually add baking powder, soda and flour; slowly add sour milk. Divide dough into 4 greased pie plates. Mix crumb ingredients until crumbly. Put crumbs over each one. Bake at 350° until a toothpick inserted near center comes out clean. When cakes are cool, cut in half, divide filling among the 4 cakes. Put top half on filling. For Filling: Mix flour or clear jel with sugar. Whisk in 1 c. milk and cook over low heat until thickened, stirring constantly. Remove from heat. In a large bowl, combine cream cheese with thickened mixture, whisk until smooth. Add remaining ingredients and mix well.

*Mrs. Freeman (Mabel) Yoder*

*If you can't sleep, don't count sheep; talk to the Shepherd.*

# Fluffy Frosting

| | |
|---|---|
| 4 Tbsp. sugar | 1 egg |
| 4 Tbsp. water | $1/2$ tsp. vanilla |
| $1/2$ c. Crisco | 2–4 c. powdered sugar |
| $1/2$ c. oleo | |

Beat sugar and water together for about 5 minutes or until syrupy. Cream Crisco and oleo together. Add egg and vanilla. Then add the syrup. Stir in powdered sugar. *This is a very fluffy frosting and will not get hard or sticky.*

*Mrs. Lonnie (Norma) Bontrager*

# Double Delight Coffee Cake

| | |
|---|---|
| 2 c. flour | 4 eggs |
| 2 tsp. baking powder | 1 c. sugar |
| 1 c. water | 1 tsp. salt |
| 2 - $3^{1}/2$ oz. boxes vanilla instant pudding | 1 tsp. vanilla |

**TOPPING:**

| | |
|---|---|
| 1 c. chopped pecans | 2 tsp. cinnamon |
| 1 c. brown sugar | |

**FROSTING:**

| | |
|---|---|
| 1 c. powdered sugar | 2 Tbsp. milk |
| 1 Tbsp. margarine | |

Mix together all batter ingredients. In a separate bowl mix topping ingredients. Pour half of batter into a 9" x 13" cake pan. Sprinkle half of topping on batter; pour in remaining batter. Top with remaining topping and bake at 350° for 40 minutes. Mix powdered sugar, margarine and milk; drizzle over cooled cake.

*Mrs. Lester (LaVerda) Yoder*

# Cowboy Cake

| | |
|---|---|
| 2 c. brown sugar | 1 tsp. soda |
| 2 c. flour | 1 egg |
| $^1/_2$ c. shortening | 2 tsp. vanilla |
| 1 c. sour milk | $^1/_2$ tsp. salt |

Mix first 3 ingredients until crumbly. Reserve $^2/_3$ c. of crumbs. Add remaining ingredients to remaining crumbs. Sprinkle reserved crumbs on top of batter and bake at 350° for 35 minutes or until done.

*Mrs. David (JoAnn) Bontrager*

# Raspberry Cream Cheese Coffee Cake

| | |
|---|---|
| $2^1/_4$ c. flour | $^1/_2$ tsp. soda |
| $^3/_4$ c. sugar | $^3/_4$ c. sour cream |
| $^3/_4$ c. oleo | 1 egg |
| $^1/_2$ tsp. baking powder | $^1/_2$ tsp. almond flavor |
| $^1/_2$ tsp. salt | |

**FILLING:**

| | |
|---|---|
| 8 oz. cream cheese | 1 egg |
| $^1/_2$ c. sugar | raspberry pie filling |

In a large bowl, combine flour and sugar. Cut in oleo as for pastry. Reserve 1 c.; set aside. Add the remaining ingredients to remaining crumbs. Spread in bottom of a 9" x 13" pan. For Filling: Beat cream cheese, sugar and egg together. Pour over batter. Spoon on raspberry filling. Sprinkle reserved crumbs on top. Bake for 30–40 minutes.

*Mrs. Dan (Esther) Miller*

---

*Praise not only pretends we are better than we are; it may help to make us better than we are.*

---

# Cream Cheese Pound Cake

| | |
|---|---|
| 8 oz. cream cheese | 6 eggs |
| 1 1/2 c. butter | 1 tsp. vanilla |
| 3 c. sugar | 3 c. all-purpose flour |

Cream first 2 ingredients together, then add sugar and beat until light and fluffy. Then add eggs, vanilla and flour; beat well. Pour batter into a bundt or angel food cake pan. Bake at 250° for 1 hour, then at 300° until done (approximately 45 minutes).

*Mrs. Allen (Elsie) Bontrager*

# Heath Bar Cake

| | |
|---|---|
| 1 box German chocolate cake mix | 8 oz. Cool Whip |
| 1 can Eagle Brand milk | butter brickle bits, Heath bits or Heath bar (broken in small pieces) |
| 1 jar Smucker's hot fudge sauce | |

Bake cake as directed on box. Remove from oven and immediately poke holes all over cake. Pour Eagle Brand milk over cake. Top with hot fudge sauce. Let cool. Spread Cool Whip over cooled cake and sprinkle with candy bar bits.

*Mrs. Levi (Carolyn) Schrock, Mrs. Glen (Ruby) Yoder*

---

*Gossip is like a balloon; it grows bigger with every puff.*

# Heath Bar Cake

1 c. brown sugar
1 c. sugar
1 tsp. vanilla
1/2 c. butter
2 c. flour (not sifted)
1 tsp. soda

1/2 tsp. salt
1 egg
1 c. milk
1 tsp. vinegar
1/2 c. pecan pieces
6 Heath bars (chopped)

Mix milk and vinegar together; set aside. Mix first 7 ingredients together until consistency like oatmeal. Reserve 1/2 c. Add egg and milk and vinegar mixture. Pour into a greased 9" x 13" pan. Sprinkle reserved crumbs, pecan pieces and chopped Heath bars on top. Bake at 350° for 30–35 minutes.

*Mrs. Raymond (LeEtta) Yoder*

# Maple Nut Cake

1/2 c. shortening
3/4 c. brown sugar
1/2 c. sugar
3 egg yolks (beaten)
1/2 tsp. maple flavoring
2 1/2 c. flour

1/4 tsp. salt
3 tsp. baking powder
1 c. milk
1/2 c. chopped nuts
3 egg whites (stiffly beaten)

## CARAMEL FROSTING:
2 c. brown sugar
1/2 c. margarine

1/2 c. milk
4 c. powdered sugar

Combine first 5 ingredients; mix well. Mix flour, salt, baking powder and nuts together. Add to first mixture alternately with milk. Beat thoroughly. Fold in stiffly beaten egg whites. For Caramel Frosting: Combine sugar, margarine and milk. Heat to boiling. Cook over low heat for 3 minutes. Stir in powdered sugar. Beat well. Spread on cake. Garnish with pecan halves.

*Mrs. Samuel (Norma) Yoder*

# Raspberry Cake

1 pkg. white cake mix
3 oz. raspberry gelatin
10 oz. frozen sweetened
raspberries (thawed,
undrained)

4 eggs
1/2 c. vegetable oil
1/4 c. hot water

**FROSTING:**

1 - 12 oz. carton frozen
whipped topping (thawed)

10 oz. frozen sweetened raspberries
(thawed, undrained)

In a large bowl, combine dry cake mix and dry gelatin. Add remaining ingredients. Beat until well blended. Pour into a greased 9" x 13" pan. Bake at 350° for 35–40 minutes. Cool, then frost. For Frosting: Mix together and refrigerate.

*Mrs. Marvin (Katie) Miller*

# Rebecca's Rhubarb Cake

1 1/2 c. diced rhubarb
2/3 c. sugar (or 1 cup)
2 c. flour
1/2 c. oil

2 tsp. soda
1 tsp. cinnamon
2 eggs
1 c. sour milk

Mix all ingredients well. Add rhubarb last. Pour into a greased 9" x 13" pan. Bake at 350° until toothpick inserted near center of cake comes out clean.

*Mrs. Paul (Rhoda) Yoder*

---

*A little girl was the only one to bring an umbrella to the
prayer meeting when they went to pray for rain.*

---

# Pumpkin Cake

2 c. sugar
1¼ c. oil
2 c. pumpkin
4 eggs (beaten)
2 c. flour
1 tsp. salt

2 tsp. cinnamon
2 tsp. soda
2 tsp. baking powder
½ c. black walnuts
½ c. shredded coconut

FROSTING:
¼ c. butter
8 oz. cream cheese
1 lb. powdered sugar

1 tsp. vanilla
½ c. black walnuts
½ c. shredded coconut

Preheat oven to 350°. In a large bowl mix first 4 ingredients. Mix flour, salt, cinnamon, soda and baking powder together. Add to first mixture. Add black walnuts and shredded coconut. Mix well. Spray two 9" cake pans with Pam. Bake for about 40–45 minutes or until a toothpick inserted near center comes out clean. For Frosting: Mix ingredients together. When cake is cooled, frost between layers, on top and sides. This makes a 2-layer cake.

*Mrs. David (JoAnn) Mast*

# Ugly Duckling Cake

1 pkg. yellow cake mix
1 - 16 oz. can fruit cocktail
2⅓ c. coconut
2 eggs
½ c. packed brown sugar

½ c. chopped nuts
½ c. butter
½ c. sugar
½ c. evaporated milk

Combine cake mix, fruit cocktail (undrained), 1 c. coconut and eggs; blend. Beat at medium speed for 2 minutes and pour into a greased 9" x 13" pan. Sprinkle with brown sugar and nuts. Bake at 325° for 45 minutes. Bring butter, sugar and milk to a boil and boil for 1 minute. Stir in remaining coconut. Spoon over warm cake. Top with whipped topping if desired.

*Mrs. Lester (Verna) Bontrager*

# Yellow Love Light Cake

2¹/₄ c. flour
3 tsp. baking powder
1 c. sugar
1 tsp. salt
¹/₃ c. vegetable oil

2 eggs (separated)
1 c. water
1 tsp. lemon flavoring
¹/₂ c. sugar

Sift flour, baking powder, 1 c. sugar and salt together. Make a well. Add in this order: oil, egg yolks, water and lemon flavoring; beat well. Beat egg whites and ¹/₂ c. sugar together. Mix in with other ingredients. Bake at 350° for 40–50 minutes.

*Mrs. Eli (Pollyanna) Miller*

The Lord is my Light and my Salvation; whom shall I fear? The Lord is the strength of my life: of whom shall I be afraid? Ps. 27:1

AMY

# Candies, Snacks, Jams, Jellies & Miscellaneous

*Forbidden fruits create many jams.*

AND THE FEAST OF HARVEST, THE FIRSTFRUITS OF THY
LABOURS, WHICH THOU HAST SOWN IN THE FIELD:
AND THE FEAST OF INGATHERING, WHICH IS IN THE
END OF THE YEAR, WHEN THOU HAST GATHERED
IN THY LABOURS OUT OF THE FIELD.
Exodus 23:16

# Hints for Candy Making

*T*emperature tests for candy making: There are two different methods of determining if candy has been cooked to the right consistency. One is by using a candy thermometer in order to record degrees; the other is to use the cold water test. The chart below will prove useful in helping to follow candy recipes.

| TYPE OF CANDY: | DEGREES: | COLD WATER |
|---|---|---|
| Fondant, Fudge | 234°–238° | Soft Ball |
| Divinity, Caramels | 245°–248° | Firm Ball |
| Taffy | 265°–270° | Hard Ball |
| Butterscotch | 275°–280° | Light Crack |
| Peanut Butter | 285°–290° | Hard Crack |
| Caramelized | 310°–321° | Caramelized |

When using the cold water test, use a fresh cupful of cold water for each test. When testing, remove the candy from the fire and pour about 1/2 tsp. of the candy into the cold water. Pick the candy up with fingers and roll into a ball if possible.

In the soft ball test the candy will roll into a soft ball which quickly loses its shape when removed from the water.

In the firm ball test the candy will roll into a firm but not hard ball. It will flatten out a few minutes after being removed from water.

In the hard ball test the candy will roll into a hard ball which has lost almost all plasticity and will roll around on a plate when removed from water.

In the light crack test it will form brittle threads which will soften on removal from water.

In the hard crack test the candy will form brittle threads in the water which will remain brittle after being removed from the water.

In caramelizing, the sugar first melts then becomes a golden brown. It will form a hard brittle ball in the cold water.

# Butter Toffee

2 c. slivered almonds
11 oz. milk chocolate
1 c. butter

1 c. sugar
3 Tbsp. cold water

Spread almonds in a pan and toast in oven at 350° for 10 minutes. Cool. Sprinkle 1 c. almonds over the bottom of jellyroll pan. Shave 1 c. of chocolate and sprinkle over almonds; set aside. In heavy saucepan, combine butter, sugar and water. Cook over medium heat until mixture reaches 270° (soft crack). Pour this over nuts and chocolate quickly. Scrape even with spatula. Sprinkle remaining almonds over this and the remaining chocolate. Chill, then break into pieces. *This tastes like Heath Toffee bars.* May use mini milk chocolate chips instead of melting chocolate. Melt in warm oven before putting on caramel layer.

*Charlene Yoder (Daughter)*

# Corn Flakes Candy

1 c. sugar
1 c. cream
1 c. light Karo
2 tsp. vanilla
2 c. Rice Krispies

2 c. corn flakes
2 c. salted peanuts (honey
   roasted are best)
1 c. Kix (optional)

Boil sugar, cream, Karo and vanilla to soft ball stage. Pour over cereal and peanuts in buttered bowl. Pour into a 9" x 13" pan. Cool and cut into 2" pieces.

*Mrs. Allen (Elsie) Bontrager*

# Crispy Nut Goodies

5 lb. white chocolate (melted)
3 c. almonds (crushed)
1 lb. coconut (toasted)

Rice Krispies
pecans

Melt white chocolate, then add almonds and coconut. Stir in Rice Krispies until the right consistency. Drop by spoonfuls onto wax paper and press a pecan in center.

*Mrs. Kenneth (Susan) Bontrager*

# Famous Candy Bars

| | |
|---|---|
| $1/2$ c. sugar | 6 c. corn flakes |
| $1/2$ c. brown sugar | 1 c. salted peanuts |
| 1 c. light corn syrup | 6 oz. semisweet chocolate chips |
| 1 c. peanut butter | 6 oz. milk chocolate chips |

In a saucepan mix sugars and syrup over low heat; bring to a boil. Boil for 1 minute. Add peanut butter and stir well. In a large mixing bowl, stir together corn flakes and salted peanuts. Add sugar mixture. Grease a 9" x 13" pan and firmly press mixture into pan. Melt chocolate chips and put on top. Cut into bars.

*Mrs. Marvin (Katie) Miller*

# Peanut Butter Bon Bons

| | |
|---|---|
| $1 1/2$ c. powdered sugar | $1/2$ c. peanut butter |
| 1 c. graham cracker crumbs (12 squares) | 1 - 6 oz. pkg. semisweet chocolate chips |
| $1/2$ c. butter or oleo | 1 Tbsp. oleo or shortening |

Mix first 4 ingredients and shape mixture into 1" balls. Heat chocolate chips with oleo or shortening. Dip balls into chocolate until coated. Place on waxed paper. Refrigerate until firm. *Yummy!*

*Mrs. Allen (Elsie) Bontrager*

# Peanut Butter Candy

| | |
|---|---|
| 1 c. peanut butter | 2 c. mini marshmallows |
| 2 lb. white chocolate | 3 c. Rice Krispies |
| 2 c. peanuts | |

Melt first 2 ingredients together. In a large bowl, mix peanuts, marshmallows and Rice Krispies. Pour the melted mixture over the dry ingredients. Drop by spoonfuls onto waxed paper.

*Mrs. Kenneth (Susan) Bontrager*

# Trash Candy

1 box bugles
$^1/_2$ box Honey Nut Cheerios
1 lb. M&M's (plain)

1 lb. dry roasted peanuts or cashews
1 small bag pretzels
2 lb. almond bark

Mix first 5 ingredients together in a 13 qt. mixing bowl. Melt almond bark and pour over ingredients in bowl. Toss until well coated. Spread on waxed paper. When chocolate is hard, break up into small pieces.

*Mrs. Marlin (Loretta) Bontrager*

# Cheese Ball Snack Mix

2 c. salted cashews
2 c. Planters crisp cheese
  ball snacks
3 c. Corn Chex
2 c. Rice Chex
2 c. small twist pretzels
2 c. chow mein noodles

1 c. butter or margarine (melted)
2 Tbsp. soy sauce
2 tsp. Worcestershire sauce
1 tsp. Lawry's seasoned salt
$^1/_2$ tsp. chili powder
$^1/_4$ tsp. hot pepper sauce

In a large bowl combine first 6 ingredients. In another bowl mix the remaining ingredients and pour over cereal mixture. Toss to coat. Pour onto 15" x 10" x 1" cookie sheets. Bake at 250° for 1 hour, stirring every 15 minutes. *This is a nice change from regular party mix!*

*Mrs. Freeman (Mabel) Yoder*

# Cheez Whiz

3 - 2 lb. boxes cheese
$^1/_2$ c. oleo

2 c. (or more) milk
$3^1/_4$ c. cream

Melt all together. Scald milk before adding to mixture. Makes 9 pts. and 1 c. *This is a good spread for church dinner.*

*Mrs. Ervin (Edna) Bontrager*

# Corny Snack Mix

3 qt. popped corn
1 - 15 oz. pkg. corn puffs

1 - 15 oz. pkg. corn chips
22—24 oz. white melting chocolate

In a large bowl combine first 3 ingredients. In saucepan, over medium-low heat melt white chocolate; stir until smooth. Pour over popcorn mixture and toss to coat. Spread into 2 - 15" x 10" x 1" pans. Cool. Store in airtight containers. Yield: 7$\frac{1}{2}$ quarts. *Yum!*

*LuAnn Yoder (Daughter)*

# Finger Jell-O

LAYER 1: (red)
6 oz. Jell-O (cherry or
  strawberry)

2 c. boiling water
1 pkg. Knox gelatin

LAYER 2: (white)
1 can Eagle Brand milk
2 c. boiling water

4 pkg. Knox gelatin

LAYER 3: (green)
6 oz. lime Jell-O
2 c. boiling water

1 pkg. Knox gelatin

Put in layers of red, white and green. Let one layer set before you put another layer on. Also cool off the mixture before pouring it on the next layer.

*Mrs. Harry (Edna Mae) Bontrager, Mrs. Daniel (Arlene) Beechy*

---

*Peace, perfect peace, our future all unknown;*
*Jesus we know and He is on the throne.*

---

# Jell-O Pinwheels

1 c. Jell-O
1 1/4 c. warm water

2 c. small marshmallows

Mix Jell-O, water and marshmallows. Cook for 1 1/2 minutes. Pour into a greased 9" x 13" pan. Refrigerate until set. Mix enough cream cheese and Cool Whip to spread over Jell-O. Loosen edges by using a knife dipped in warm water. Starting at one end, roll up tightly. With seam-side down, cut into 1/2" slices. Serve immediately or refrigerate in covered dish until ready to serve.

*Mrs. Nelson (Irene) Miller*

# Popcorn Balls

2 c. sugar
1 c. light corn syrup
3 Tbsp. vinegar
1/2 tsp. salt

2 Tbsp. margarine
1/2 tsp. soda
6 qt. popped corn (slightly salted)

Cook sugar, Karo, vinegar, salt and margarine in a large saucepan. Boil until soft ball stage. Remove from heat and stir in soda. Stir until almost done foaming. Pour over popped corn. Stir well. Then with buttered hands form balls and store in an airtight container.

*Mom (Rosa) Bontrager*

# Puppy Chow

1 - 12 oz. box Corn or
   Rice Chex
2/3 c. creamy peanut butter

1 - 12 oz. bag chocolate chips
1/2 c. margarine
3 c. powdered sugar

Melt chocolate chips, peanut butter and margarine in a saucepan over low heat. Stir until smooth. Pour over Corn or Rice Chex and stir until all is covered. Put the powdered sugar in a clean grocery bag and pour in the chocolate-covered Chex. Close bag and shake until all is covered. *Delicious! Tastes like candy bars.*

*Sister (Elvesta) Bontrager*

# Tasty Party Mix

1 box Cheerios
1 box Kix
1 box Chex
1 bag pretzels
1 jar peanuts
3 c. oleo

$^3/_4$ c. Worcestershire sauce
1 Tbsp. salt
1 Tbsp. seasoned salt
1 Tbsp. garlic salt
1 Tbsp. Alpine Touch
1 Tbsp. onion salt

Combine cereals, pretzels and peanuts in a large bowl. Melt oleo; add Worcestershire sauce and seasonings; pour over cereals, stirring to coat evenly. Pour on cookie sheets and toast at 250° until crunchy again.

*Mrs. James (Sara Marie) Yoder*

# Trail Mix

16 oz. milk chocolate M&M's
10 oz. peanut butter chips
3 oz. chow mein noodles

$1^1/_2$ c. chocolate-coated raisins
$1^1/_4$ c. peanuts

In a large bowl, combine all ingredients; mix well. Store in an airtight container. Yield: 8 cups.

*Mrs. Freeman (Mabel) Yoder*

# Trash Bag Treats

1 box bugles
1 box pretzel sticks
1 box Crispix
1 box fish crackers
2 cans mixed nuts
1 box Rice Chex

1 box Cheez-Its crackers
$^1/_2$ c. margarine (melted)
6 oz. popcorn oil
1 pkg. Hidden Valley Ranch
    dressing mix

Pour all snacks into trash bag. Add dressing mix and toss well. Mix margarine and oil. Add to cereals. Mix well. Shake bag 3 to 4 times, being careful not to break cereal. Store in airtight container. This takes 3 to 4 days to set up. Sizes of boxes and cans may vary. May add or omit anything to suit your taste.

*Mrs. Eli (Pollyanna) Miller, Mrs. Vernon (Nelda) Miller*

# Apple Butter

3 c. sugar
1 gal. sliced or quartered apples
  (unpeeled)

2 tsp. cinnamon, *optional*

Put sugar and apples in a large pot with lid (8–10 qt. pot is big enough). Don't remove lid! Let set overnight. The next morning turn burner on; bring to boiling and turn down so it will keep boiling. Boil for 3 hours. Put through a Victorio strainer. Add cinnamon if you wish. Put in jars and hot water bathe for 30 minutes. Very important not to turn burner too high and not take lid off at all!

*Mrs. Darrell (Rosa) Troyer*

# Apple Butter

4 qt. applesauce (unsweetened)
1 c. vinegar
7 c. brown sugar

1 Tbsp. ground cloves
2 Tbsp. cinnamon

Combine all ingredients in a large roaster. Put uncovered in oven at 350° for 3 hours, stirring every hour. If you make a double batch, cook for 5 hours. A single batch makes 5 quarts.

*Mrs. Allen (Rosemary) Bontrager*

# Easy Apple Butter

26 c. applesauce
$13^1/_2$ c. sugar
4 tsp. cinnamon
$^1/_2$ tsp. ground cloves

$^1/_2$ c. water
$^1/_2$ c. strong vinegar
pinch of salt

Mix all ingredients together well. Put in a large roaster and cook in oven at 200°–325° for $3^1/_2$ hours, stirring well every 15 minutes. Makes about 14 pints. Red hots may be added when finished to give a more red color.

*Mrs. Vernon (Nelda) Miller*

# Church Peanut Butter

5 lb. peanut butter
3 lb. marshmallow creme
3 c. boiling water

*2 c. brown sugar
2 c. Karo
1 c. margarine

Boil water, brown sugar, Karo and margarine together; add peanut butter and marshmallow creme. *Irene uses 4 more cups brown sugar and only ¹/₂ c. margarine. Spread on bread.

*Mrs. Vern (Irene) Schlabach, Mrs. Samuel (Norma) Yoder*

# Delicious Bread Spread

2 c. brown sugar
1 c. cream
1 tsp. vanilla

pinch of salt
*1 qt. Karo
3 - 13 oz. cans marshmallow creme

Cook first 4 ingredients until soft ball stage. Remove from stove and immediately add Karo. Cool, then add marshmallow creme. This makes 1 Fix 'n Mix bowl full (32 cups). *Rosa adds 2 qt. Karo.

*Mrs. Allen (Elsie) Bontrager, Mrs. Darrel (Rosa) Troyer*

# Peach Spread

4 c. peaches
1 - 20 oz. can crushed
   pineapple

7 c. sugar
2 - 3 oz. pkg. orange Jell-O

Boil peaches, pineapple and sugar together rapidly for 15 minutes. Add Jell-O. Put into jars and seal.

*Mrs. David (Mary Lou) Whetstone*

---

*One secret of patience is having something to do while you are waiting.*

# Peanut Butter Syrup

2 c. sugar
2 c. brown sugar
$^1/_2$ c. light Karo
2 c. boiling water

1 Tbsp. maple flavoring
$2^1/_2$ lb. peanut butter
1 qt. marshmallow creme

Mix first 5 ingredients together and bring to a boil. Remove from heat; cool. Add peanut butter and marshmallow creme. *This is a spread used at Amish church services.* Spread on bread. Batches may be doubled. Variations: Maple flavoring and Karo may be omitted.

*Mom (Elsie) Yoder, Mrs. Wilbur (Waneta) Nisley*

# Pineapple Zucchini Jam

2 c. crushed pineapple
1 c. grated zucchini
1 box Sure-Jell

$4^1/_2$ c. sugar
$^1/_4$ c. candied cherries (cut in small pieces), *optional*

Put pineapple, zucchini and Sure-Jell in pan; stir together, then turn on heat and bring to a boil. Boil for 1 minute. Keep stirring and add sugar with cherries. Bring to a boil and boil for 1 minute, stirring constantly. Skim off foam. Place in pint jars and seal.

*Mrs. Ervin (Edna) Bontrager*

# Zucchini Butter

4 c. peeled, cubed zucchini
2 c. sugar
$^1/_4$ c. vinegar
1 tsp. cinnamon

1 tsp. allspice
1 Tbsp. lemon juice
$^1/_2$ c. red hots

Cook zucchini with small amount of water. When soft, put through a blender or Salsa Master to make it real fine. Add sugar, vinegar, cinnamon, allspice and lemon juice to zucchini and put in kettle. Boil on low heat until thickened. Add red hots and continue to cook and stir until dissolved. Put into hot jars and seal. Tastes like apple butter.

*Mrs. Freeman (Mabel) Yoder*

# Zucchini Jam

| | |
|---|---|
| 6 c. peeled & grated zucchini | 2 Tbsp. lemon juice |
| 1 c. water | 20 oz. crushed pineapple (drained) |
| 6 c. sugar | 2 - 3 oz. pkg. apricot Jell-O |

Cook zucchini and water together over medium heat; bring to a boil. Reduce heat and cook for another 6 minutes. Add sugar, lemon juice and pineapple; bring to a boil. Cook for 6 minutes longer. Add dry Jell-O and mix well. Pour into prepared jelly jars and seal.

*Mom (Elsie) Yoder*

# Rhubarb Jelly

| | |
|---|---|
| 5 c. rhubarb (cut up fine) | 2 c. crushed pineapple |
| 5 c. sugar | 6 oz. strawberry Jell-O |

Mix first 3 ingredients together and let set overnight. The next morning cook until tender (about 20 minutes). Then mix in 6 oz. strawberry Jell-O.

*Mrs. Fred (LeEtta) Yoder*

# Strawberry Butter

| | |
|---|---|
| 8 oz. cream cheese | 1 tsp. vanilla |
| $^1/_2$ c. butter (softened) | 1 c. fresh strawberries (pureed) |
| 1 c. powdered sugar | |

In a mixing bowl, beat cream cheese and butter until smooth. Gradually add sugar and vanilla; mix well. Stir in strawberries. Cover tightly and refrigerate for several hours before using. I omit the butter as we like it better that way. Try it on pancakes, waffles, toast or use as a dip with Ritz crackers. *Very delicious!*

*Mrs. Omer (Mabel) Schwartz*

# Sandwich Spread

6 red peppers
6 green peppers
6 large cucumbers
6 green tomatoes
6 onions
10 carrots
10 sticks celery

$^1/_2$ c. salt
water
2 pt. vinegar
5 c. sugar
1 Tbsp. turmeric
1 qt. prepared mustard
1 c. flour

Grind vegetables together and add salt and a little water. Let set for 2 hours; drain and add vinegar. Cook for 20 minutes. Mix sugar, turmeric, mustard and flour together. Add to vegetables. Cook well, stirring often. Put into jars and seal.

*Mrs. Orla (Ruby) Raber*

# Syrup for Bread

4 c. brown sugar
1 c. water

5 c. light Karo syrup

Cook for 10 minutes. Cook in a large kettle. This boils over easily; medium heat is best. This is a very good spread on bread. A good honey substitute. Cook no longer than 10 minutes or it will get stiff too easily. After cooking you may add 1 tsp. vanilla or maple flavoring.

*Mrs. Freeman (Mabel) Yoder*

# Grape Wine

8 c. fresh grape juice
3 c. water
1 c. boiling water

$^3/_4$ tsp. yeast
$^1/_4$ c. warm water
4 c. sugar

Dissolve sugar in 1 c. boiling water, then add 3 c. water and grape juice. Dissolve yeast in $^1/_4$ c. warm water. Mix all together then pour into a gallon jug with a narrow neck. Put an airlock on top so juice can ferment. This can be bought from winery catalogs or specialty shops.

*Mom (Rosa) Bontrager*

# Popsicles

2 c. boiling water
1 pkg. Kool-Aid (any flavor)
1 c. sugar

1 box (8 Tbsp.) Jell-O (any flavor)
2 c. cold water

Mix boiling water and Jell-O. Add sugar and Kool-Aid. Stir in cold water. Pour into popsicle trays and freeze. *A cool treat for the whole family on a warm summer day!*

*Mrs. Orla (Ruby) Raber*

# Marshmallow Creme

2 c. sugar
2$^1/_2$ c. corn syrup
1 c. water

$^1/_2$ c. warm corn syrup
3–4 egg whites
1 tsp. vanilla

Mix first 3 ingredients and cook to 242° (med. hard ball). While this is cooking, place warm corn syrup and egg whites in an 8-qt. mixing bowl. Beat slowly until mixed, then beat hard until light and fluffy. Pour the first mixture into this, in a fine stream. When all mixed, beat again with beater (beat hard) for 3 minutes. Add vanilla. Store.

*Mrs. John (Christina) Yoder*

# To Clean Stainless Steel

1 c. bleach
1 c. powdered Tide or
   liquid soap

$^1/_2$ c. lye
2–3 gal. hot water

Fill the plastic tub with 2 batches of this recipe. Take all handles and knobs off kettles. Soak for 10–20 minutes. Then wash in hot soapy water and it will shine. May also use it on glass, silverware, plastic, Melmac and granite. Do not use it on aluminum pots and pans. Use rubber gloves in the cleaner water.

*Mrs. Allen (Elsie) Bontrager, Mrs. Levi (Elsie) Lambright*

# Houseplant Food

1 gal. water
1 tsp. baking powder
1 tsp. epsom salt

1 tsp. saltpeter
$^1/_2$ tsp. clear ammonia (household)

Mix all ingredients together and use it to water your houseplants.

*Mrs. Dean (Rebecca) Troyer*

# Homemade Spray-N-Wash

Wisk
ammonia

water

Mix equal parts of Wisk, ammonia and water. Put in spray bottle and spray on soiled clothes. Soak in warm water then wash as usual. *I have been using this for quite a few years and it works great! I like it especially in the summertime when the clothes get extra dirty.*

*Mrs. David (Rachel) Plank*

# Homemade Pedialyte

4 tsp. sugar
$^1/_2$ tsp. soda
$^1/_2$ tsp. salt

$^1/_4$ tsp. salt substitute
3 c. hot water

Mix well and chill or cool it enough to put into a baby bottle. Jell-O may be added for flavor and to thicken it if you'd rather feed it as Jell-O dessert. Give this to children with diarrhea or for vomiting to prevent dehydration.

*Mrs. Paul (Rhoda) Yoder*

---

*Grace humbles a man without degrading him,
and exalts him without inflating him.*

---

# Homemade Noodles

2 c. egg yolks
1½ c. boiling water

1 Tbsp. oil
9 c. flour (scant)

Beat egg yolks with egg beater, then add boiling water and oil. Stir in flour (all at once), and mix with hands. This takes very little kneading. Cut into chunks and flour cut ends. Put through Noodle Chef and flour each slab and put through Noodle Chef again. *A very easy and never-fail recipe.* Variations: Waneta does not use oil and uses 4 lb. flour.

*Mom (Elsie) Yoder, Mrs. Wilbur (Waneta) Nisley*

# Brine to Cure Ham or Bacon

1 gal. water
1 pt. Tender Quick
1 c. brown sugar

1 Tbsp. (heaping) black pepper
2 tsp. soda
1 Tbsp. liquid smoke

Bring all ingredients to a boil and pour over meat. Let soak in brine for approximately 1 week for bacon and 2 weeks for ham.

*Mrs. Samuel (Wilma) Miller*

# Turkey Brine

1 c. Tender Quick
1½ c. *sugar cure

1½ gal. water
¼ c. liquid smoke

Mix together well. Let turkey soak in this for 2–3 days in cool place. Make enough to cover turkey. Turn twice a day. This makes the turkey very tender and tasty. *You may use store-bought sugar cure or make your own.

**SUGAR CURE:**
1 c. salt
1 Tbsp. red pepper

1 Tbsp. brown sugar
2 Tbsp. black pepper

*Mrs. Gerald (Darla) Yoder*

# Edible Play Dough

1 c. crunchy peanut butter
$^1/_2$ c. honey

2 c. powdered sugar
$^1/_2$–1 c. Rice Krispies or raisins

Blend first 2 ingredients well, then add remaining ingredients. Serve with rolling pins and cookie cutters. *Eat freely. Children love it!*

*LuAnn Yoder (Daughter)*

# Fruity Play Dough

$2^1/_2$ c. flour
$^1/_2$ c. salt
1 Tbsp. alum
2 small pkg. Kool-Aid (any flavor)

2 Tbsp. oil
2 c. boiling water

Combine dry ingredients. Add oil and water. Stir with a spoon until mixture is cool enough to knead. Knead in a little more flour if it's sticky. Store in airtight container. *Smells great!*

*Mrs. David (Rachel) Plank*

# Play Dough

1 c. flour
1 c. water
2 Tbsp. vegetable oil

$^1/_2$ c. salt
2 Tbsp. cream of tartar
food coloring

Mix first 5 ingredients and bake for 5–10 minutes at 350°. Divide into 4 balls and color with food coloring. *Easy and long lasting!*

*Mrs. Lonnie (Norma) Bontrager, Mrs. Jonathan (Lou Ida) Miller*

---

*Troubles, like babies, grow larger by nursing them.*

# Notes

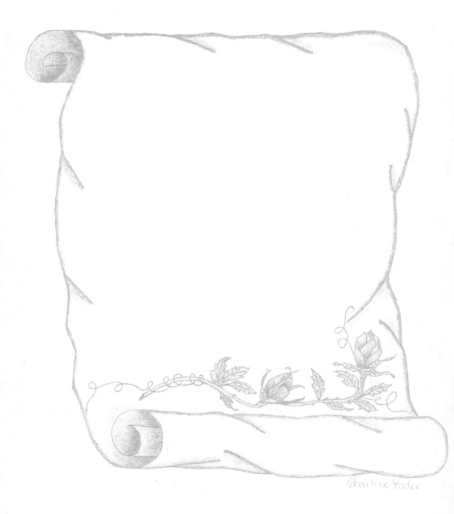

# Canning & Freezing

*Prayer is the key to heaven,*
*but faith unlocks the door.*

*Kind words can be short*
*and easy to speak,*
*but their echos are*
*truly endless.*

PRAISE YE THE LORD. PRAISE THE LORD, O MY SOUL.
WHILE I LIVE WILL I PRAISE THE LORD: I WILL SING
PRAISES UNTO MY GOD WHILE I HAVE ANY BEING.
PSALM 146:1–2

# Ma's Bowl of Sunshine

When I was just a growin' lad,
    Oh, what an appetite I had!
To smell the things my ma was cookin'—
    The biscuits buttered steamin' hot,
The soup abubblin' in the pot,
    The crullers sprinkled with a lot
O' sugar, brown an' temptin' lookin';
    To see Ma spread the cloth so white
An' gently smooth it out just right
    Was such an appetizin' sight
To wait we weren't hardly able;
    But 'fore we'd get a bite or sup
An' fore she'd lay a plate or cup
    She'd have to go an' gather up
A bowl o' sunshine for the table.
    Some pansies from the middle bed,
Nasturtium yellow, flecked with red,
    Or golden glow with heavy head,—
Just flowers, —an' yet it seemed so funny,
    Black clouds might come to spoil your view,
You might be feelin' mad clean thru',
    But when them blossoms smiled at you
The whole wide world grew fair and sunny.
    There ain't a silken shaded light
In any cabaret tonight
    Can lure a failin' appetite
Like my ma's golden flowers;
    They seemed to lay your meanness bare,
An' like that sundial over there
    They spread their message everywhere,—
Let's only count the sunny hours!—
    *Submitted by Mrs. Ervin (Anna Mary) Miller*

# Chunky Beef Soup to Can

2¹/₂ gal. water
³/₄ c. beef base
2 large cans beef broth
¹/₂ c. butter
4 qt. tomato juice
1³/₄ c. sugar
¹/₄ c. salt
4 qt. carrots
2 qt. green beans
3 qt. peas
4 qt. potatoes
2 large onions
2 qt. flour (scant) or 2 c. Perma-Flo
  or clear jel
8 lb. hamburger
salt & pepper to taste

Brown hamburger in frying pan with onions and season with salt and pepper; set aside. Heat water, beef base, beef broth, butter, tomato juice, sugar and salt to boiling. Dice vegetables then add to soup mixture. Take flour or Perma-Flo and add enough cold water to make a smooth paste to thicken soup. Now add hamburger to soup. Fill quart or pint jars and pressure can for 1 hour at 10 lb. pressure. Use less flour or Perma-Flo for a thinner soup.

*Mrs. Gerald (Darla) Yoder, Mrs. Joe (Karen) Graber*

# Homemade Salami

5 lb. hamburger
5 tsp. salt
2¹/₂ tsp. coarse pepper
2¹/₂ tsp. garlic salt
2¹/₂ tsp. whole mustard seed
2¹/₂ tsp. liquid smoke

Mix all ingredients together in bowl. Cover and refrigerate. Knead well for 5 minutes, once a day for 3 days. On the 4th day, divide into 6 or 7 rolls. Lay on broiler rack and bake in oven for 9 hours at 160°–200°, turning after 4¹/₂ hours. Remove and put on paper towels to remove grease. Roll in plastic wrap and refrigerate or freeze. Keeps in refrigerator for 3–4 weeks. Note: Hamburger should not be lean.

*Mrs. David (JoAnn) Mast*

*The best gift you can give to others is being a good example.*

# Beef Chunks

20 lb. beef (cut into 1" cubes)
11 oz. Tender Quick
2 tsp. soda
1 c. brown sugar
1 qt. water

Boil water, brown sugar, soda and Tender Quick until all is dissolved. Cool. Then pour over stew chunks and add enough water to cover. Stir and let set 1–2 weeks. When ready to can chunks, drain and wash chunks in fresh water. Put in quart jars and pressure can at 10 lb. for 1 1/2 hours.

*Mom (Rosa) Bontrager*

# Barbecue Beef for Canning

2 c. raw hamburger
2 c. beef bones (cook &
   pick off meat & grind)
1/2 c. chopped onions
1/2 c. chopped celery
1 Tbsp. prepared mustard
2 Tbsp. brown sugar
2 Tbsp. Worcestershire sauce
3/4 c. ketchup
1 tsp. salt
1/2 tsp. pepper

Fry meat with onions and celery until browned. Remove from stove and add remaining ingredients; mix well. Barbecue sauce may be added to suit taste. Add beef broth to mixture until it is the consistency to spread on buns. Fill glass jars only to 2" from the top. Process in hot water bath for 1 1/2 hours. Heat when ready to serve.

*Mrs. Samuel (Norma) Yoder, Mrs. Vernon (Nelda) Miller*

# Beef Bologna

50 lb. ground hamburger
1 c. brown sugar
1 Tbsp. black pepper
1 Tbsp. garlic salt
3 Tbsp. liquid smoke
2 c. Tender Quick
4 1/2 c. flour
1 gal. water

Mix all ingredients together and put in glass jars. Makes approx. 30 quarts. Cold pack for 2 hours.

*Mrs. Toby (Vera) Yoder*

# Chicken Bologna

35 lb. chicken
1 lb. Tender Quick
2 Tbsp. black pepper

1 c. sugar
2 tsp. garlic powder
3 Tbsp. liquid smoke

Grind chicken and Tender Quick together. Grind twice. Then add remaining ingredients and mix well; grind again. Put in jars and let set for 24 hours. Then process 1 hour at 10 lb. pressure. Or put in cloth bags 3¹/₂" in diameter and desired length. Set in hot water (170°–175°) for 3 hours. Less for smaller bags. Wrap and freeze.

*Mrs. Mervin (Emma) Yoder*

# Venison Bologna

50 lb. ground beef or venison
15 lb. ground pork
1¹/₂ lb. Tender Quick
3 Tbsp. black pepper
1 Tbsp. saltpeter
1 Tbsp. garlic powder
3 qt. water
2¹/₂ lb. white soda crackers
  (crushed)

2 c. brown sugar
2 Tbsp. liquid smoke
3 Tbsp. sweet basil
2 Tbsp. ground coriander seed,
  *optional*
2 Tbsp. table salt, *optional*

Soak crackers with the water. Then mix with meat and seasonings. Let set for 24 hours. Put in jars and pressure can for 1¹/₂ hours at 10 lb. pressure. I like to add 10 lb. extra pork.

*Mrs. Freeman (Mabel) Yoder*

---

*God didn't comfort us to make us comfortable*
*but to make us comforters.*

---

# Jerky

| | |
|---|---|
| 7 lb. meat | 4 Tbsp. seasoned pepper or |
| 3 c. water | Hickory Burger seasoning |
| 2 Tbsp. garlic salt | 14 Tbsp. liquid smoke |
| 3 Tbsp. garlic powder | 12 Tbsp. Worcestershire sauce |
| 5 Tbsp. salt | 3 c. soy sauce |
| 3 Tbsp. onion powder | 3 Tbsp. black pepper |

Cut meat into ¹/₈" and ¹/₄" strips. Marinate in refrigerator overnight (2 nights for hot and spicy). Put in oven at 150°–170° for about 6 hours. Put tinfoil on oven racks and lay meat on foil, then put the liquid mixture in cake pan and put it beneath the rack and let simmer as meat drys. This keeps it from getting so hard.

*Mrs. Chris (Esther) Bontrager*

# Meat Loaf to Can

| | |
|---|---|
| 15 lb. ground beef | ³/₄ c. salt |
| 4 slices bread | 1 pkg. crackers |
| 3 c. oatmeal | 4 eggs |
| onion (cut up), *optional* | |

Mix well, then pack into jars, being careful not to get them too full. Cold pack for 2 hours. Makes 10–12 quarts.

*Mrs. Levi (Elsie) Lambright*

---

*DELIVERANCE—We are like a postage stamp . . . we may get licked, depressed, stuck in a corner, and sent from post to post, but we will always succeed and arrive at the right place if only we stick to it.*

---

# Red Beets to Can

red beets
*4 c. sugar
1¹/₂–2 c. vinegar
1¹/₂–2 c. hot water

1 c. water (which beets were cooked in for more color)
1 Tbsp. salt

Boil beets; pour off hot water and slip off skins. To pressure boil: Boil
them at 10 lb. pressure for 15 minutes. Cut into bite-size chunks and
put in jars. Mix remaining ingredients together. Stir well to dissolve
sugar. Pour over beets and water bathe for 10 minutes. *Erma uses one
cup less sugar and all brown.

*Mrs. Calvin (Erma) Schmucker, Mrs. James (Sara Marie) Yoder*

# To Freeze Corn

8 c. corn (cut off cobs)
¹/₂ c. butter
1 Tbsp. salt

1 c. water
1 Tbsp. sugar

Cook all together; boil for 5 minutes. Cool; put in containers and freeze.

*Mrs. James (Sara Marie) Yoder*

# Pork 'n Beans to Can

8 lb. navy beans
¹/₃ c. salt
¹/₂ tsp. pepper
1 tsp. ground cinnamon
1 large onion (chopped)
3 c. sugar

4 qt. tomato juice
4 c. brown sugar
1 tsp. prepared mustard
32 oz. ketchup
4 lb. wieners
4 Tbsp. cornstarch or Perma-Flo

Soak navy beans in water overnight; drain. Cover with fresh water in
large kettle and cook until soft. Preheat wieners in separate kettle, cool
and slice desired amount into the bottom of jars. Combine everything
else in a kettle over medium heat; bring to a boil. Mix cornstarch or
Perma-Flo with a small amount of cold water. Add to boiling mixture
and boil until thickened. Drain water from beans; add sauce and ladle
into jars. Pressure can 10 lb. for 30–40 minutes. Browned hamburger
may be used instead of wieners. Yield: 16 qt.

*Mrs. Freeman (Mabel) Yoder*

# Pork 'n Beans to Can

2 c. navy beans (uncooked)
1 c. brown sugar
2 Tbsp. prepared mustard
4 tsp. garlic salt

$^1/_2$ lb. bacon or wieners
2 Tbsp. hickory smoke
salt to taste

Soak beans overnight, put in bowl and cover with water. Next morning, cook beans until soft. Add sugar, mustard, garlic salt, bacon or wieners, hickory smoke and salt. Mix all together, put in jars and pressure cook for 20 minutes at 10 lb. pressure. When you open it to serve, add a little cream.

*Mrs. Samuel (Wilma) Miller, Mrs. Orva (Marietta) Yoder*

# Pizza Sauce

3 gal. tomato juice
2 Tbsp. parsley
3 onions & green peppers
1 c. sugar
$^1/_2$ c. salt

1 Tbsp. paprika & chili powder
1 tsp. red pepper
2 Tbsp. garlic
2 Tbsp. oregano

Thicken with clear jel; boil well. Cold pack for 10 minutes.

*Mrs. Menno (Ruby) Mullet*

# Pizza Sauce

$^1/_2$ bu. tomatoes
2–3 garlic buds
3 lb. onions
4 bell peppers
8 - 12 oz. cans tomato paste

1 Tbsp. sweet basil
1 Tbsp. oregano
$1^3/_4$ c. sugar
$^1/_2$ c. salt (scant)

Cook tomatoes and garlic together until soft, then strain. Chop onions and peppers, then cook in vegetable oil until soft. Put all ingredients together and cook for 15 minutes. Put in jars and seal. Makes 32 pints.

*Mrs. Lester (Verna) Bontrager*

# Homemade Ketchup

2 gal. tomato juice
2 c. vinegar
8 Tbsp. salt (scant)
$1/4$ tsp. cinnamon oil
$1/4$ tsp. clove oil

4 onions (chopped)
8 c. sugar
8 Tbsp. Perma-Flo
cold water

Mix first 6 ingredients together and boil down $1/3$. Skim off onions. Then put in sugar and bring to boil again. Make a paste of Perma-Flo and cold water; stir in until it boils again. Use more Perma-Flo if you want thicker ketchup. Bottle and seal.

*Mrs. Orla (Ruby) Raber*

# Salsa

14 lb. tomatoes
$2^1/2$ lb. onions
10 green peppers
6 jalapeño peppers
1 c. vinegar
$1/3$ c. sugar

$1/4$ c. salt
$1^1/2$ tsp. cumin
3 cloves garlic
2 Tbsp. chili powder
2 tsp. oregano

Cut tomatoes in bite-sized pieces; heat through and add other vegetables (cut up) and spices. Cook for 45 minutes, thicken with 1 c. clear jel (mixed with 1 c. water). Process 20 minutes at 10 lb. pressure. Makes 20–21 pints.

*Mrs. Daryl (Marsha) Miller*

---

*Children are like sponges. They absorb all your strength and leave you limp. But give them a squeeze and you get it all back.*

---

# Seasoning for Tomato Juice

| | |
|---|---|
| 1/2 c. celery salt | 3 Tbsp. sugar |
| 1/2 c. onion salt | 2 Tbsp. pepper |
| 2 Tbsp. garlic salt | 1 c. table salt |

Mix all together and add 1 level tsp. to each qt. of tomato juice when canning. May also be used for vegetable soup.

*Mrs. Levi (Elsie) Lambright*

# Variety Sauce

| | |
|---|---|
| 1 gal. tomato juice | 1 tsp. cinnamon |
| 2 Tbsp. salt | 1 tsp. dry mustard |
| 3 c. sugar | 1/4 tsp. red pepper |
| 3 large onions (finely diced) | 6 Tbsp. cornstarch |
| 1 1/2 c. vinegar | |

Cook first 8 ingredients for 1 hour then add cornstarch mixed with water. Cook for 10 minutes longer. Put into jars and seal. May use Therma-Flo instead of cornstarch. May use this as spaghetti sauce or ketchup. I use it mostly as ketchup.

*Mrs. Marvin (Katie) Miller*

# V-8 Juice

| | |
|---|---|
| 1 peck ripe tomatoes | 2 Tbsp. salt |
| 3 large green peppers | 1 1/2 c. sugar |
| 1 small stalk celery | 2 Tbsp. celery seed |
| 2 large onions | 1 Tbsp. parsley flakes |
| 3 garlic buds | |

Cook tomatoes, peppers, celery, onions and garlic buds until soft; put through strainer. Add salt, sugar, celery seed and parsley flakes. Heat again and pour into jars and seal. Excellent to drink when chilled. Parsley flakes and celery seed may be put in a cloth bag.

*Mrs. Leland (Orpha) Yoder*

# Million Dollar Pickles

4 qt. sliced cucumbers
8–10 small onions
$1/2$ c. salt
2 c. vinegar
4 c. sugar

$1/2$ tsp. celery seed
1 tsp. turmeric
2 tsp. mustard seed
1 tsp. mixed pickling spice

Slice cucumbers and onions. Place in large bowl. Sprinkle salt on top and cover with water; let set overnight. The next morning, drain. Combine vinegar, sugar and spices in large kettle; bring to a boil. Put in jars and cold pack for 15 minutes.

*Mrs. Levi (Carolyn) Schrock*

# Bread & Butter Pickles

6 qt. sliced cucumbers
6 sliced onions

$1/2$ c. salt

Mix these ingredients together and cover with water. Allow to set for 3 hours; drain. Boil the following ingredients together.

4 c. vinegar
2 c. water
6 c. sugar

$1/2$ c. mustard seed
1 Tbsp. celery seed
$1^{1}/2$ Tbsp. turmeric

Add cucumbers and onions. Heat, but do not boil. Can while hot.

*Mrs. Wilmer (Marilyn) Schmucker*

# Mixed Pickles

3 qt. cauliflower
3 qt. carrots
3 qt. very small cucumbers
4 c. water

4 c. vinegar
6 c. sugar
2 Tbsp. celery seed
3 Tbsp. turmeric

Boil cauliflower and carrots until tender. Do not cook cucumbers. Put all vegetables together. Heat water, vinegar, sugar, celery seed and turmeric together. Pour over vegetable mixture. Put in jars and hot water bathe for 5 minutes. Variation: Other vegetables like lima beans, corn, onions and celery may be used.

*Mom (Elsie) Yoder*

# Mixed Pickles

celery
carrots
cauliflower
broccoli
onions

corn
beans
cucumbers
peppers

Boil all vegetables until tender except cucumbers and peppers. Put all vegetables in a large bowl. Mix the following ingredients together in a kettle.

5 c. sugar
3 c. water
2 tsp. turmeric

2 c. vinegar
$^1/_2$ tsp. celery seed
4 Tbsp. pickling spice

Bring to boil then thicken a bit with cornstarch. Pour over vegetables. Put in jars and hot water bathe for 15 minutes. Yield: Approx. 4 qt.

*Mrs. Ivan (Inez) Yoder*

# Red Hot Pickles

2 gal. large cucumbers
   (peeled & sliced lengthwise)
8 qt. water
2 c. pickling lime
1 c. vinegar
3 Tbsp. red food coloring
1 Tbsp. alum
3 c. water

1 Tbsp. salt
3 c. vinegar
10 c. sugar
8 sticks cinnamon
$1^1/_4$ c. red hots
1 c. sugar
$^1/_2$ c. vinegar

Peel and slice cucumbers lengthwise. Remove seeds and cut into bite-sized pieces. Soak 24 hours in 8 qt. water and pickling lime. Drain and rinse well. Soak in cold water for 3 hours. Drain and simmer in 1 c. vinegar, red food coloring, alum and enough water to cover cucumbers for 2 hours of simmering. Drain. Mix 3 c. water, salt, 3 c. vinegar, 10 c. sugar, cinnamon and red hots. Bring to a boil and pour over cucumbers. Drain and reheat every 24 hours for 3 days. Add 1 c. sugar and $^1/_2$ c. vinegar if your syrup gets low. On the fourth day, pack pickles in prepared jars. Reheat syrup, pour over pickles. Now cold pack (using warm water) for 5 minutes. *We call these candy pickles; they are so good!*

*Mrs. Glen (Ruby) Yoder, Mrs. Calvin (Martha Sue) Lehman*

# Refrigerator Pickles

1 c. vinegar
1 Tbsp. salt
2 c. white sugar

1 c. sliced onions
6 c. sliced cucumbers

Mix vinegar, salt and sugar together. Heat, cool, and pour over onions and cucumbers. These will keep up to 2 months in the refrigerator.

*Mrs. Joseph (Barbara) Bontreger*

# The Best Dill Pickles

In a quart jar put $1/2$ tsp. alum and 1 head fresh dill or 1 heaping tsp. dill weed. Add sliced cucumbers to fill jar. Boil 1 qt. vinegar, 3 qt. water and $1/2$ c. canning salt. Pour over cucumbers. Seal. In about 3 months you'll have the best dill pickles ever. *I sell them at craft shows. This recipe always produces crisp, delicious pickles.*

*Mrs. Noah (Verena) Schwartz*

# Apple Pie Filling

7 c. sugar
2 c. clear jel
3 tsp. salt

6 tsp. cinnamon
4 Tbsp. lemon juice or ReaLemon
vanilla, *optional*

Heat 7 qt. water in an 8-qt. pot. Mix all above ingredients together and add water to moisten. Stir into boiling water. Cook until it bubbles then pour over the following.

4 ice cream pails peeled, diced apples (16–18 qt.)

Put in jars and process 20 minutes in hot water bath. Yield: Approx. 18 qt.

*Mrs. David (Arlene) Chupp, Mrs. Calvin (Erma) Schmucker*

# Fruit Cocktail to Can

| | |
|---|---|
| 3 gal. Baby Gold peaches | $^1/_2$ gal. red seedless grapes |
| 2 gal. pears | 1 gal. pineapple chunks |
| 1 gal. green seedless grapes | orange juice |

Wash and peel peaches. Dice to bite-sized pieces. Wash grapes. Place peaches and grapes in a 13-qt. mixing bowl. Add pineapple. Wash and peel pears last to avoid discoloration. Dice to bite-sized pieces and add to rest of ingredients. Mix gently. Put in jars. Fill jars with orange juice instead of sweet syrup. Process in water bath for 15 minutes. If you prefer firmer peaches use less time or just to boiling point. Then let set for approximately 10 minutes before removing from water (other varieties of peaches may also be used such as Loring, but do not process longer than a few minutes).

*Mrs. David (Mary Lou) Whetstone*

# Canning Strawberries

| | |
|---|---|
| 4 pt. strawberries (whole or slightly mashed) | 1 tsp. cornstarch |
| | 1 tsp. sugar |
| 1 c. sugar | water |
| 1 Tbsp. vinegar | |

Put first 3 ingredients in a kettle and bring to a boil. Thicken with a thin paste made of cornstarch, sugar and a little water. Let boil 5–10 minutes. Can open kettle.

*Mrs. Ivan (Inez) Yoder*

---

*Don't lament because your neighbor's garden surpasses yours. Keep hoeing.*

# Rhubarb Tapioca

8 c. water
1/2 tsp. salt
1 c. baby pearl or
   granulated tapioca

4 c. (or more) rhubarb (cut up)
1 c. water
3.4 oz. strawberry Jell-O
2 1/2 c. sugar

Cook 8 c. water, salt and tapioca over medium heat until tapioca is dissolved; set aside. Boil rhubarb and 1 c. water together slowly for 20 minutes; drain slightly. Add Jell-O and sugar. Mix all ingredients together and stir well. Put in jars and seal. No need to water bathe. Variation: May add several Tbsp. lemon Jell-O instead of all strawberry. *A real treat in wintertime to add whipped cream to a quart of rhubarb!*
    *Mrs. Willis (Mary) Bontrager, Mrs. Vern (Irene) Schlabach*

# How to Can Rhubarb

3 qt. rhubarb
2 qt. water
2 c. pineapple tidbits
1 tsp. lemon flavor

5 c. sugar
6 Tbsp. strawberry Jell-O
1 c. tapioca or 1 1/2 c. clear jel
   (mixed with a little cold water)

Cook rhubarb, water and pineapple until rhubarb is soft. Stir in tapioca or clear jel. When that is cooked, add lemon flavor, sugar and Jell-O; let cook for 3 minutes. Then can, open kettle. Let water boil about 15–20 minutes.

    *Mrs. Levi (Elsie) Lambright*

# Canning Rhubarb

6 qt. boiling water
7 Tbsp. minute tapioca,
   *optional*
4 1/2 c. Perma-Flo

6 c. sugar
7 Tbsp. cherry Jell-O
10 qt. rhubarb (cut up)
1–2 Tbsp. cinnamon, *optional*

Stir tapioca (if using) into boiling water. Next thicken with Perma-Flo. Stir in sugar and Jell-O. Pour thickened mixture over rhubarb. Put into jars and hot water bathe for 15–20 minutes. The cinnamon adds a good flavor.
    *Mrs. Ivan (Inez) Yoder*

# To Freeze Rhubarb for Pies

Wash and cut up **rhubarb** in small pieces and let dry. Put 2 c. rhubarb in one baggie and freeze. That is enough for 1 pie. *Very good in wintertime!*

*Mrs. Dean (Rebecca) Troyer*

# Frozen Peaches

**17–20 lb. fresh peaches**
**7 c. sugar**

**12 oz. frozen orange juice concentrate**

Slice peaches. Stir sugar and orange juice together; pour over sliced peaches and mix well. Put in freezer containers and freeze.

*Mrs. Lavern (Martha) Yoder, Mrs. Chris (Esther) Bontrager*

# Grape Juice to Can

**3 c. Concord grapes**

**1$^{1}/_{4}$ c. sugar**

Put grapes in quart jar. Put sugar into a 2-c. measuring cup and fill with very hot water to dissolve sugar. Pour over grapes. Process 10 minutes in boiling water bath. When ready to serve, drain off juice and discard grapes. Add water to make 2 quarts juice. Let set 2 weeks after canning before drinking. *Enjoy!*

*Mrs. Dean (Rebecca) Troyer*

---

*We worship a God who is greater than any of our problems,*
*and He is still on the throne in 2002.*

---

# Cookies &
# Bars

*Contentment in life consists not in great wealth, but in simple wants.*

FOR I HAVE LEARNED IN WHATSOEVER STATE I AM,
THEREWITH TO BE CONTENT. PHILIPPIANS 4:11B

HE GIVES FOOD TO ALL FLESH FOR HIS STEADFAST
LOVE ENDURES FOREVER.
PSALM 136:25

# Cookie Hints

- When using brown sugar in a recipe, always press the brown sugar firmly into the measuring cup.
- Grease the cookie sheet once—before you begin to bake—no need to grease for the rest of the batch of dough.
- Baked cookies freeze well and can be stored for several months. Pack as airtight as possible. When ready to use, thaw in refrigerator and warm in oven for a few minutes. They will taste fresh-baked.
- After melting chocolate over hot water or in microwave, cool before adding to batter.
- Heavy, shiny cookie sheets are best for baking. When using lightweight sheets, reduce oven temperature slightly.
- When sprinkling sugar on cookies, put sugar in shaker first. Dry Jell-O may be added to sugar for variation.
- Before rolling, chill cookie dough in refrigerator for 30–60 minutes. Less dusting flour or powdered sugar will be needed. Too much flour rolled into cookies can cause them to be tough.
- To cream butter or margarine, allow to reach room temperature. While this requires planning ahead, melting the shortening would make the batter too liquidy.
- When baking cookies, use center shelf of oven only. Sheets on two levels will cause uneven distribution of heat.
- Place a piece of fresh baked bread in the cookie jar to keep the cookies soft and chewy.
- Many cookie recipes call for too much sugar. You can cut down on the sugar as much as half, particularly if you are using raisins, dates, chocolate chips, etc.
- When making filled cookies, use a melon ball cutter. Scoop out dough and you have a round ball.
- Cut bar cookies or rolled cookies with a pizza cutter.
- Use the doughnut cutter for rolled cookies for the children. Hole in the center is great for little ones to hold.
- When rolling out sugar cookies, use powdered sugar instead of flour.
- If you put marshmallows in the refrigerator the night before you use them, they won't stick to the shears.
- To powder sugar: When you run out of powdered sugar, blend 1 c. granulated sugar and 1 Tbsp. cornstarch in blender at medium speed for 2 minutes.
- Add 2 eggs and $1/2$ c. cooking oil to any flavor cake mix and you have a quick batch of cookies. Raisins, nuts or coconut may be added, if desired. Drop by teaspoonfuls onto slightly-greased cookie sheets. Bake at 350° for 8–10 minutes.
- Cookies that are too crisp may have too much sugar in the dough.
- Cookies that are too soft usually have too much liquid in proportion to the flour.

# Butterscotch Delights

2$^1$/$_2$ c. sugar
2$^1$/$_2$ c. brown sugar
1 c. pre-creamed shortening
1 c. butter (softened)
5 eggs
2 Tbsp. vanilla
$^1$/$_4$ c. milk

5 c. quick oats
3 tsp. soda
2$^1$/$_2$ tsp. baking powder
2 tsp. salt
5 c. flour
powdered sugar

Mix sugars, shortening, butter, eggs and vanilla. Beat until fluffy. Then mix in milk and quick oats. Add soda, baking powder, salt and flour; mix well. Shape into balls. Roll in powdered sugar and press down slightly on greased cookie sheets. Bake at 375° until lightly golden. *Delicious!*

*Sister (Elvesta) Bontrager*

# Cake Mix Cookies

1 cake mix (any flavor)
1 egg
2 c. Cool Whip

1 Tbsp. flour (a little rounded)
powdered sugar

Mix first 4 ingredients together and roll in powdered sugar. Bake at 350° for 10–15 minutes. Takes 3 batches to fill a Fix 'n Mix bowl.

*Mrs. Toby (Vera) Yoder, Mrs. Darrell (Erma) Yoder*

# Chewy Sorghum Cookies

5 c. sugar
4 eggs
3 c. Crisco or margarine
8 tsp. soda (dissolved in 1 c. buttermilk or sour milk)

1 c. sorghum
4 tsp. cinnamon
2 tsp. baking powder
1 tsp. salt
12 c. flour

Mix in order given. This makes a stiff dough. Roll in small balls and dip in sugar. Do not press. Bake at 350° until done. Do not overbake!

*Mrs. Harley (Martha) Raber*

# Chocolate Banana Cookies

1 c. sugar
2 eggs
1 c. mashed bananas
2¹/₂ c. flour
2 tsp. salt

²/₃ c. shortening
1 tsp. vanilla
1 tsp. soda
2 tsp. cocoa

FROSTING:
2 Tbsp. butter (softened)
3 Tbsp. warm water

1 Tbsp. cocoa
2 c. powdered sugar

Beat sugar and shortening until light and fluffy. Add eggs and vanilla; beat well. Add bananas. Sift dry ingredients and add to mixture. Drop by teaspoonfuls onto cookie sheet 2" apart. Bake at 350° for about 10 minutes. Cool and frost. Yield: 4–5 dozen.

*Mrs. Wayne (Marilyn) Yoder*

# Chocolate Chip Cookies

6 eggs
2 c. butter-flavored Crisco
1 c. sugar
2 c. brown sugar
1 Tbsp. vanilla

4 tsp. cream of tartar
4 tsp. soda
1 tsp. salt
7 c. flour
1 lb. chocolate chips

Cream Crisco and sugars together. Add eggs and vanilla. Mix dry ingredients and add to rest of mixture. Mix well and add chocolate chips. Bake at 350° until a little golden brown. Do not overbake!

*Mrs. Orla (Ruby) Raber, Mrs. Daryl (Marsha) Miller*

---

*Forgiveness is the fragrance that the violet sheds
on the heel that crushes it.*

---

# Chocolate Chip Cookies

| | |
|---|---|
| 2 c. butter | 5 c. oatmeal (grind or put through |
| 2 c. sugar | blender) |
| 2 c. brown sugar | 1 tsp. salt |
| 4 eggs | 2 tsp. soda |
| 2 tsp. vanilla | 2 tsp. baking powder |
| 4 c. flour | chocolate chips as desired |

Blend butter and sugars thoroughly. Add eggs, one at a time, and beat well. Add other ingredients. Dough may be chilled. *A good cookie!* Lou Ida uses 1 c. more oatmeal, 1 c. less flour and all brown sugar. She shapes the dough into balls and rolls them in powdered sugar before baking.

*Mrs. David (Arlene) Chupp, Mrs. Jonathan (Lou Ida) Miller*

# Chocolate Chip Jumbo Cookies

| | |
|---|---|
| 2 c. brown sugar | 1 tsp. salt |
| 2 c. sugar | 2 c. oatmeal |
| 2 c. butter (melted) | 2 c. corn flakes (slightly crushed) |
| 4 eggs | 12 oz. chocolate or butterscotch |
| 2 tsp. vanilla | chips |
| 4 c. flour | 1 c. walnuts or peanuts (chopped) |
| 2 tsp. soda | 1 c. raisins or dates, *optional* |
| 2 tsp. baking powder | 1 c. macaroon coconut |

Blend first 5 ingredients in a large bowl. Sift flour, soda, baking powder and salt together, then add to first mixture; mix well. Add remaining ingredients, mixing well after each addition. Drop with ice cream scoop onto greased cookie sheet. Do not put more than 6 on a cookie sheet. Bake at 350° for approximately 13 minutes.

*Mrs. David (JoAnn) Mast*

*We can't reach new horizons if we're afraid to leave the shore.*

# Chocolate Chip Treasure Cookies

1½ c. graham cracker crumbs
½ c. flour
2 tsp. baking powder
14 oz. Eagle Brand milk
½ c. butter (softened)

1½ c. coconut
2 c. chocolate chips
1 c. walnuts
¼ tsp. salt

In a small bowl, mix graham crackers, flour and baking powder. In a large bowl, beat Eagle Brand milk and butter until smooth. Add graham cracker mixture and mix well. Stir in salt, coconut, chocolate chips and walnuts. Bake at 375° for 9–10 minutes.

*Mrs. Joseph (Barbara) Bontrager*

# Chocolate Chip Oatmeal Cookies

3¾ c. unsifted flour
  (all-purpose)
3 tsp. soda
3 c. butter or oleo
¾ c. sugar
2¼ c. brown sugar
  (firmly packed)

9 oz. vanilla instant pudding
6 eggs
10½ c. quick oatmeal
3 c. chocolate chips or raisins

Mix flour with baking soda. In large bowl, combine butter or oleo with sugars and vanilla pudding. Beat until smooth and creamy. Beat in eggs. Gradually add flour mixture. Stir in oatmeal and chocolate chips (batter will be stiff). Drop by rounded teaspoons onto ungreased baking sheet. Bake at 375° for 10–12 minutes.

*Mrs. Floyd (Marietta) Troyer*

*A journey of a thousand miles begins with a single step.*

# Cream Wafers

1 c. butter
2 c. brown sugar
4 eggs
2 tsp. vanilla
4 Tbsp. cream

2 tsp. soda
1 tsp. baking powder
$^1/_2$ tsp. salt
5 c. flour

FILLING:
8 Tbsp. butter
4 Tbsp. cream

4 c. powdered sugar
2 tsp. vanilla

Mix wafer ingredients well. Drop by teaspoonfuls onto greased and floured cookie sheets and flatten them. These are best when rolled out and cut, or using a cookie press. Bake at 350°. For Filling: Melt butter, then add cream. Bring almost to a boil. Add powdered sugar and vanilla. Mix and spread between cookies.

*Mrs. Samuel (Viola) Miller*

# Crunchy Double Chip Cookies

$1^3/_4$ c. flour
$^1/_2$ tsp. salt
1 tsp. baking powder
$^1/_2$ tsp. soda
1 c. sugar
1 c. margarine or butter
(softened)

2 eggs
1 tsp. vanilla
8 c. corn flakes (crushed to 5 c.)
$^1/_2$ c. milk chocolate chips
$^1/_2$ c. peanut butter chips

Stir eggs, sugar, vanilla and salt together; beat well. Mix in all remaining ingredients except corn flakes; stir well. Mix in 3 c. corn flakes gently. Reserve 2 c. corn flakes in a small bowl. Shape dough into small balls and roll in corn flakes. Flatten slightly and place on greased cookie sheets. Bake at 350°.

*Sister (Elvesta) Bontrager*

*The middle letter of pride is "I".*

# Date-Filled Oatmeal Cookies

**FILLING:**

| | |
|---|---|
| 2 c. sugar | 2 Tbsp. flour |
| 2 c. ground dates | 2 c. water |

Mix together in a saucepan. Cook over medium heat for 15 minutes. Cool.

**DOUGH:**

| | |
|---|---|
| 2 lb. oleo | 4 tsp. baking powder |
| 6 c. brown sugar | 2 tsp. salt |
| 8 eggs (beaten) | 2 tsp. soda |
| 4 tsp. vanilla | 10 c. quick oats |
| 8 c. flour | |

Cream oleo and brown sugar together; add eggs and vanilla. Stir together, then add dry ingredients. Mix well and chill for 1 hour. Bake at 350°. Put filling between baked cookies. Are best when several days old.

*Mrs. Marvin (Katie) Miller, Mrs. Reuben (Alma) Miller*

# Favorite Chocolate Chip Cookies

| | |
|---|---|
| 1 c. butter or margarine (softened) | 2 eggs |
| 1/4 c. sugar | 2 1/4 c. flour |
| 3/4 c. brown sugar | 1 tsp. soda |
| 1 tsp. vanilla | 12 oz. chocolate chips |
| 4 oz. instant vanilla pudding | 1 c. nuts, *optional* |
| | 1/2 tsp. salt |

Combine butter, sugars, vanilla and pudding in a large bowl. Beat until smooth and creamy. Beat in eggs; gradually add flour, soda, salt, chips and nuts. Batter will be stiff. Drop by teaspoonfuls onto ungreased cookie sheets. Bake at 375° for 8–10 minutes. Variations: May add 1/2 tsp. cream of tartar.

*Mrs. Calvin (Martha Sue) Lehman, Mrs. Larry (Mary) Troyer*

# Irresistable Peanut Butter Cookies

$2^1/_4$ c. peanut butter
$1^1/_2$ c. Crisco (no substitute other than butter Crisco)
$3^3/_4$ c. firmly packed brown sugar
$^1/_2$ c. milk (scant)

3 Tbsp. vanilla
3 eggs
$5^1/_4$ c. all-purpose flour
$2^1/_4$ tsp. salt
$2^1/_4$ tsp. baking soda
1 c. M&M's or chocolate chips

Mix all ingredients together. Drop by teaspoonfuls onto ungreased baking sheets. Flatten slightly with a fork. Bake at 375° for 7–8 minutes until lightly brown or beginning to set. Cool for 2 minutes before removing from sheet.

*Mrs. Ray (Irene) Mullett*

# Jell-O Cookies

$^1/_2$ c. sugar
3 oz. Jell-O (any flavor)
$^1/_2$ c. butter
$^1/_2$ tsp. salt
2 eggs

$^1/_2$ tsp. almond flavoring, *optional*
1 tsp. vanilla
$^1/_2$ c. milk
1 tsp. soda
2 c. flour

Cream sugar, Jell-O, butter, salt and eggs. Add flavorings and milk. Then add soda and flour. Drop onto cookie sheet. Bake at 350°. Frost while still warm.

*Mrs. Wilmer (Marilyn) Schmucker*

*Brighten your day,*
*Lighten your way,*
*And lessen your care*
*With daily prayer.*

# Just Perfect Cookies

3 c. brown sugar
2 c. sugar
2$^1$/$_2$ c. Wesson oil
6 eggs (beaten)
1 Tbsp. vanilla
1 Tbsp. lemon flavoring

2 c. sour cream
1 c. milk
3 tsp. soda
6 tsp. baking powder
11 c. flour

Combine sugars, oil and eggs; beat well. Add sour cream, milk and flavorings, then dry ingredients. Refrigerate overnight and roll out. Bake at 350°.

*Mrs. Wilbur (Alta) Beechy*

# Lemon Sugar Cookies

2 eggs
1$^1$/$_2$ c. sugar
1 c. Crisco (or oleo)
1 c. milk
3 tsp. lemon extract

4 c. flour
2 tsp. baking powder
1 tsp. soda
$^1$/$_4$ tsp. salt

Beat eggs for 1 minute. Add sugar and shortening and beat for 1 minute. Add lemon extract and milk, then dry ingredients. Drop by teaspoonfuls onto cookie sheet. Flatten with glass dipped in sugar. Bake at 350° for about 10 minutes. Frost with lemon-flavored, powdered sugar icing.

*Mrs. Ervin Lee (Lydia) Yoder*

---

*It is in loving, not in being loved, the heart is blessed.*
*It is in giving, not in seeking gifts, we find our quest.*
*Whatever be your longing or your need, that give;*
*So shall your soul be fed and you indeed shall live.*

---

# Little Debbie Cookies

3 c. margarine (melted)
6 c. brown sugar
8 eggs
1 Tbsp. vanilla
8 c. quick oats

6 c. flour
3 tsp. soda
2 tsp. salt
4 tsp. cinnamon
1 tsp. nutmeg

FILLING:
4 egg whites (beaten)
2 c. Crisco

6 c. powdered sugar
2 Tbsp. vanilla

In a large bowl, combine the first 4 ingredients and mix well. Stir in the quick oats. Add rest of ingredients in order given and mix well. Chill dough an hour before baking. Drop by teaspoonfuls onto lightly greased cookie sheets. Bake at 325°–350° for 10–12 minutes. Cool, then spread filling between 2 cookies. Yield: Approximately 4 dozen double cookies. *These have always been great sellers at bake sales!*

Mrs. Dennis (Mary) Bontrager, Mrs. Daniel (Arlene) Beechy

# Molasses Cookies with Chocolate Chips

2 c. shortening
2 c. brown sugar
2 eggs
$1/2$ c. molasses
$1/2$ c. milk
5 c. flour

4 tsp. soda
1 tsp. cloves
2 tsp. cinnamon
2 tsp. ginger
12 oz. chocolate chips

Combine shortening, brown sugar, eggs, molasses and milk; mix well. Add dry ingredients and chocolate chips. Chill dough. Roll into balls and coat with granulated sugar before baking. Bake at 350° for 10 minutes.

Mrs. Mervin (Pauline) Ropp

*For every minute you are angry you lose sixty seconds of happiness.*

# Molasses Snaps

| | |
|---|---|
| 1 c. sugar | 1 tsp. salt |
| 3 c. brown sugar | 3 tsp. ground ginger |
| 1 c. pre-creamed shortening | 1 1/2 tsp. cinnamon, *optional* |
| 2 c. margarine or butter (softened) | 1 tsp. ground cloves, *optional* |
| | 9 c. flour |
| 5 eggs | 1 c. sugar |
| 1 c. baking molasses | 2 tsp. cinnamon |
| 7 tsp. soda | |

Combine last 2 ingredients in a small bowl; set aside. Combine sugars, shortenings, eggs and molasses; beat well. Add soda, salt, spices and flour; mix thoroughly. Shape dough into balls and roll in sugar and cinnamon mixture. Bake at 350°. *These cookies are similar to the Honey Sugar Snaps in Vol. I Cookbook. Great to dip in cappuccino, coffee or milk!*

*Mrs. Freeman (Mabel) Yoder, Mom (Rosa) Bontrager*

# Monster Cookies

| | |
|---|---|
| 12 eggs | 1 lb. butter |
| 2 lb. brown sugar | 3 lb. peanut butter |
| 1 Tbsp. vanilla | 18 c. oatmeal |
| 1 Tbsp. corn syrup | 1 lb. chocolate chips |
| 8 tsp. soda | 1 lb. M&M's |

Mix in a very large bowl in order given. Drop by teaspoonfuls onto cookie sheets and flatten. Preheat oven to 350°. Do not overbake. No flour needed but you may add 1–2 c. for a firmer cookie.

*Mrs. Menno (Ruby) Mullet, Sister (Elvesta) Bontrager*

---

*All that you do, do with your might;*
*Things done in halves are never done right.*

---

# Never-Fail Sugar Cookies

2 c. vegetable oil
2 c. sugar
4 eggs
2 tsp. soda
6 tsp. baking powder

1 tsp. salt
2 c. buttermilk
4 tsp. vanilla
6$^{1}/_{2}$ c. flour

In a large mixing bowl beat vegetable oil, sugar and eggs together. Add remaining ingredients. Bake at 400° for 8–10 minutes. Vera uses only 3 tsp. baking powder and 1$^{1}/_{4}$ c. vegetable oil and only 1$^{1}/_{2}$ c. milk.

*Mrs. Larry (Rose) Mullett, Mrs. Toby (Vera) Yoder*

# Oatmeal Pudding Cookies

2 c. margarine (softened)
1$^{1}/_{2}$ c. brown sugar
$^{1}/_{2}$ c. sugar
2 small pkg. instant
   pudding (vanilla or
   butterscotch)
4 eggs (beaten)

1 tsp. vanilla
7 c. quick oats
1–2 c. raisins or chocolate chips
2$^{1}/_{2}$ c. flour
2 tsp. baking soda
$^{3}/_{4}$ tsp. baking powder
1 tsp. salt

Mix flour with soda and baking powder. Combine margarine, sugars and pudding; beat until smooth. Beat in eggs. Add vanilla. Add flour mixture and salt. Stir in quick oats and raisins or chocolate chips. Drop by teaspoonfuls onto cookie sheets. Bake at 350° for 10–12 minutes. Esther uses butter-flavored Crisco instead of margarine, $^{1}/_{2}$ c. more brown sugar and only half as much quick oats.

*Mrs. Lavern (Martha) Yoder, Mrs. Wilbur (Esther) Yoder*

---

*Make new friends but keep the old;*
*New ones are silver, old ones are gold.*

---

# Oatmeal Raisin Cookies

4 c. oleo (melted)
6 c. brown sugar
8 eggs
4 tsp. vanilla
2 tsp. salt

4 tsp. baking powder
4 tsp. soda
12 c. oatmeal
5 c. flour (more if needed)
4 c. raisins (heated & drained)

Mix all ingredients together and bake at 375°.

*Mrs. Mervin (Emma) Yoder*

# Peanut Butter Blossom Cookies

14 oz. Eagle Brand milk
3/4 c. peanut butter
1 egg

1 tsp. vanilla
2 c. biscuit baking mix

Mix all ingredients well and shape into small balls and roll in granulated sugar. Bake at 350° for 6–8 minutes. Remove from oven. Immediately place a Hershey's kiss on top of each cookie. Press down gently. Remove from baking sheet immediately.

*Mrs. Larry (Rose) Mullett*

# Peanut Butter Cookies

1¹/₃ c. shortening or butter
4 eggs
2 c. brown sugar
2 c. sugar
1¹/₃ c. peanut butter

1 tsp. salt
5¹/₂ c. flour
8 tsp. baking powder
1 tsp. soda
2 tsp. vanilla

Cream shortening or butter, eggs, sugars, peanut butter and salt. Add remaining ingredients. Bake at 350° on greased cookie sheets.

*Mom (Rosa) Bontrager*

---

*A loving heart makes happiness.*

# Peanut Butter Round-Up Cookies

| | |
|---|---|
| 1 c. shortening | 2 c. flour |
| 1 c. brown sugar | 2 tsp. soda |
| 3/4 c. sugar | 1/2 tsp. salt |
| 1 c. creamy peanut butter | 1 c. quick oats |
| 2 eggs | |

Beat shortening and sugars together until creamy. Add eggs and peanut butter; beat well. Stir flour, soda and salt together. Add to creamed mixture, mixing well. Stir in quick oats. Shape into balls and put on cookie sheet. Press down with fork. Bake at 350°.

*Mrs. Dean (Rebecca) Troyer, Mrs. Levi (Elsie) Lambright*

# Pumpkin Cookies

| | |
|---|---|
| 3/4 c. lard | 1 tsp. soda |
| 2 c. pumpkin | 2 tsp. cinnamon |
| 2 c. sugar | 1 c. raisins |
| 4 c. flour | 1 c. nuts |
| 1 tsp. baking powder | |

**ICING:**

| | |
|---|---|
| powdered sugar | butter |
| milk | maple flavoring |

Cream lard, pumpkin and sugar together. Sift flour, baking powder, soda, and cinnamon together and add to first mixture. Stir in raisins and nuts. Drop onto greased and floured cookie sheet. Bake at 375°. While still warm ice with icing. *A good recipe to use when you don't have any eggs.*

*Mrs. Reuben (Martha) Yoder, Mrs. Willis (Mary) Bontrager*

---

*It is one of the most beautiful compensations of this life that we cannot sincerely help another without also helping ourselves.*

---

# Soft Sugar Cookies

2 c. brown sugar
2 c. sugar
2 c. butter or shortening
2½ c. sour cream or sour milk
1½ c. sweet milk
8 eggs (well beaten)

8 tsp. baking powder
8 tsp. soda
10 c. flour
2 Tbsp. vanilla, maple flavoring
 and/or lemon extract, *optional*
2 tsp. salt

Cream sugars and butter or shortening together. Add remaining ingredients. Drop onto cookie sheets and sprinkle a little sugar on top of each cookie. Bake at 350°. Norma uses 12 c. flour and 4 c. brown sugar.

*Mrs. Harry (Edna Mae) Bontrager, Mrs. Samuel (Norma) Yoder*

# Sour Cream Chocolate Cookies

½ c. butter or margarine
 (softened)
¾ c. sugar
½ c. brown sugar (packed)
1 egg
½ c. sour cream
1 tsp. vanilla extract

1¾ c. all-purpose flour
½ c. baking cocoa
1 tsp. baking powder
½ tsp. baking soda
¼ tsp. salt
1 c. semisweet chocolate chips
½ c. vanilla or white chips

In a mixing bowl, cream butter and sugars. Beat in egg, sour cream and vanilla. Combine dry ingredients; gradually add to the creamed mixture. Stir in chips. Drop by rounded tablespoons 2" apart onto greased baking sheets. Bake at 350° for 12–15 minutes or until set. Cool for 2 minutes before removing to wire racks to cool completely. Yield: About 3 dozen.

*Mrs. Mervin (Ruth) Yoder*

*Smile, and give your frown a rest.*

# Soft Oatmeal Cookies

1 c. oil
2 eggs
1¼ c. sugar
⅓ c. molasses
1¾ c. flour
1 tsp. soda

1 tsp. salt
1 tsp. cinnamon
2 c. quick oats
1 c. raisins
½ c. nuts

Mix first 4 ingredients. Sift together and add flour, soda, salt and cinnamon. Mix and add raisins, nuts, and oats. Drop by teaspoonfuls onto greased cookie sheet. Bake for 10 minutes at 400°. Yield: 5 dozen.

*Mrs. Levi (Elsie) Lambright*

# Strawberry Creme Cookies

1 c. butter or margarine
  (softened)
1 c. sugar
3 oz. cream cheese
1 egg

1 Tbsp. vanilla
2½ c. flour
¼ tsp. salt
½ tsp. baking powder
strawberry jam (room temperature)

Cream butter or margarine, sugar and cream cheese together. Add egg and vanilla; mix well. Add dry ingredients. Chill dough. Shape into 1" balls and place on ungreased cookie sheet. Using floured thimble, press a dent in center of cookie and fill with ½ tsp. jam. Bake at 350° for 10–12 minutes. Top with your favorite icing, leaving center with jam exposed.

*Mrs. Sam (Viola) Miller*

*Worry is like a rocking chair. It gives you something to do but gets you nowhere.*

# Vanilla Chip Cookies

| | |
|---|---|
| 1 c. shortening | 3 c. flour |
| 1/2 c. butter (softened) | 2 tsp. soda |
| 2 c. brown sugar | 1/2 tsp. salt |
| 2 eggs | 2 c. vanilla or white chips |
| 1 tsp. vanilla extract | 1/2 c. chopped pecans |
| 1 tsp. maple flavoring | |

FROSTING:

| | |
|---|---|
| 1/4 c. butter or margarine (softened) | 1 tsp. maple flavoring |
| 4 c. powdered sugar | 4–6 Tbsp. milk |
| | 3 1/2 c. pecan halves |

Cream shortening, butter and brown sugar. Add eggs and beat well. Beat in flavorings. Add flour, soda and salt gradually to creamed mixture. Stir in chips and pecans. Drop by tablespoonfuls onto ungreased cookie sheets. Bake at 350° for 8–10 minutes. Cool. For Frosting: Cream all ingredients together and beat until fluffy. Add more milk if needed to reach spreading consistency. Frost each cookie and top with a pecan half.

*Charlene Yoder (Daughter)*

# Banana Bars

| | |
|---|---|
| 1/2 c. margarine | 2 ripe bananas (mashed) |
| 2 c. sugar | 1 tsp. soda |
| 2 eggs | 1/2 c. nuts |
| 3/4 c. sour milk | 1 tsp. vanilla |
| 2 c. flour (scant) | 1/4 tsp. salt |

Cream margarine and sugar; add eggs. Dissolve soda in sour milk. Add to creamed mixture. Stir in remaining ingredients. Bake at 350° for 25 minutes or until done.

*Mrs. Mervin (Pauline) Ropp*

# Apple Squares

| | |
|---|---|
| 3 c. flour | 2 tsp. baking powder |
| 1 c. oleo | 1 egg |
| 3 Tbsp. sugar | milk |
| 1/2 tsp. salt | |

FILLING:

| | |
|---|---|
| 10 apples (peeled & shredded) | 3 Tbsp. flour |
| 1 1/2 c. sugar (white) | a little vinegar & water |
| 2 tsp. cinnamon | oleo |
| pinch of salt | |

Put egg in a cup and fill up with milk (same as for pie dough). This dough is quite similiar to pie dough. Roll out half of dough and put on a big cookie sheet. For Filling: Mix everything together well except apples and oleo. Then add apples and pour over bottom crust. Roll out remaining dough and put on top. Pinch sides together like a pie and poke holes in top. Put dabs of oleo between layers to prevent from running over. Bake until apples look done or crust is browned. When cooled, frost with your favorite white frosting. *A quick way to make apple pie!*

*Mrs. Omer (Mabel) Schwartz*

# Butterscotch Zucchini Bars

| | |
|---|---|
| 3 eggs | 1 tsp. salt |
| 2/3 c. vegetable oil | 1 tsp. baking powder |
| 2 c. sugar | 2 c. shredded zucchini (packed) |
| 2 tsp. vanilla | 1/2 c. brown sugar |
| 2 1/2 c. flour | 1 c. butterscotch chips |
| 1 tsp. soda | |

Beat eggs, oil, sugar and vanilla together. Mix in flour, soda, salt and baking powder. Stir in zucchini. Pour into a greased 10" x 15" x 1" pan. Mix brown sugar and butterscotch chips together and sprinkle over batter. Bake at 350° for approx. 30 minutes or until toothpick inserted near center comes out clean.

*Mrs. Mervin (Emma) Yoder*

# Caramel Pecan Dream Bars

18 oz. yellow cake mix
$^1/_3$ c. butter (melted)
2 eggs (divided)
14 oz. sweetened
   condensed milk

1 tsp. vanilla
1 c. chopped pecans
$^1/_2$ c. toffee bits

In a large bowl, combine cake mix, butter and 1 egg. Mix vigorously until crumbly. Press into a 9" x 13" greased pan. In a small bowl, beat remaining egg, sweetened condensed milk and vanilla until blended. Stir in pecans and toffee bits. Pour over crust in pan; spread to cover. Bake at 350° for 25–30 minutes or until light golden brown. Center may appear loose, but will set upon cooling. Allow bars to cool completely before cutting. Yield: 24 bars.

*Mrs. Ervin (Anna Mary) Miller*

# Can't Leave Alone Bars

1 yellow cake mix
2 eggs
$^1/_3$ c. vegetable oil

$^1/_2$ c. butter
1 c. chocolate chips
14 oz. Eagle Brand milk

Mix cake mix, eggs and oil. Press into bottom of a 9" x 13" pan, reserving $^3/_4$ c. for the top. Melt butter, chocolate chips and Eagle Brand milk. Pour over crust. Put small dabs of reserved crust over top. Bake at 350° for 35–40 minutes.

*Mrs. Eugene (Ruth) Yoder, Mrs. Wilbur (Waneta) Nisley*

---

*To err is human; to blame it on others is even more human.*

---

*Don't begin the day with a sigh, or you may end it with a downpour.*

# Cheerio Bars

$^1/_2$ c. butter or oleo (melted)
white or yellow cake mix
$1^1/_2$ c. mini marshmallows
1 c. chocolate chips

1 c. butterscotch chips
1 c. Cheerios
14 oz. can sweetened condensed
   milk

Melt butter or oleo and mix with cake mix. Pat into a 9" x 13" pan. Top with marshmallows, chocolate and butterscotch chips and Cheerios. Pour sweetened condensed milk over top. Bake at 350° for 30 minutes or until golden brown. *These bars are delicious!*

*Sister (Elvesta) Bontrager*

# Cheese Cake Bars

5 Tbsp. butter
$^1/_3$ c. brown sugar
1 c. flour
$^1/_4$ c. chopped nuts
8 oz. pkg. cream cheese
   (softened)

$^1/_2$ c. sugar
1 egg
2 Tbsp. milk
1–2 Tbsp. lemon juice
$^1/_2$ tsp. vanilla

Cream butter; stir in brown sugar until fluffy. Beat in flour and nuts. Press mixture into bottom of an ungreased 8" x 8" x 2" pan, reserving 1 cup. Bake at 350° for 12 minutes. Beat cream cheese and sugar together. Add remaining ingredients. Mix well and pour over baked layer. Sprinkle remaining 1 cup mixture over top. Bake at 350° for 25 minutes. Cool and cut into small bars.

*Mrs. Harley (JoAnna) Miller*

---

*If you think you don't have much to be thankful for,*
*why not be thankful for some of the things you don't have?*

---

# Chocolate Chip Blonde Brownies

³/₄ c. margarine
2 c. brown sugar
2 eggs
2 tsp. vanilla
2 c. flour

1 tsp. baking powder
¹/₂ tsp. soda
³/₄ tsp. salt
³/₄ c. chopped dates, *optional*
³/₄ c. chocolate chips

Heat margarine and sugar until melted, stirring constantly. Cool slightly. Add eggs and vanilla; beat well. Sift together and add dry ingredients. Blend in dates and chocolate chips. Pour into a greased 11" x 15" pan. Bake at 350° for 20–25 minutes. Do not overbake. Cut into squares.

*Mrs. Floyd (Marietta) Troyer, Sister (Elvesta) Bontrager*

# Chocolate Peanut Squares

1 c. margarine (divided)
6 - 1 oz. squares Baker's
   semisweet chocolate morsels
   (divided)
1 c. coconut
1¹/₂ c. graham cracker crumbs

¹/₂ c. chunky peanut butter
2 - 8 oz. pkg. cream cheese
   (softened)
1 c. sugar
1 tsp. vanilla

Melt ³/₄ c. margarine and 2 oz. chocolate squares, stirring often. Stir in graham cracker crumbs, coconut and peanut butter. Press into bottom of a 9" x 13" pan. Chill for 30 minutes. Mix cream cheese, sugar and vanilla until well blended. Spread over crust. Chill for 30 minutes. Melt remaining margarine and chocolate squares. Spread over cream cheese layer. Chill and cut into squares. Yield: 4 dozen.

*Mrs. Levi (Elsie) Lambright*

---

*Every good deed is an example. So is every bad one.*

---

# Coffee Bars

**DOUGH:**

$1^1/_2$ c. sugar
2 eggs (beaten)
$^1/_2$ c. oleo (softened)
$1^1/_3$ c. milk

$3^1/_2$ c. flour
4 tsp. baking powder
pinch of salt

**FILLING:**

$^1/_2$ c. oleo
1 c. brown sugar
4 Tbsp. flour

3 tsp. cinnamon
4 Tbsp. water

**CARAMEL ICING:**

$^1/_2$ c. butter
$^1/_3$ c. cream

1 c. brown sugar
2 c. powdered sugar

Beat first 4 dough ingredients together. Add remaining ingredients. Mix well and spread dough onto a large jellyroll pan. For Filling: Boil all ingredients together. Pour onto dough in pan and spread evenly. Bake at 350° for 30 minutes. Frost with Caramel Icing when bars are cool. For Caramel Icing: Melt butter and sugar together. Boil for 2 minutes, stirring constantly. Add cream and bring to a boil. Cool, then add powdered sugar. Drizzle or spread over bars. May put chopped pecans over top.

*Mrs. Ray (Irene) Mullett*

# Coffee Bars

2 eggs
2 c. brown sugar
$^1/_2$ c. sugar
1 c. warm coffee
3 c. all-purpose flour

1 c. vegetable oil
1 tsp. soda
1 tsp. vanilla
1 tsp. salt

Mix all ingredients together and spread onto a 10" x 15" x 2" cookie sheet. Top with nuts and chocolate chips. Bake at 350° for 20–25 minutes. *Very simple and delicious!* No frosting needed.

*Mrs. Toby (Vera) Yoder*

# Cream Cheese Brownies

| | |
|---|---|
| $1/2$ c. oleo (melted) | 1 c. flour |
| 1 oz. baking chocolate | $1/2$ c. nuts |
| 1 c. sugar | 1 tsp. vanilla |
| 2 eggs | 1 tsp. baking powder |

Melt oleo with chocolate. Add remaining ingredients and mix. Spread into loaf pan. Pour filling on top and bake at 350°.

**FILLING:**

| | |
|---|---|
| 6 oz. cream cheese | 2 Tbsp. oleo |
| $1/4$ c. sugar | 2 Tbsp. flour |
| 1 egg | $1/2$ c. nuts |

**FROSTING:**

| | |
|---|---|
| 2 oz. cream cheese | 2 Tbsp. cocoa |
| 2 Tbsp. oleo | milk |
| 2 c. powdered sugar | |

Mix frosting ingredients, adding enough milk till the right spreading consistency. Frost brownies.

*Mrs. Samuel (Wilma) Miller*

---

*Greet the dawn with enthusiam and you may*
*expect satisfaction at sunset.*

---

*Old Age: When the gleam in your eye is just the sun on your bifocals.*

# Crispy Date Bars

1 c. flour
1/2 c. brown sugar
1 c. margarine (divided)
1 c. chopped dates
1/2 c. sugar
1 egg (beaten)

2 c. Rice Krispies
1 c. chopped nuts
1 1/2 tsp. vanilla (divided)
2 c. powdered sugar
3 oz. cream cheese (softened)

Mix flour, brown sugar and 1/2 c. margarine together until crumbly. Press into a 9" x 9" pan. Bake at 375° for 10–12 minutes or until golden brown. Combine dates, sugar and 1/2 c. margarine in a saucepan. Cook over medium heat until it boils, stirring constantly. Simmer for 3 minutes. Blend 1/4 of mixture into beaten egg; return to saucepan. Cook just until bubbly, stirring constantly. Remove from heat, stir in Rice Krispies, chopped nuts and 1 tsp. vanilla. Spread this mixture over baked crust. Cool completely. Combine powdered sugar, cream cheese and 1/2 tsp. vanilla. Spread over Rice Krispie mixture. These should be refrigerated. Yield: 12–15 bars.

*Mrs. Ervin (Anna Mary) Miller*

# Delicious Chocolate Chip Bars

1 c. butter
1/2 c. sugar
1 1/2 c. brown sugar
3 eggs (separated)
1 Tbsp. water
2 c. flour

1/4 tsp. salt
1/4 tsp. soda
1 tsp. baking powder
1 1/2 tsp. vanilla
1 c. chocolate chips

Cream butter, sugar and 1/2 c. brown sugar together. Then add egg yolks and water; beat well. Combine flour, salt, soda, baking powder and 1 tsp. vanilla; mix well with creamed mixture. Spread in a greased 9" x 13" cake pan. Put chocolate chips over batter. Beat egg whites stiff with remaining brown sugar and vanilla. Spread over dough and bake at 350° for 25 minutes.

*Mrs. Darrell (Erma) Yoder*

# Four-Layer Bars

1 chocolate or yellow cake mix
$1/2$ c. butter or margarine
  (melted)
1 egg (beaten)

3 c. mini marshmallows
1 c. chocolate chips or M&M's
$1/2$ c. peanuts or pecans (chopped)

Mix first 3 ingredients together and spread in a 9" x 13" x 2" baking pan. Bake at 375° for 20 minutes. Immediately sprinkle with mini marshmallows, chocolate chips or M&M's and peanuts or pecans. Return to oven for 4 minutes. Cool completely before cutting.

*Mrs. Wilbur (Alta) Beechy*

# Fudge Brownies

2 c. sugar
$1^1/3$ c. all-purpose flour
$3/4$ c. cocoa
1 tsp. baking powder
$1/2$ tsp. salt

$1/2$ c. chopped nuts
$2/3$ c. vegetable oil
4 eggs (lightly beaten)
2 tsp. vanilla

Combine sugar, flour, cocoa, baking powder, salt and nuts; set aside. Combine oil, eggs and vanilla. Add to dry ingredients. Do not overmix. Spread into a 13" x 9" x 2" baking pan. Bake at 350° for 20–25 minutes.

*Mrs. Calvin (Martha Sue) Lehman*

# Granola Bars

$1/2$ c. margarine
1 c. brown sugar
$2/3$ c. peanut butter
$1/2$ c. honey

2 tsp. vanilla
5 c. granola
2 c. small chocolate chips

Melt margarine and add brown sugar, peanut butter, honey and vanilla. Heat slowly until melted. Cool. In a bowl combine granola and chocolate chips and pour first mixture over this. Press into a $10^1/2$" x 18" cookie sheet. Bake at 350° for 20 minutes. Bars will not look done. Cut before cool.

*Mrs. John (Elsie) Yoder*

# Marshmallow Fudge Bars

3/4 c. flour
2 Tbsp. cocoa
1/4 tsp. baking powder
1/4 tsp. salt
1/2 c. shortening

3/4 c. sugar
2 eggs
1 tsp. vanilla
12 large marshmallows

FROSTING:
1/2 c. brown sugar
1/4 c. water
2 heaping Tbsp. cocoa

3 Tbsp. butter
1 tsp. vanilla
1 1/2 c. powdered sugar

Sift flour, cocoa, baking powder and salt together. Combine shortening and sugar. Cream well. Blend in eggs, one at a time. Add dry ingredients. Add vanilla and spread in a greased 9" x 13" pan. Bake at 350° for 15–20 minutes until done. Remove from oven and cover top with marshmallows (cut in half). Return to oven for 3 minutes (until marshmallows are soft). For Frosting: Combine first 3 ingredients and bring to a boil. Boil for 3 minutes. Add butter and vanilla. Cool. When cooled blend in powdered sugar. Spread over marshmallows and cut into bars. Variation: Marietta adds several Tbsp. coffee to frosting.

*Mrs. Daniel (LeAnn) Yoder, Mrs. Floyd (Marietta) Troyer*

# Oatmeal Apple Butter Bars

1 c. old-fashioned oats
1 c. quick oats
3/4 c. brown sugar
1 c. flour

1/4 tsp. salt
1/2 tsp. cinnamon
3/4 c. butter (softened)
1 1/2 c. apple butter

Combine first 6 ingredients and add butter. Mix until crumbly. Put half of mixture (2 c.) into a 9" square pan. Spread apple butter evenly over crumb layer. Sprinkle remaining crumbs over top. Press down gently. Bake at 350° for 30–35 minutes or until golden.

*Mrs. Floyd (Darlene) Yoder*

# PayDay Bars

| | |
|---|---|
| 16 oz. dry roasted peanuts | 3 Tbsp. margarine |
| 1 pkg. Reeses peanut butter chips | 1 can sweetened condensed milk |
| | 2 c. mini marshmallows |

Spread half of peanuts in bottom of a 9" x 13" pan. Melt peanut butter chips with margarine. Remove from heat; add sweetened condensed milk; stir well. Add marshmallows. Stir just until marshmallows are coated; do not melt. Pour on top of peanuts. Pat down with buttered hands. Add remaining peanuts on top and press into filling. Tastes like a PayDay candy bar!

*Amy Yoder (Daughter)*

# Peanut Butter Oatmeal Bars

| | |
|---|---|
| $2/3$ c. margarine or butter | 1 tsp. vanilla |
| $1/4$ c. chunky peanut butter | 4 c. quick oats |
| 1 c. brown sugar | $1/2$ tsp. salt |
| $1/4$ c. light corn syrup | |

TOPPING:

| | |
|---|---|
| 1 c. milk chocolate chips | $1/3$ c. peanut butter |
| $1/2$ c. butterscotch chips | |

Combine butter, peanut butter, brown sugar, corn syrup and vanilla; gradually add oats and salt. Press into a 9" x 13" x 2" greased pan. Bake at 375°–400° for 12–14 minutes or until edges are golden brown. Cool for 5 minutes. For Topping: Melt chips and peanut butter over low heat. Stir until smooth and spread over slightly cooled bars. Cool completely before cutting.

*Mrs. Freeman (Mabel) Yoder*

---

*The best helping hand you can find is at the end of your arm.*

# Rhubarb Squares

**CRUST:**

2 c. flour

1 c. margarine

**FILLING:**

5 c. rhubarb

2 c. sugar

1 c. cream

5 Tbsp. flour

6 egg yolks

2 tsp. vanilla

**TOPPING:**

6 egg whites (beaten)

3/4 c. brown sugar

2 tsp. vanilla

Mix crust ingredients and press into a cake pan and bake until light brown. Cook filling ingredients and put on crust. Mix topping ingredients and pour over filling. Bake at 350° until golden.

*Mrs. David (Arlene) Chupp*

# Salted Peanut Bars

2/3 c. brown sugar

1/4 c. sugar

1/2 c. butter or oleo (melted)

1 tsp. vanilla

2 eggs

1/2 tsp. salt

1/2 tsp. baking powder

1/4 tsp. soda

1 1/2 c. flour

miniature marshmallows

2 c. Rice Krispies

2 c. salted peanuts

**TOPPING:**

12 oz. chocolate, butterscotch
   or peanut butter chips

2/3 c. Karo

1/2 c. butter

Mix first 9 ingredients together and put in a 12" x 17" cookie sheet. Bake at 350° for 12–15 minutes. Cover with miniature marshmallows and return to oven until marshmallows look puffy. Remove from oven and pour mixture of Rice Krispies and salted peanuts on top. For Topping: Melt chips, Karo and butter together and put on top of Rice Krispie mixture.

*Mrs. John (Elsie) Yoder*

# Sour Cream Raisin Bars

**CRUMBS:**

$1^3/_4$ c. oatmeal

$1^3/_4$ c. flour

1 c. brown sugar

1 tsp. soda

1 c. oleo

**FILLING:**

4 egg yolks

$1^1/_4$ c. sugar

1 Tbsp. cornstarch

2 c. sour cream

2 c. raisins

Pat $^2/_3$ of crumbs in bottom of a 9" x 13" pan. Bake at 350° for 15–20 minutes. Cool. For Filling: Boil all ingredients for 5–10 minutes, stirring constantly. Pour over crumbs. Cover with remaining crumbs. Bake for 20 minutes. Variation: May add 1 tsp. baking powder to crust.

*Mrs. Dan (Esther) Miller, Mrs. Allen (Rosemary) Bontrager*

# Toffee Nut Bars

**CRUST:**

$^1/_2$ c. margarine or butter

$^1/_2$ c. brown sugar

1 c. flour

**TOPPING:**

2 eggs (well beaten)

1 c. brown sugar (packed)

1 tsp. vanilla

2 Tbsp. flour

1 tsp. baking powder

$^1/_2$ tsp. salt

1 c. moist coconut

1 c. cut-up almonds (or other nuts)

For Crust: Mix margarine or butter and brown sugar thoroughly. Stir in flour. Press into a 9" x 13" baking pan. Bake at 350° for 10 minutes. For Topping: Beat eggs well. Stir in brown sugar and vanilla. Mix and stir in flour, baking powder, salt, coconut and almonds. Return to oven and bake 25 minutes longer or until topping is golden brown. Cool slightly, then cut into bars.

*Mrs. Menno (Ruby) Mullet*

# Tropical Pineapple Coconut Bars

**BASE:**

1 pkg. yellow cake mix
1$^1$/$_2$ c. quick oats

$^1$/$_2$ c. butter (softened)
1 egg

**FILLING:**

$^1$/$_2$ c. flour
$^1$/$_2$ tsp. nutmeg
14 oz. can sweetened
   condensed milk

8 oz. can crushed pineapple
   (well drained; reserve juice)

**TOPPING:**

1 c. chopped nuts
1 c. coconut

1 c. white vanilla chips

**GLAZE:**

1 c. powdered sugar

4–6 tsp. reserved pineapple juice

In a large bowl combine all base ingredients at low speed until crumbly.
Reserve 1$^1$/$_2$ c. of mixture. Press the rest into a greased 9" x 13" pan.
Combine all filling ingredients and pour over crust. Add all topping
ingredients to reserved crumb mixture. Sprinkle over filling. Bake at
350° for 30–40 minutes or until golden brown. Cool. Combine glaze
ingredients, adding more pineapple juice if necessary for desired consistency. Drizzle over cooled bars.

*Mrs. Eugene (Ruth) Yoder*

# No-Bake Bars

4 c. Cheerios
2 c. Rice Krispies
2 c. dry roasted peanuts
2 c. M&M's

1 c. light corn syrup
1 c. sugar
1$^1$/$_2$ c. creamy peanut butter
1 tsp. vanilla

In a large bowl, combine first 4 ingredients; set aside. In a saucepan,
bring corn syrup and sugar to a boil. Cook and stir until sugar is dissolved. Remove from heat; stir in peanut butter and vanilla. Pour over
cereal mixture and toss evenly to coat. Spread on greased 15" x 10" x 1"
baking pan.

*Mrs. Perry (Rosemary) Miller*

# Mud Hen Bars

1/2 c. shortening
1 c. sugar
3 eggs (separate 2)
1 1/2 c. flour
1 tsp. baking powder

1/4 tsp. salt
1 c. nuts
1/2 c. chocolate chips
1 c. mini marshmallows
1 c. brown sugar

Cream shortening and sugar. Beat in 1 whole egg and 2 egg yolks. Sift flour, baking powder and salt together. Combine the two mixtures; blend thoroughly. Spread batter into a 9" x 13" pan. Sprinkle nuts, chocolate chips and marshmallows over the batter. Beat the 2 egg whites stiff. Fold in brown sugar. Spread over top of bars. Bake at 350° for 30–40 minutes. Cut into bars.

*Mrs. Fred (LeEtta) Yoder*

# No-Bake Granola Bars

2 1/2 c. Rice Krispies
2 c. quick oats
1/2 c. raisins, *optional*
1/2 c. brown sugar

1/2 c. Karo
1/2 c. peanut butter
1 tsp. vanilla
1/2 c. chocolate chips

Combine first 3 ingredients in a bowl and set aside. In a heavy saucepan bring Karo and brown sugar to a boil over medium heat. Remove from heat and stir in peanut butter and vanilla until well blended. Pour over cereal mixture and stir until coated. Let set for 10 minutes, then stir in chocolate chips and press into a 9" x 13" pan.

*Mrs. Toby (Vera) Yoder, Mrs. Ferman (LuEtta) Miller*

---

*A smile is a frown turned upside down.*

---

# Desserts

*Happiness comes from feeling deeply,
enjoying simply and thinking freely.*

THEREFORE BEING JUSTIFIED BY FAITH, WE HAVE PEACE
WITH GOD THROUGH OUR LORD JESUS CHRIST: BY
WHOM ALSO WE HAVE ACCESS BY FAITH INTO THIS
GRACE WHEREIN WE STAND AND REJOICE IN HOPE
OF THE GLORY OF GOD.
ROMANS 5:1–2

*B*anish the future; live only for the hour and its allotted work. Think not of the amount to be accomplished, the difficulties to be overcome, but set earnestly at the little task at your elbow, letting that be sufficient for the day; for surely our plain duty is "not to see what lies dimly at the distance, but to do what lies clearly at hand."

*Submitted by Mrs. Ervin (Anna Mary) Miller*

*W*e shall steer safely through every storm as long as our heart is right, our intention fervent, our courage steadfast, and our trust fixed on God.

*B*ecause my faith in God is strong,
My life is filled with hope.
When problems rise and threaten me
He gives me strength to cope.

I won't lose heart or be depressed,
Because God's love is true;
And He will help me find success
In everything I do.

*Submitted by Mrs. Glenn (Polly) Yoder*

# Apple Goodie

<sup>1</sup>/<sub>2</sub> c. sugar

2 Tbsp. flour

<sup>1</sup>/<sub>4</sub> tsp. salt

1 tsp. cinnamon

1<sup>1</sup>/<sub>2</sub> qt. apples (sliced)

**TOP PART:**

1 c. oatmeal

1 c. brown sugar

1 c. flour

<sup>1</sup>/<sub>4</sub> tsp. soda

<sup>1</sup>/<sub>3</sub> tsp. baking powder

<sup>2</sup>/<sub>3</sub> c. butter

Mix sugar, flour, salt and cinnamon. Add to apples and mix. Place in a 9" x 13" cake pan. Mix all ingredients of top part until crumbly. Put on top of apples and pat firmly. Bake at 350° until brown and crust is formed. Serve with milk or cream.

*Mrs. John (Christina) Yoder*

# Quick Cobbler

2 eggs (beaten)

<sup>1</sup>/<sub>2</sub> c. butter or margarine
    (melted)

<sup>1</sup>/<sub>4</sub> tsp. salt

1<sup>1</sup>/<sub>2</sub> c. flour

<sup>3</sup>/<sub>4</sub> c. milk

1 c. sugar

1 tsp. vanilla

2 tsp. baking powder

1 qt. fruit (any kind)

<sup>1</sup>/<sub>2</sub> c. sugar

1 Tbsp. flour

Put fruit in cake pan. Add <sup>1</sup>/<sub>2</sub> c. sugar mixed with 1 Tbsp. flour. Mix remaining ingredients together and pour evenly over fruit mixture. Bake at 350° for approximately 45 minutes.

*Mrs. Mervin (Ruth) Yoder*

---

*The secret of happy living is not to do what you like,*
*but to like what you do.*

---

# Fruit Crunch

1 c. flour
1 c. sugar
$^1/_2$ tsp. salt
2 tsp. baking powder

2 Tbsp. butter
1 egg (beaten)
1 qt. blueberry, raspberry or cherry
    pie filling or peaches*

Pour pie filling or peaches into a 9" x 13" pan. Mix remaining ingredients in order given. Spoon onto pie filling or peaches. Dough will be thick and sticky. For a more crumbly top add $^1/_2$ c. more flour and sugar. * When using peaches, drain juice off peaches, then mix 1 Tbsp. flour with $^1/_2$ c. peach juice and pour over peaches in pan before topping with dough. Bake at 400°-425° for 30-40 minutes. Serve warm with milk.

*Mrs. Eli (Martha) Mullet*

# Apple Fritters

$1^1/_2$ c. flour
2 Tbsp. sugar
2 tsp. baking powder
$^1/_2$ tsp. salt

1 egg (beaten)
$^1/_4$ c. milk
4 medium apples (chopped)

SAUCE:
1 Tbsp. butter
1 c. water
1 c. sugar

1 tsp. vanilla
1 Tbsp. cornstarch

Mix together and drop by spoonfuls into hot oil or shortening. For Sauce: Brown butter and add water. Bring to a boil. Mix sugar, vanilla and cornstarch together. Mix into water. Pour over fritters and serve while hot.

*Mrs. Eli (Martha) Mullet*

*Courage is just fear that holds on a little longer.*

# Apple Pizza

pie dough
2/3 c. sugar
1/2 c. flour
1/2 c. chopped nuts

1/4 c. butter
2 tsp. cinnamon
4 med. apples (peeled & sliced)

GLAZE:
1 c. powdered sugar
1 tsp. vanilla

1 tsp. water

Spread a thick layer of pie dough in bottom of a greased cookie sheet. Mix sugar, flour, chopped nuts, butter and cinnamon together. Layer apples on dough and sprinkle with sugar mixture. Bake at 350° for 45 minutes. Drizzle with glaze.

*Mrs. Reuben (Alma) Miller*

# Apple Torte

2 c. flour
1 c. brown sugar
3/4 c. butter
8–10 apples (peeled & sliced)

1 c. water
3/4 c. sugar
1 Tbsp. cornstarch

Mix flour, brown sugar and butter together. Put half of this mixture in bottom of a 9" x 13" pan, reserving the rest for the top. Combine water, sugar and cornstarch in a saucepan and boil until thick. Then stir this mixture into the apples and pour into pan. Put remaining crumbs on top. Bake at 350° for 30–40 minutes. You may mix red hots (cinnamon candy) with the apples and sprinkle butterscotch chips and walnuts on top if desired. *Very good when served warm with milk or ice cream!*

*Mrs. Leland (Orpha) Yoder*

---

*Those who hope in the Lord renew their strength.*

---

# Dressing for Apple Salad

1 pt. water
2 Tbsp. butter or oleo
1 c. sugar
$^1/_3$ c. flour or Perma-Flo

2 Tbsp. water
1 egg (beaten)
1 tsp. vanilla (or any flavor you
   desire)

Bring water and butter or oleo to boiling point. Mix remaining ingredients and add to boiling water; bring to boil again. Remove from heat and cool. Use this dressing on cubed apples, miniature marshmallows, pineapples, nuts, bananas, cheese and chopped celery. Add or omit anything you wish. Variation: Erma adds 2 tsp. vinegar to sauce, 1 more c. sugar and some orange drink mix for more flavor.

*Mrs. Mervin (Pauline) Ropp, Mrs. Calvin (Erma) Schmucker*

# Angel Food Cake Trifle Pudding

1 angel food cake (cut up in bite-sized pieces)

FILLING:
2 - 8 oz. pkg. cream cheese
2 c. powdered sugar
1 c. sour cream

$^1/_2$ tsp. vanilla
$^1/_4$ tsp. almond flavoring
1 c. whipping cream

TOPPING:
4 c. water
1 pkg. strawberry or
   raspberry Kool-Aid
$1^1/_4$ c. sugar

$^1/_2$ c. clear jel
1 pkg. strawberry Jell-O
strawberries

For Filling: Cream together cream cheese and powdered sugar. Add sour cream, vanilla and almond flavoring. Whip cream and fold into cream cheese mixture. For Topping: Cook first 4 ingredients together until thick then add strawberry Jell-O. Add strawberries after it is cooled. Layer in a bowl: angel food cake, filling and then topping. Fix by layers.

*Mrs. Wilbur (Waneta) Nisley*

# Almond Delight Dessert

$1/3$ c. peanut butter
1 c. milk chocolate chips

3 c. Almond Delight cereal
1 gal. vanilla ice cream (softened)

Melt peanut butter and chocolate chips over low heat. Add cereal and stir until coated. Mix this together with ice cream. Put in a dish. Cover and freeze. May use frosted flakes cereal instead of Almond Delight cereal; less expensive and delicious!

*Mrs. Samuel (Viola) Miller*

# Simple Pudding

CRUST:
2 c. crushed graham crackers
1 Tbsp. brown sugar

$1/4$ c. butter (melted)

TOPPING:
3 c. whipping cream (whipped)
$1^1/2$ c. water
1 can sweetened condensed
    milk

2 - 3 oz. pkg. instant pudding
    (vanilla or butter pecan*)

Mix all crust ingredients together and press into a 9" x 13" pan, reserving a little for the top. For Topping: Mix pudding with water; let set 5 minutes. Whip the cream and mix into sweetened condensed milk and pudding mixture. Pour over graham cracker crumbs and sprinkle reserved crumbs on top. *May use chocolate pudding with Oreo cookies instead of graham crackers, which is very good!

*Mrs. Leland (Orpha) Yoder, Mom (Elsie) Yoder*

---

*Happiness is not a station you arrive at, but a manner of traveling.*

# Banana Pudding

3 - 3¹/₂ oz. pkg. instant
   vanilla pudding
5 c. milk
8 oz. sour cream

12 oz. Cool Whip or 8 oz. whipping cream, whipped to stiff peaks
2 - 8 oz. boxes vanilla wafers
9–12 bananas (sliced)

In a large bowl, blend pudding mix in milk with wire whisk. Add sour
cream and half of whipped topping; mix well and set aside. In a large,
deep bowl, alternate wafers, bananas and pudding mixture in layers.
Top with reserved whipped topping and additional banana slices, if
desired. Refrigerate. Hint: If milk is unpasteurized, heat it first, then
cool. Your pudding will stay better longer.

*Mrs. Harley (JoAnna) Miller*

# Toffee Coffee Dessert

¹/₄ c. sugar
1 Tbsp. (rounded) cornstarch
1 Tbsp. instant coffee
1 Tbsp. butter
1¹/₄ c. milk (divided)
1 tsp. vanilla
14 oz. sweetened condensed
   milk

2 c. Rich's topping
12 Oreo cookies or chocolate
   sandwich cookies
12 oz. English Heath toffee bits
caramel & chocolate ice cream
   topping

In a medium saucepan, heat 1 c. milk to boiling point. In the meantime, combine sugar, cornstarch and coffee. Mix in ¹/₄ c. milk and slowly
add to hot milk, stirring constantly. Bring to a boil and boil for 1 minute.
Remove from heat; add butter and vanilla. Cool completely and add
sweetened condensed milk. Whip Rich's topping and fold into mixture.
Add Heath bits. Crush Oreo cookies into a 10" pie plate. Pour first
mixture over Oreo cookies. Swirl with caramel and chocolate ice cream
topping. Freeze 8–12 hours before serving. *A great make-ahead dessert
that tastes like a Heath Toffee Blizzard!*

*Mrs. Freeman (Mabel) Yoder*

# Toffee Lover's Dream

**CRUST:**

$^1/_2$ c. margarine

1 c. flour

$^1/_2$ c. brown sugar

**FILLING:**

8 oz. cream cheese

2 c. Cool Whip

1 c. powdered or granulated sugar

**TOPPING:**

$2^1/_2$ c. milk (scalded*)

$^1/_2$ c. instant vanilla pudding

$^1/_4$ c. instant butterscotch
   pudding

1 tsp. butter pecan flavoring

1 c. *(plus)* toffee bits

2 c. Cool Whip

chocolate shavings or 1 finely
   chopped Hershey bar

For Crust: Cut margarine into flour and brown sugar until crumbly. Press into a greased 9" x 13" pan. Bake at 350° for 10–15 minutes or until golden. Cool. For Filling: Whip together and spread on crust. For Topping: Scald and cool milk (unless you use pasteurized, then scalding is not necessary). Blend in puddings and flavoring. Spread on filling mixture. Sprinkle 1 c. toffee bits on top. When pudding is set, top with Cool Whip and garnish with a generous amount of toffee bits and chocolate shavings. Refrigerate at least 6 hours before serving.

*Mrs. Lester (Verna) Bontrager*

# Butterscotch Pudding

1 Tbsp. butter

2 c. brown sugar

$^1/_2$ c. boiling water

$^1/_2$ tsp. soda

pinch of salt

2 eggs (beaten)

2 c. flour

2 c. sugar

cold water

3 pt. boiling water

vanilla

Brown butter in saucepan; add brown sugar, $^1/_2$ c. boiling water and soda. Boil to 250° and add salt. Mix beaten eggs, flour and 2 c. sugar with a small amount of cold water. Then add 3 pt. boiling water. Add to first mixture and bring to a boil. Add vanilla. This is very good to layer with angel food cake or a white cake, crumbled, butterscotch pudding and then whipped cream.

*Mrs. Orva (Marietta) Yoder*

# Caramel Dumplings

**SYRUP:**

1 1/2 c. brown sugar

4 Tbsp. butter

1 c. water

1/8 tsp. salt

**DUMPLINGS:**

2 c. flour

1/2 tsp. salt

4 Tbsp. sugar

3 tsp. baking powder

4 Tbsp. butter

1 egg

1 c. milk

Combine syrup ingredients and boil for 1 minute. Pour into cake pan.
For Dumplings: Mix dry ingredients, cut in butter, mixing with knife.
Add egg and milk. Mix just enough to hold together. Drop by tablespoonfuls into syrup. Bake at 350° for 20 minutes. This is good to eat
warm with milk. Variation: Wilma drops dough into boiling sauce instead of baking them.

*Mrs. Orva (Marietta) Yoder, Mrs. Samuel (Wilma) Miller*

# Cherry Crumb Dessert

1/2 c. butter or margarine
    (chilled)

18–12 oz. yellow cake mix

21 oz. can cherry or
    blueberry pie filling

1/2 c. chopped walnuts

In a mixing bowl, cut butter into cake mix as for pastry dough; set aside
1 c. Pat remaining crumbs onto the bottom and 1/2" up the sides of a
greased 13" x 9" x 2" baking pan. Spread pie filling over crust. Combine the walnuts with reserved crumbs; sprinkle over top. Bake at 350°
for 30–35 minutes. Serve warm with whipped cream or ice cream if
desired. Yield: 12–16 servings.

*Mrs. Levi (Elsie) Lambright*

---

*Children need more models than they need critics.*

# Chocolate Peanut Butter Dessert

CRUST:
2 c. flour          4 Tbsp. sugar
1 c. oleo           1 tsp. salt

CRUMBS:
2 c. powdered sugar    $^2/_3$ c. peanut butter

PUDDING:
6 c. milk           1 tsp. salt
4 eggs (beaten)     5 Tbsp. cornstarch
$1^1/_2$ c. sugar       2 Tbsp. flour
4 Tbsp. cocoa       whipped cream (for top)

For Crust: Blend ingredients until crumbly. Press into a cake pan. Bake at 325° for 30–35 minutes. Cool. For Crumbs: Mix ingredients together until crumbly. For Pudding: Heat 4 c. milk. Mix sugar, cocoa, salt, cornstarch and flour. Add beaten eggs and 2 c. cold milk. Add to boiling milk and cook. Cool. Line baked and cooled crust with crumbs. Add cooled pudding. Top with whipped cream and sprinkle with more crumbs.

*Mrs. Joe (Karen) Graber*

# Chocolate Tapioca

6 c. boiling water      1 c. milk
1 tsp. salt             $^1/_2$ c. white sugar
$1^1/_2$ c. tapioca         $^1/_4$ c. cocoa
2 c. brown sugar        2 large containers Cool Whip
2 eggs (beaten)         mini chocolate chips
$^1/_4$ c. cornstarch

Cook boiling water, salt and tapioca together until tapioca is clear (approximately 15–20 minutes). Add brown sugar. Mix eggs, cornstarch, milk, sugar and cocoa. Stir into tapioca; bring to boil and remove from heat and cool. Mix in Cool Whip and mini chocolate chips.

*Mrs. Reuben (Alma) Miller*

# Black Raspberry Tapioca

3 qt. black raspberry juice
2 c. fine pearl tapioca
2 c. sugar
3/4 c. raspberry Jell-O
(or berry Kool-Aid)

16 oz. whipped topping
4 - 8 oz. pkg. cream cheese
(softened)

Heat berry juice to boiling and add tapioca. Cook until clear and add sugar and Jell-O. Cool. Mix cream cheese and whipped topping and add to cooled tapioca.

*Mrs. Joseph (Barbara) Bontreger*

# Pearl Tapioca Fruit

1/2 c. baby pearl tapioca*
4 c. water
2/3 c. sugar

3 oz. flavored gelatin
2–3 c. frozen fruit or berries

*Baby pearl tapioca can be found in bulk food stores. Soak tapioca in water for several hours or overnight. Add sugar and cook for about 5 minutes until clear. Remove from heat. Add gelatin, stirring until dissolved. Cool. Fold in frozen fruit or berries and chill thoroughly. Use the same flavor gelatin as fruit you choose, or a flavor to complement fruit. Some suggestions for fruit: Strawberries, peaches, raspberries, pineapple, bananas or oranges.

*Mrs. Floyd (Marietta) Troyer*

# Tapioca Dessert

5 c. water
1 tsp. salt
1 c. tapioca

3/4 c. Jell-O (your choice)
Cool Whip

Boil water and salt together. Add tapioca. Cook for 20 minutes and let set covered for 15 minutes. Stir in Jell-O. Cool. Mix in as much Cool Whip as you please and serve. Keeps well. Fruit may be added such as oranges (cut up) when using orange Jell-O, etc.

*Mrs. Paul (Rhoda) Yoder*

# Orange Tapioca

8 c. boiling water
1 c. tapioca
pinch of salt
1 small box instant vanilla
    pudding

6 oz. orange Jell-O
1 c. sugar
whipped topping (whipped)

Cook water and tapioca together slowly until tapioca is clear. Mix salt, vanilla pudding, orange Jell-O and sugar together; add to boiling tapioca and cook for 1 minute. Cool and add whipped cream as desired.

*Mrs. Omer (Mabel) Schwartz*

# Fluffy Tapioca Pudding

3 Tbsp. minute tapioca
3 Tbsp. sugar
1 egg (separated)
1/8 tsp. salt

2 c. milk
1 tsp. vanilla
2 Tbsp. sugar

Mix tapioca, sugar, egg yolk, salt, milk and vanilla together in a saucepan. Let set for 5 minutes. Then bring to a boil and boil for 6–8 minutes. Beat egg white until foamy then add sugar and beat until soft peaks form. Add to tapioca mixture, stirring quickly until blended. Cool. Serves 5.

*Mrs. Mervin (Pauline) Ropp*

---

*Bad habits are like a comfortable bed,*
*easy to get into, but hard to get out of.*

---

# Floating Raspberry Dessert

**CRUST:**

1 c. flour
<br>¹/₂ c. butter

¹/₂ c. brown sugar
<br>¹/₂ c. chopped nuts

**SECOND LAYER:**

25 large marshmallows
<br>²/₃ c. milk

²/₃ c. whipped cream

**TOP LAYER:**

1 large box raspberry Jell-O
<br>2 c. water

1 qt. fresh or frozen raspberries

For Crust: Mix all ingredients and press into a 9" x 13" pan. Bake at 350° for 10 minutes. Let cool. For Second Layer: Melt marshmallows in milk. When cool, fold in whipped cream. Put over crust and place in refrigerator until set. Do not add top layer until it is set. For Top Layer: Prepare by mixing Jell-O, water and raspberries together. When syrupy, pour over second layer and chill until solid. May be topped with whipped cream.

*Mrs. Raymond (LeEtta) Yoder*

# Cinnamon Pudding

1 c. sugar
<br>2 Tbsp. margarine (softened)
<br>2 c. flour
<br>2 tsp. baking powder
<br>2 tsp. ground cinnamon

1 c. milk
<br>1¹/₂ c. brown sugar
<br>1¹/₂ c. water
<br>2 Tbsp. butter or margarine
<br>¹/₂ c. chopped walnuts

Cream sugar and margarine together. Sift flour, baking powder and ground cinnamon together. Add to margarine mixture alternately with milk. Pour into a greased 8" x 12" baking pan. Combine brown sugar, water and butter in saucepan. Heat to boiling. Then pour over batter in dish. Sprinkle walnuts over all. Bake at 350° for approximately 40 minutes. Serve warm with whipped cream. Yield: 8 servings.

*Mrs. Floyd (Marietta) Troyer*

# Cottage Cheese Pudding

3 oz. lime or orange Jell-O
1 c. boiling water
1 c. cream (whipped)

1/2 c. drained pineapple
1 c. cottage cheese
1/4–1/2 c. sugar

Stir Jell-O and boiling water together. When it starts to thicken add remaining ingredients.

*Mrs. Jonathan (Lou Ida) Miller*

# Cream Cheese Dessert

6 oz. Jell-O (any flavor)
2 c. boiling water
16 oz. cream cheese

2 c. powdered sugar
5 c. Cool Whip

Stir Jell-O and boiling water together. Set aside until partially set. Mix remaining ingredients together and blend into partially set Jell-O. Yield: 1 round Jell-O mold.

*Mrs. Allen (Rosemary) Bontrager*

# Cream Cheese Salad

1 lb. marshmallows
1/2 c. milk
3 - 3 oz. pkg. cream cheese
1 pt. cottage cheese
1 - No. 2 can crushed pineapple
   (drained)

chopped nuts
1 small jar maraschino cherries
   (cut up)
1 pt. whipped cream

Melt marshmallows and milk in double boiler. Then add cream cheese and cottage cheese. Stir until melted. Cool a little, then add pineapple, chopped nuts and maraschino cherries. Cool a while longer, then fold in whipped cream. Let set. *Delicious!*

*Mrs. Perry (Rosemary) Miller*

# Frozen Cream Cheese Salad

1 pkg. graham crackers
$1/4$ c. oleo (melted)
$1/4$ c. sugar
3 eggs (separated)
8 oz. cream cheese

$1^{1}/_{2}$ c. sugar
$1/2$ tsp. salt
1 tsp. vanilla
16 oz. Cool Whip

Crush graham crackers fine. Add oleo and $1/4$ c. sugar. Line bowl with $3/4$ of the crumbs, reserving the rest for the top. Cream egg yolks, cream cheese, $1^{1}/_{2}$ c. sugar, salt and vanilla. Fold in stiffly beaten egg whites and Cool Whip. Pour into a dish and top with crumbs. Freeze overnight. Yield: 1 oblong Tupperware container.

*Mrs. Samuel (Wilma) Miller*

# Tropical Pudding

2 Tbsp. cornstarch or clear jel
2 eggs (beaten)
1 c. orange juice, pineapple
    juice or other fruit juice*

1 c. sugar
juice of 2 lemons, or ReaLemon
whipped cream
fruit of your choice

*If using other fruit juice add some orange Jell-O. Mix first 5 ingredients together and bring to a boil. Cool. Add whipped cream and fruit of your choice. Good with marshmallows, pineapple and bananas.

*Mrs. David (Arlene) Chupp*

---

*Favor is deceitful, and beauty is vain:*
*but a woman that feareth the Lord, she shall be praised.*
*Proverbs 31:30*

---

# Cream Puff Dessert

| | |
|---|---|
| 1 c. water | 1 large box instant vanilla pudding |
| 1/2 c. butter | 8 oz. cream cheese |
| 1 c. flour | 8 oz. Cool Whip |
| 5 eggs | chocolate syrup |

Combine water, butter and flour in saucepan. Boil until thick. Remove from heat and add eggs, one at a time, beating after each egg. Spread on greased jellyroll pan. Bake at 425° for 12–20 minutes. Prepare pudding as directed on box. Add cream cheese. Beat until smooth, spread over crust. Top with Cool Whip. Drizzle with chocolate syrup when ready to serve.

*Mrs. Marlin (Loretta) Bontrager*

# Eagle Brand Pudding

| | |
|---|---|
| graham cracker crumbs | 3 c. water |
| 1/2 c. oleo (melted) | 2 c. whipped topping |
| 2 boxes instant vanilla pudding | 2 c. sweetened condensed milk |
| 1 box butterscotch pudding | |

Crush graham crackers and mix with melted oleo. Press into the bottom of a 9" x 13" pan, reserving some crumbs for the top. Mix remaining ingredients together and pour over the crumbs in pan. Sprinkle with remaining crumbs.

*Mrs. Larry (Mary) Troyer*

---

*There's only one way to fail, and that's to quit.*

---

*Let me win; but if I cannot win,*
*let me be brave in the attempt.*

# Date Pudding

| | |
|---|---|
| 1 c. dates | 1$^1$/$_3$ c. flour |
| 1 c. boiling water | 1 tsp. soda |
| $^1$/$_2$ c. sugar | $^1$/$_2$ tsp. baking powder |
| $^1$/$_2$ c. brown sugar | $^1$/$_2$ tsp. salt |
| 1 egg | $^1$/$_2$ c. nuts (walnuts or pecans) |
| 2 tsp. oleo (melted) | |

SAUCE:

| | |
|---|---|
| 1$^1$/$_2$ c. brown sugar | 1$^1$/$_2$ c. boiling water |
| 2 tsp. oleo | |

Combine dates and boiling water. Let set until cool. Cream sugars, egg and oleo. Add flour, soda, baking powder and salt; mix well. Stir in cooled date mixture and nuts. For Sauce: Mix all ingredients and pour into bottom of cake pan. Spread dough on top. Bake at 350° for 30 minutes or until cake is done. Cake and sauce may be made separately and sauce thickened with perma-flo. Fix in layers with whipped cream.

*Mrs. Wilmer (Marilyn) Schmucker*

# Graham Cracker Custard

CRUST:

| | |
|---|---|
| 18 graham crackers | $^1$/$_2$ c. butter |
| $^1$/$_4$ c. sugar | |

CUSTARD:

| | |
|---|---|
| $^3$/$_4$ c. milk | $^1$/$_2$ c. sugar |
| 3 eggs (separated) | $^3$/$_4$ c. whipping cream (whipped) |
| 1 pkg. lemon or orange Jell-O | |

Crush crackers; add butter and sugar. Line a dish with crumbs, reserving some for the top. For Custard: Bring milk to a boil. Add egg yolks and sugar. Remove from heat and add Jell-O. Allow to cool and set partly, then fold in egg whites (beaten stiff) and whipped cream. Pour into dish lined with crumbs. Sprinkle with remaining crumbs and chill.

*Mrs. Menno (Ruby) Mullet*

# Graham Cracker Pudding

1 box graham crackers
8 oz. cream cheese
2 small pkg. or ²/₃ c. instant
   vanilla pudding

3¹/₂ c. milk (scalded & cooled)
9 oz. Cool Whip (may use other
   whipped topping)

FROSTING:
2 Tbsp. vegetable oil
3 Tbsp. cocoa
2 tsp. light Karo
2 tsp. vanilla

3 Tbsp. butter (softened)
1¹/₂ c. powdered sugar
3 Tbsp. milk

Butter the bottom of a 9" x 13" pan. Line with whole graham crackers. Mix pudding with milk. Add Cool Whip and cream cheese. Pour half of mixture over crackers, then place second layer of crackers over pudding. Pour remaining pudding over this. Cover with more crackers. Refrigerate for 2 hours, then frost. For Frosting: Beat all ingredients until smooth. Spread over pudding. Refrigerate for 24 hours.

*Mrs. Wilbur (Waneta) Nisley*

# Old-Fashioned Graham Cracker Pudding

16 graham crackers (crushed)
¹/₃ c. brown sugar
6 Tbsp. butter
whipped topping
7 c. milk
1 c. sugar
¹/₂ c. brown sugar

²/₃ c. cornstarch or clear jel
4 egg yolks (beaten)
1 tsp. salt
1 c. cold milk
2 Tbsp. butter
2 tsp. vanilla

Mix first 3 ingredients together and toast lightly in oven. Cool. In a large saucepan heat 7 c. milk. Mix sugars, cornstarch and salt. Gradually add egg yolks and cold milk. Whisk until smooth. Add to almost boiling milk, stirring until thickened. Remove from heat and add butter and vanilla. Cool slightly and cover with plastic wrap and cool in refrigerator. Layer in large bowl in this order: Cracker crumbs, pudding, whipped topping. Repeat layers ending with cracker crumbs.

*Mrs. Vern (Irene) Schlabach*

# Paradise Dessert

18 graham crackers (crushed)
$1/4$ c. butter (melted)
1 c. powdered sugar
1 egg
1 c. cream (whipped)
1 c. pineapple & mandarin
   oranges (drained) (or use
   other fruit)

8 oz. cream cheese
$1/4$ tsp. salt
$1/4$ c. chopped nuts
2 Tbsp. sugar

Cream melted butter, powdered sugar and egg together. Crush graham crackers. Spread $1/3$ of them in dish. Pour in butter mixture. Use another $1/3$ of crumbs on top. Mix whipped cream, drained fruit, cream cheese, salt, chopped nuts and sugar. Pour over crumbs. Add remaining crumbs on top.

*Mrs. Glenn (Polly) Yoder*

# Jeweled Crunch Jell-O

1 small box lime Jell-O
1 c. pineapple (drained)
$1/4$ c. mayonnaise
$1/2$ c. celery (finely chopped)
$1/2$ c. chopped pecans

8 oz. cream cheese (softened)
5 - 3 oz. pkg. Jell-O (orange, grape,
   strawberry, berry blue & lemon)
   (or any other flavors you desire)
$1^1/2$ c. water for each box of Jell-O

Mix lime Jell-O as directed on box. Let partially set, then add pineapple and pour into a cut glass bowl. Refrigerate until set. Meanwhile combine next 4 ingredients and mix until cream cheese is smooth. Then spoon carefully and evenly over set lime Jell-O. Refrigerate. Fix 5 kinds of Jell-O, each in a separate bowl. Stir until Jell-O is dissolved. Then pour each into an 8" x 8" pan and let set. Cut each flavor into squares. Then arrange on top of cream cheese layer, interchanging colors until slightly rounded above the bowl. Store any leftover Jell-O for another use. *Very pretty!*

*Mrs. Freeman (Mabel) Yoder*

# Jell-O Pudding

6 oz. box Jell-O (any flavor)
2 c. boiling water
8 oz. cream cheese

1 c. sugar
2 c. ready to whip topping

Mix Jell-O and boiling water. Let cool. Do not let the Jell-O set; just cool. Cream together cream cheese and sugar; add Jell-O, then fold in whipped topping. If you want to put in layers, just let the first layer set for approximately $^1/_2$ hour. Then use different flavor Jell-O for the next layer. The different colors make it look nice! *Delicious!*

*Mrs. Gerald (Darla) Yoder*

# Layered Rhubarb Dessert

4 c. rhubarb (diced)
1 c. sugar
3 oz. strawberry Jell-O
$^1/_2$ box (2 c.) white or
    yellow cake mix

$^1/_3$ c. butter (melted)
1 c. water

Layer first 4 ingredients in a 9" x 13" pan. Drizzle butter over top. Pour water over all. Bake at 350° for 1 hour.

*Mrs. Perry (Rosemary) Miller*

# Rhubarb Butter Crunch

$4^1/_2$ c. rhubarb (cut up)
$1^1/_2$ c. sugar
$4^1/_2$ Tbsp. flour
$1^1/_2$ c. brown sugar

$1^1/_2$ c. quick oats
$2^1/_4$ c. flour
$1^1/_8$ c. butter

Combine rhubarb, sugar, and $4^1/_2$ Tbsp. flour and place in a 9" x 13" baking dish. Combine brown sugar, oats and flour; cut in butter. Sprinkle over rhubarb mixture. Bake at 375° for 40 minutes. Serve hot or cold. Serve with milk or ice cream.

*Mrs. James (Sara Marie) Yoder*

## Lemon Sherbet Dessert

3 eggs (separated)          1 c. heavy cream (whipped)
$^1/_2$ c. sugar                      $^3/_4$ c. graham cracker crumbs
lemon flavoring or vanilla

Beat egg yolks until thick. Gradually beat in sugar. Add lemon flavoring or vanilla. Fold in cream and stiffly beaten egg whites. Cover bottom of pan (an oblong Tupperware works well) with half cup of graham cracker crumbs. Pour in sherbet mixture. Top with remaining crumbs. Put in freezer. This is best if frozen hard. This is nice for company as you can make it ahead . . . *almost tastes like ice cream.*

*Mrs. David (Rachel) Plank*

## Pineapple Fluff

1 lb. marshmallows              1 tsp. vanilla
1 c. whipping cream (whipped)  $^1/_2$ c. milk
1 c. crushed pineapple          dash of salt

Melt marshmallows with milk in double boiler. Add pineapple and cool. Add vanilla, salt and whipped cream. Cover bottom of pan with crushed graham crackers., Pour mixture over cracker crumbs. Sprinkle crumbs on top. Chill before serving.

*Mrs. Mervin (Ruth) Yoder*

---

*Happiness is contagious. Be a carrier.*

---

*It takes less time to do something right than to
explain why you did it wrong.*

# Sweet Pineapple Treat

1 - 20 oz. can sliced pineapple
14 oz. can sweetened
   condensed milk

8 oz. Cool Whip
1 small jar maraschino cherries

Place unopened can of sweetened condensed milk in a 10-qt. pot and fill with water. When water starts boiling, turn burner down between low and medium and boil for 3 hours (don't let water get low because can will explode if there is no water left). Let milk set until cooled. Arrange sliced pineapple on a plate or individual plates. Open each end of can (cooked milk can) with can opener. Take one lid off and use the other one to push out the caramel. Dip a sharp knife in hot water to slice caramel and place on pineapple that was placed on plate. Put Cool Whip on caramel and cherries on top of Cool Whip. It is a good idea to cook 1–6 cans sweetened condensed milk at a time. Keeps a long time.

*Mrs. Darrel (Rosa) Troyer*

# Orange Squares

2 c. flour
1/2 c. brown sugar
1 c. butter or margarine
1/2 c. nuts
1 can crushed pineapple

1/3 c. orange Jell-O (or any flavor)
8 oz. cream cheese
1 c. sugar
2 c. whipped topping

Mix first 4 ingredients together and press into a 9" x 13" pan. Bake in moderate oven for 15–20 minutes or until golden brown. Set aside and let cool. Drain pineapple and add water to make 1 c. juice (if needed). Bring to boil. Remove from heat and add Jell-O. Set aside to cool. Cream together cream cheese and 1 c. sugar; add whipped topping. Add Jell-O and juice mixture to this, blending well. Fold in pineapple and spread onto cooled crust. Chill until firm before serving.

*Mrs. Reuben (Martha) Yoder*

---

*The secret of getting ahead is getting started.*

# Peach Delight

**CRUST:**

1 c. flour

$^1/_2$ c. pecans

$^1/_2$ c. margarine or butter

Mix and press into a 9" x 13" pan. Bake at 350° for 15 minutes. Cool. Mix the following and spread over crust.

**SECOND LAYER:**

8 oz. cream cheese

1 c. whipped topping

$^1/_2$ c. powdered sugar

**TOP LAYER:**

1 c. sugar

3 (level) Tbsp. clear jel

2 c. water

$^1/_8$ tsp. salt

$^1/_3$ c. peach or orange gelatin

3–4 c. fresh peaches (cut up)

Mix sugar and clear jel; add water and salt; bring to a boil, stirring constantly until thickened. Add peach or orange gelatin. Cool. Add peaches. Spread on second layer.

*Mrs. Harley (Martha) Raber*

# Peach Pudding

8 oz. cream cheese

1 can sweetened condensed
  milk

1 large Cool Whip

2 qt. drained peaches (cut up)

graham cracker crust

Mix cream cheese and sweetened condensed milk. Then add Cool Whip and peaches. Pour onto graham cracker crust. Sprinkle some graham cracker crumbs on top.

*Mrs. Eli (Martha) Mullet*

---

*God has two dwellings—one in heaven
and the other in a meek and thankful heart.*

# Pumpkin Chiffon Pudding

1 c. brown sugar
2 Tbsp. gelatin
$^1/_2$ tsp. salt
1 tsp. cinnamon
5 eggs (separated)
$1^1/_2$ c. milk

$2^1/_2$ c. pumpkin
1 tsp. vanilla
1 tsp. lemon
whipped cream
$^1/_3$ c. sugar

In a saucepan combine brown sugar, gelatin, salt, cinnamon, vanilla and lemon. Combine egg yolks (slightly beaten) and milk; stir into brown sugar mixture; add pumpkin. Cook and stir until mixture comes to a boil. Remove from heat and chill until mixture mounds slightly when spooned. Beat egg whites until soft peaks form. Gradually add sugar, beating till stiff peaks form. Fold pumpkin mixture into egg whites. Chill until firm. Top with whipped cream.

*Mrs. Mervin (Pauline) Ropp*

# Pumpkin Dessert

**FIRST LAYER:**
1 c. flour
$^1/_2$ c. oleo

$^1/_2$ c. nuts (pecans)

**SECOND LAYER:**
8 oz. cream cheese
1 c. powdered sugar

1 c. Cool Whip

**THIRD LAYER:**
1 c. pumpkin
$^1/_2$ c. sugar
2 Tbsp. flour (heaping)
2 eggs
4 c. milk

dash of nutmeg
1 tsp. cinnamon
1 tsp. vanilla
2 small boxes vanilla pudding
   (not instant)

Mix first layer ingredients together and press into a 9" x 13" cake pan. Bake at 350° for 15 minutes. Cool. Mix second layer ingredients well and spread on first layer. Beat third layer ingredients together well. Cook until thick. Stir occasionally until cool. Pour over layers in cake pan. Top with Cool Whip.

*Mrs. Harley (JoAnna) Miller*

# Strawberry Champagne

| | |
|---|---|
| 8 oz. cream cheese | 1 qt. strawberries |
| 3/4 c. sugar | 8 oz. Cool Whip |
| 2 mashed bananas | |
| 1 - 15 oz. can crushed pineapple | |

Mix all together and freeze. Very good in mold with cottage cheese.

*Mrs. Marlin (Loretta) Bontrager*

# Strawberry Cheesecake

| | |
|---|---|
| 1/2 c. margarine | 8 oz. cream cheese (softened) |
| 2 1/2 c. crushed graham crackers | 1 c. sugar |
| 3 oz. strawberry Jell-O | 1 tsp. vanilla |
| 1 c. boiling water | 12 oz. Cool Whip |

Melt margarine and mix to crushed graham crackers. Spread in bottom of pan. Dissolve Jell-O in hot water. Chill, but don't let set up. In a mixing bowl, place cream cheese, sugar and vanilla. Beat until smooth. Add chilled Jell-O and blend well. Fold in Cool Whip and spoon on crust. Refrigerate for 3 hours before serving. Other flavors of Jell-O may be used.

*Mrs. Perry (Rosemary) Miller*

---
*It's not the hours you put in, but what you put in the hours that counts!*
---

---
*Remember, our tongues are in a wet place and likely to slip.*
---

# Strawberry Yum-Yum

1 c. flour
1/2 c. butter
1/4 c. brown sugar
1/2 c. nuts (chopped)
1 c. sugar

2 tsp. lemon juice
3 c. partially frozen strawberries
2 c. whipped topping
2 egg whites

Mix the first 4 ingredients until crumbly and press into a 9" x 13" x 2" pan. Bake at 350° for 20–25 minutes. Cool and break into crumbs; set aside. Next, combine the egg whites and lemon juice, sugar, and strawberries. Beat at medium speed for 15–20 minutes. Fold strawberry mixture into whipped topping. Put half of the crumbs into the bottom of a 9" x 13" x 2" greased pan. Spread strawberry mixture over crumbs and top with remaining crumbs. Freeze. Cut into squares and serve.

*Mrs. Samuel (Norma) Yoder*

# Pretzel Fruit Pizza

2 1/2 c. finely crushed pretzels
2/3 c. brown sugar
1 c. butter
1 - 14 oz. can sweetened
  condensed milk

1 tsp. ReaLemon
2 c. whipping cream
7 c. (approx.) assorted fruit
  (mandarin oranges, blueberries,
  strawberries, grapes, apples etc.)

In a bowl combine pretzels and sugar. Cut in butter until coarse crumbs form. Press into a 10" x 15" x 1 1/2" cookie sheet. Bake at 350° for 10 minutes or until set. Cool. Combine milk, ReaLemon and whipped topping. Spread over crust. Chill well, then add assorted fruit. *A favorite of ours!*

*Mrs. Freeman (Mabel) Yoder*

---

*If happiness existed 24 hours a day, how could one recognize and appreciate it?*

# Supreme Fruit Pizza

**CRUST:**
1 box yellow or lemon cake mix
2/3 c. graham cracker crumbs

1/2 c. margarine (melted)
1 egg (beaten)

**FILLING:**
8 oz. cream cheese (softened)
1/2 c. powdered sugar

2 c. nondairy topping or 16 oz. Cool Whip

**TOPPING:**
2 c. pineapple juice
1/2 c. sugar

1 Tbsp. clear jel or Perma-Flo mixed with a small amount of water

For Crust: Combine ingredients and press into a greased 10" x 15" x 2" pan. Bake at 325°–350° for 12–15 minutes. This crust always stays soft. Cool. For Filling: Whip the topping and gently fold in cream cheese and powdered sugar. Layer onto cooled crust. For Topping: In saucepan cook pineapple juice and sugar; mix in clear jel and boil until thickened. Cool and add **1 tsp. margarine** and **1 Tbsp. ReaLemon juice.** Mix sauce with various fresh fruits, sliced bananas, seedless grapes, apples, strawberries, etc., and spread over filling. *The best!*

*Mrs. Samuel (Viola) Miller*

# Butter Pecan Ice Cream

1 small box vanilla instant pudding
1 small box butter pecan instant pudding
1/2 tsp. maple flavoring
1/2 c. sugar

1 (heaping) Tbsp. oleo (melted)
2/3 c. brown sugar
1/2 c. pecans
1 small can sweetened condensed milk or rich cream

Mix first 6 ingredients together, then add pecans and sweetened condensed milk. Put in freezer and add whole milk to make freezer 2/3 full. Yield: 1 gallon.

*Mrs. Kenneth (Susan) Bontrager*

# Blueberry Cheesecake Ice Cream

8 oz. cream cheese (softened)
1½ c. sugar
6 eggs (beaten)
2 c. cream
1 - 6 oz. pkg. instant vanilla
  pudding

1 tsp. salt
vanilla
6 c. milk
3 c. blueberry pie filling

CRUMBS:
¾ pkg. graham crackers
1 Tbsp. sugar

6 Tbsp. butter (melted)

Beat cream cheese and sugar together. Add eggs, cream, instant pudding, salt and vanilla. Pour in milk and blueberry filling. Freeze and add crumbs when finished, turning a few times to mix in crumbs.

*Mrs. Joseph (Barbara) Bontreger*

# 6-Qt. Freezer Ice Cream

2½ c. sugar
½ c. instant clear jel
½ c. instant vanilla pudding
  or your favorite flavor
2 qt. cold milk

6 eggs (beaten)
2 c. cream
1 tsp. vanilla
¾ tsp. salt

Mix sugar, instant clear jel and pudding; set aside. Mix milk and eggs, then take a wire whisk and beat in sugar mixture. Add salt and vanilla; add cream. Pour into a 6-qt. ice cream freezer and freeze.

*Mom (Elsie) Yoder*

---

*The best way to remember people is in prayer.*

---

# Homemade Ice Cream

2 - 3 oz. boxes instant
   pudding (any flavors)
4–5 c. milk*
2 c. cream

1 c. brown sugar
$^1/_4$ c. sugar
2 eggs

Beat pudding and milk together; set aside. Beat the cream until stiff, then add sugars and eggs. Beat thoroughly, then add pudding mixture and beat again until well blended. Pour in can and freeze. This fills a 1-gal. freezer. *If using unpasteurized milk it is best to heat milk and cool before mixing with pudding.

*Mrs. Samuel (Wilma) Miller*

# Ice Cream

7 c. milk
2 c. sugar
2 (rounded) Tbsp. flour
$^1/_2$ tsp. salt

4 eggs
2 Tbsp. vanilla flavoring
1 pt. cream

Heat milk. Mix sugar, flour, salt and eggs (beaten until light). Add to milk and boil. Then add vanilla and cream when cool. Freeze in 1-gal. hand freezer.

*Mrs. Floyd (Marietta) Troyer*

---

*Things work out best for those who make the best
of the way things work out.*

---

*The greatest sum in addition is to count your blessings.*

# Health Section

BELOVED, I WISH ABOVE ALL THINGS THAT THOU MAYEST
PROSPER AND BE IN HEALTH, EVEN AS THY
SOUL PROSPERETH.
III JOHN 2

THEN SHALL THY LIGHT BREAK FORTH AS THE MORNING
AND THINE HEALTH SHALL SPRING FORTH SPEEDILY: AND
THY RIGHTEOUSNESS SHALL GO BEFORE THEE; THE GLORY
OF THE LORD SHALL BE THY REWARD.
ISAIAH 58:8

## Face Life with a smile

There's a lot of joy in living,
If we face life with a smile;
Take time to do some kindness,
And go the second mile.

For the greatest joy is giving,
And it all comes back to you
When you add a little sunshine
To all you say and do.

Before the day has ended
Try to do a worthwhile thing,
Help to ease another's burdens
And make a sad heart sing.

You will find each new tomorrow
Will be happy from the start
If you only will remember
Keep a smile within your heart!

by Lonnie Yoder, 11 years old

Charlene Yoder

*But they that wait upon the Lord shall renew their strength; they shall mount up with wings as eagles; they shall run, and not be weary; and they shall walk, and not faint.*
*Isaiah 40:31*

# Whole Wheat Bread

2 eggs
2 Tbsp. salt
$^1/_2$ c. honey or sorghum
   molasses
$^1/_2$ c. lard

$3^1/_2$ c. warm water
$1^1/_2$ Tbsp. yeast
Montana Wheat Prairie Gold
   whole wheat flour

Combine eggs, salt, honey or sorghum, lard and water. Add yeast and enough flour to make a stiff dough. L t rise until doubled. Punch down and let rise again. Divide into 3 loaves. Bake at 350° for approx. 35–40 minutes.

*Mrs. Vern (Irene) Schlabach*

# Sugar-Free Whole Wheat Bread

3 Tbsp. yeast
1 c. molasses or honey
$^1/_2$ c. oil
$^1/_2$ c. lard
2 Tbsp. salt

1 c. potato flakes, *optional*
6 c. hot tap water
4 c. hi-gluten flour
approx. 12 c. fresh ground wheat
   flour (hard white)

Mix molasses, oil, lard, salt and potato flakes. Add hot water to dissolve. Add 6 c. wheat flour; beat well with egg beater. Mix yeast with hi-gluten flour and stir in. Finish with wheat flour. Let rise 3 times at 1-hour intervals. The third time divide into 6 loaves. Bake at 350° for 35–40 minutes.

*Mrs. Mervin (Emma) Yoder*

---

*One talent that should be buried is faultfinding.*

---

*The soul would have no rainbows if the eyes possessed no tears.*

# 100% Whole Wheat Bread

| | |
|---|---|
| 5 c. warm water | $^3/_4$ c. canola oil |
| 3 Tbsp. yeast | $^3/_4$ c. honey |
| $^1/_2$ c. gluten | 2 Tbsp. lemon juice |
| 13 c. fresh ground wheat flour | 1 Tbsp. salt |

Mix warm water, yeast, gluten and 7 c. of the flour together. Mix well and let set until risen. Add remaining ingredients and mix well. Then divide into 5 loaves. Let rise in pans. Bake at 325° for 23–25 minutes. Note: Using a mixer improves the texture. A nice soft bread which we like better than white bread.

*Mrs. Joe (Karen) Graber*

# Our Favorite Whole Wheat Bread

| | |
|---|---|
| 1 Tbsp. yeast* | $^1/_4$ c. safflower oil |
| $3^1/_2$ c. warm water | 2 Tbsp. lecithin |
| 1 Tbsp. salt | $^1/_2$ c. honey |
| 1 Tbsp. vinegar | 8–9 c. whole wheat flour |
| 2 Tbsp. blackstrap molasses | |

Dissolve yeast in $3^1/_2$ c. warm water. (*If using instant yeast there is no need to dissolve it in water.) Add remaining ingredients, kneading in enough flour until it no longer sticks to your hands, but you still have a soft dough. Let rise, punching down every 20 minutes for 3 hours. Divide into 4 bread pans. Let rise for 1 hour or until double in size. Bake at 350° for 30 minutes. Note: I sometimes increase amount of yeast then shorten rising time. In my trials and errors of making 100% whole wheat bread, I settled with this recipe, and we still love it after 10 years! It hardly ever fails.

*Mrs. Lloyd (Mary Etta) Miller*

---

*Kindness is the oil that takes the friction out of life.*

# Applesauce Raisin Bread

| | |
|---|---|
| 1 c. applesauce (unsweetened) | 1 tsp. cinnamon |
| $^1/_2$ c. polyunsaturated oil | $^1/_2$ tsp. cloves |
| $^1/_2$ c. sugar or honey (scant) | $^1/_2$ tsp. nutmeg |
| 1$^3/_4$ c. flour (sifted) | 1 slightly beaten egg or 2 egg |
| $^1/_2$ tsp. soda | whites or 1 egg substitute |
| $^1/_2$ tsp. salt substitute | 1 c. raisins |

Mix applesauce, oil and sugar. Sift in flour, soda, salt substitute, cinnamon, cloves and nutmeg; mix well. Add egg and raisins. Mix, then pour into a greased and floured 8" x 4" loaf pan. Bake at 325° for 1 hour and 20 minutes or until loaf springs back when lightly touched.

*Mrs. Freeman (Mabel) Yoder*

# Banana Chocolate Chip Bread

| | |
|---|---|
| 1$^1/_2$ c. flour | 2 eggs |
| 1$^1/_2$ tsp. baking powder | $^1/_2$ c. vanilla yogurt or $^1/_4$ c. oil |
| $^1/_2$ tsp. soda | (scant) |
| $^1/_2$ tsp. salt | 2 Tbsp. butter (melted) |
| $^1/_2$ tsp. cinnamon | 3 large ripe bananas |
| $^1/_2$ c. sugar | $^1/_2$ c. mini chocolate chip morsels |

In medium bowl combine dry ingredients. Beat eggs, yogurt or oil and butter; mix with dry ingredients. Add bananas and chips. Bake in an 8" x 4" pan at 350° for 50–55 minutes. Uses less sugar than regular banana bread.

*Mrs. Freeman (Mabel) Yoder*

---

*Every day may not be good, but there's something good in every day.*

# Molasses Oat Bread

4 c. boiling water
2 c. old-fashioned oats
1 c. molasses
3 Tbsp. canola oil

$^1/_4$ c. sugar
3 tsp. salt
1 Tbsp. yeast
9–10 c. flour

Mix first 6 ingredients together. Cool to 110°–115°. Add yeast; mix well. Add flour to form a soft dough. Knead 6–8 minutes. Cover and let rise in a warm place until doubled (about 1$^1/_2$ hours). Punch dough down and divide into 3 loaves. Place in 3 greased bread pans. Cover and let rise until double. Bake at 350° for 40–45 minutes or until golden brown. Remove from pans to cool.

*Mrs. Freeman (Mabel) Yoder*

# Delicious Whole Wheat Pastry Crust

2 c. whole wheat pastry flour
  (sifted)
1 tsp. salt

$^3/_4$ c. butter (scant)
4–5 Tbsp. ice water
2 Tbsp. wheat germ

Sift flour and salt. Add wheat germ. With pastry blender, blend in butter. Sprinkle ice water over mixture and blend with fork. Pastry should be just moist enough to hold together. Makes 2 single crusts.

*Mrs. Lloyd (Marietta) Miller*

# Oatmeal Crust

3 c. oatmeal
1 c. whole wheat flour
  (pastry works best)

1 c. butter, margarine or lard
1 c. brown sugar
1$^1/_2$ tsp. salt

Bake at 400° for 15 minutes or until light brown. A quick and easy crust for pies or tortes.

*Mrs. David (Arlene) Chupp*

# Oat Crackers

3 c. quick oats
2 c. whole wheat flour
  (pastry is best)
1 tsp. salt

1 c. wheat germ
1 Tbsp. honey
$^3/_4$ c. oil
1 c. warm water

Mix all ingredients together and roll out thin on cookie sheets. Sprinkle with salt; cut into squares. Bake at 325° until light brown (about 30 minutes).

*Mrs. David (Arlene) Chupp*

# Oatmeal Pancakes

2 c. white flour
2 c. whole wheat flour
2 c. quick oats
1 Tbsp. baking powder
1 Tbsp. soda

1 Tbsp. salt
3 eggs (separated)
$^1/_2$ c. cooking oil
about 5 c. sweet milk

Mix dry ingredients thoroughly. Add egg yolks, oil and milk (lukewarm) and mix. Fold in beaten egg whites. Bake on ungreased griddle, turning once.

*Mrs. Mervin (Emma) Yoder*

# Diabetic Fruit Bars

$^1/_2$ c. dates
$^1/_2$ c. prunes
$^1/_2$ c. raisins
1 c. water
$^1/_2$ c. margarine
2 eggs

1 tsp. soda
$^1/_4$ tsp. salt
1 c. flour
1 tsp. vanilla
$^1/_2$ c. chopped nuts

Boil first 4 ingredients together and add margarine. Mix eggs, soda, salt, flour, vanilla and nuts together. Add batter to fruit mixture. Bake in 7" x 11" pan at 350° for 25 minutes. If you want spicy bars, add $^1/_2$ tsp. cinnamon and $^1/_4$ tsp. nutmeg.

*Mrs. Marvin (Katie) Miller*

# Honey Bars

| | |
|---|---|
| 7 c. flour | 1 pkg. chocolate chips, *optional* |
| 1 c. lard | 2 eggs (beaten) |
| 2 c. sugar | 1 c. honey |
| 1 tsp. salt | $1^1/_2$ Tbsp. soda |
| 1 lb. raisins | $^1/_4$ c. boiling water |

Mix first 4 ingredients like pie dough. Cook raisins in as little water as possible and cool. Then mix to crumbs. Add chocolate chips if desired. Add remaining ingredients. Put dough in large container and let set overnight or longer, covered. Make long rolls about $^1/_2$" thick and 2–$2^1/_2$" wide on cookie sheets. Garnish tops with an egg and a little water beaten together. Bake at 350°–375° until firm. Remove from oven and let set a little before cutting.

*Mrs. Ivan (Inez) Yoder*

# Fruit Cobbler

| | |
|---|---|
| 1 qt. fruit (your choice & sweetened to taste) | 2 Tbsp. cooking oil |
| | 1 c. honey or sorghum |
| 3 c. whole wheat pastry flour | 2 Tbsp. melted butter |
| 1 tsp. salt | 1 egg |
| 3 tsp. baking powder | milk (enough to make a nice dough) |

Put fruit of your choice in a 9" x 13" pan. Dot with dough and bake at 350° for 30 minutes. Serve with milk while still warm.

*Mrs. David (Arlene) Chupp*

# Honey Pecan Pie

| | |
|---|---|
| 1 - 9" pastry shell | $^1/_2$ tsp. salt |
| $1^1/_2$ c. honey (light honey tastes better) | 3 eggs |
| | 1 c. chopped pecans |
| $^1/_4$ c. butter | |

Cream together honey, butter and salt. Beat in eggs, one at a time. Add pecans and beat well. Pour into pastry shell. Bake at 350° for 1 hour and 10 minutes.

*Mrs. John (Christina) Yoder*

# Sugar-Free Apple Pie

9" pastry shell with top
4 c. sliced & peeled apples
   (sweet varieties are best)
$^1/_2$ c. frozen apple juice
   concentrate (undiluted)

2 tsp. tapioca or cornstarch or flour
$^1/_2$ tsp. lemon juice
1 tsp. cinnamon, nutmeg or apple
   pie spice

Mix apples, apple juice concentrate, tapioca or cornstarch or flour and spice; stir until apples are well coated. Add lemon juice to keep apples lighter colored. Pour into the pastry-lined pie pan and top with a second crust. Seal the edges and cut slits in the top crust to allow steam to escape. Bake at 425° for 40–45 minutes until golden brown.

*Mrs. David (JoAnn) Bontrager*

# Sun Gold Cake

1 c. maple syrup or honey
4 eggs (separated)
1 c. butter (softened)
1 c. milk

3 c. whole wheat flour
3 tsp. baking powder
pinch of salt
1 tsp. vanilla

Mix all ingredients well, folding in beaten egg whites last. Bake at 350° in a 9" x 13" pan for 30 minutes. *Makes a delicious shortcake!*

*Mrs. Lloyd (Mary Etta) Miller*

# Whole Wheat Crazy Cake

5 c. whole wheat pastry flour
$1^1/_2$ c. raw sugar
2 tsp. salt
4 Tbsp. cocoa or 2 tsp.
   cinnamon & 1 tsp. cloves

3 tsp. soda
3 c. water
1 c. canola oil
3 Tbsp. vinegar
3 tsp. vanilla, *optional*

Note: Mix this cake—do not beat it! Mix first 5 ingredients well. Make nest in center and add water, oil, vinegar and vanilla. Bake in a 9" x 13" pan for 40–45 minutes or until wooden toothpick inserted near center comes out clean.

*Mrs. Christy (Anna) Bontrager*

# Minute Bran Muffins

$^1/_2$ c. very hot water
$1^1/_2$ c. wheat bran
$^1/_2$ c. raisins
1 egg
$^1/_3$ c. honey
2 tsp. grated orange rind

$^1/_2$ c. chopped walnuts
1 tsp. salt
$1^1/_4$ tsp. soda
1 c. buttermilk
$1^1/_2$ c. whole wheat flour

Pour very hot water over wheat bran and raisins; set aside. Beat egg and honey together. Add salt, nuts and orange rind. Dissolve baking soda in the buttermilk. Add into batter along with flour and whip together. Pour into muffin tin. Bake at 375° for 10–20 minutes.

*Mrs. Ervin (Anna Mary) Miller*

# Oat Muffins

2 c. Post oat flakes
$1^1/_4$ c. flour
$^1/_4$ c. brown sugar
1 Tbsp. baking powder
dash of salt substitute

$^1/_4$ c. Egg Beaters
1 c. skim milk
3 Tbsp. oil
$^1/_4$ tsp. cinnamon

Mix $1^1/_2$ c. cereal with flour, brown sugar, baking powder and salt substitute. Combine Egg Beaters, milk and oil; add flour mixture and mix just enough to moisten flour. Fill greased muffin pan about $^2/_3$ full. Combine remaining oats cereal and cinnamon. Sprinkle over muffins. Bake at 400° for 15 minutes or until muffins spring back when lightly touched. Note: Remove from pan before completely cooled.

*Mrs. Freeman (Mabel) Yoder*

---

*The language of friendship is not words, but meaning.*

# Molasses Cookies

2 c. oil
3 c. molasses
1 tsp. salt
2 Tbsp. baking soda

1 Tbsp. ginger
1 Tbsp. cinnamon
1 c. water
8 c. whole wheat flour

Chill dough for several hours. Roll 1/4" thick. Cut in a round shape. Glaze with beaten egg. Bake for 10 minutes at 350°. This is a soft cookie. Note: When storing, put plastic wrap between layers to keep cookies from sticking together.

*Mrs. Lloyd (Mary Etta) Miller*

# Soft Molasses Cookies

2 c. sorghum molasses
3 tsp. soda
1 c. shortening (or use canola
    oil & add some more flour)
2 c. oatmeal

3 eggs (beaten)
2 tsp. vanilla
5 c. whole wheat pastry flour or
    enough to make a soft dough

Mix molasses and soda until fluffy. Add remaining ingredients. Bake at 400°.

*Mrs. David (Arlene) Chupp*

# Sugar-Free Banana Oat Cookies

3 c. rolled oats
1/2 tsp. salt
1/2 tsp. cinnamon or
    1/4 tsp. allspice

1/4 c. oil (canola)
3/4 c. sliced bananas
3/4 c. chopped pecans or walnuts

Preheat oven to 400°. Mix oatmeal, salt and cinnamon. Add oil and toss to coat; set aside for several minutes. Mash bananas with a fork. Add nuts and bananas to oat mixture and mix well. Using a 1/4 c. measuring cup, scoop 6 mounds of dough onto each of 2 unoiled cookie sheets. Flatten cookies to about 5" across with a fork or spatula. Bake on high rack for 10 minutes. Remove from oven and flatten each cookie with a fork. Return to oven and bake for another 8–10 minutes. You may add a little Birch sweetener to sweeten more, unless using ripe bananas (these help sweeten it). *Enjoy!*

*Mrs. Gerald (Darla) Yoder*

# Wheat Germ Crunchies

| | |
|---|---|
| 2 c. whole wheat flour | 2 c. coconut |
| 1 c. wheat bran | 3 c. oatmeal |
| 1 c. wheat germ | 1 tsp. salt |
| 1$^{1}/_{2}$ c. margarine (melted) | 1$^{1}/_{2}$ tsp. vanilla |
| 2 c. brown sugar | 1$^{1}/_{2}$ tsp. maple flavoring |
| 3 eggs (beaten) | 2 tsp. cinnamon |
| 3 tsp. baking powder | 1 c. sunflower seeds |

Mix all together in a large bowl. Bake on 2 cookie sheets at 350° for 30 minutes. Do not overbake!

*Mrs. Samuel (Wilma) Miller*

# Golden Granola

| | |
|---|---|
| 20 c. quick oats | 2 c. brown sugar or 1 c. honey |
| 2 c. shredded coconut | 1 c. maple syrup |
| 4 c. sunflower seeds | 3 Tbsp. maple flavoring |
| 2 c. butter | 3 Tbsp. vanilla |
| 1 c. cold water | 3 c. raisins, *optional* |

Place first 3 ingredients in a large bowl. Melt butter in saucepan. Remove from heat. Add cold water (if using honey use only $^{1}/_{2}$ c.), brown sugar or honey, maple syrup and flavorings. Pour onto oatmeal mixture and mix immediately. Spread into baking pans and toast to a golden brown, stirring occasionally. Add raisins after granola is done and still hot. Bake at 375° for 30 minutes approximately.

*Mrs. Ervin (Anna Mary) Miller*

---

*Why not wear a smile? It's just about the only thing that isn't taxed.*

# Granola Bars

2 - 10 oz. pkg. mini
   marshmallows
$^1/_4$ c. honey
$^1/_4$ c. peanut butter
$^1/_4$ c. vegetable oil
$^3/_4$ c. butter

5 c. quick oats
$4^1/_2$ c. Rice Krispies
1 pkg. crushed graham crackers
$1^1/_2$ c. coconut
1 c. chocolate chips

Melt first 5 ingredients together in a saucepan. In a large bowl, mix together the remaining ingredients. Stir all together and press into 2 large cookie sheets. Cool.

*Mrs. Christy (Anna) Bontrager*

# Granola Cereal

10 c. quick oats
3 c. crushed graham crackers
1 c. raw sugar
2 c. shredded unsweetened
   coconut
1 tsp. salt

1 c. crunchy peanut butter
$1^1/_2$ c. butter
2 c. raw wheat germ
1 c. flax seed meal
$^1/_2$ c. sesame seeds
2 c. chopped walnuts

Mix dry ingredients well. Melt peanut butter and butter in a small saucepan. Pour over dry ingredients and mix well until not lumpy. Divide into 2 stainless steel bowls or roasters. Bake at 250° until light brown, stirring every 15 minutes. Cool and store in airtight containers.

*Mrs. Christy (Anna) Bontrager*

*The hardships of life build the soul,*
*yet most of us strive for an easy life.*

# Yogurt

| | |
|---|---|
| 1 gal. milk | 4 Tbsp. plain yogurt |
| 2 Tbsp. gelatin | 1$^1$/$_2$ c. sugar or $^3$/$_4$ c. honey or |
| $^1$/$_2$ c. cold water | maple syrup |
| 2 Tbsp. vanilla | |

Heat milk to 190°. While heating, soak gelatin in cold water. Add to milk when it reaches 190°. Then cool to 130°. Add vanilla, plain yogurt and sugar or honey or maple syrup. Beat until smooth. Cover and put in oven with just the pilot light on overnight or 7–8 hours. Chill. Any pie filling, preserves or peanut butter may then be added. Dark cherry and strawberry pie filling are very good. Plain yogurt is a good sour cream substitute.

*Mrs. Lloyd (Mary Etta) Miller, Mrs. Vern (Irene) Schlabach*

# Quick Orange Gelatin Dessert

| | |
|---|---|
| 3 Tbsp. unflavored gelatin | 12 oz. can frozen orange juice |
| $^1$/$_2$ c. cold water | (no sugar added) |
| 2 c. boiling water | 4 c. fruit (peaches, bananas, pine- |
| 2 c. cold water or fruit juice | apples, etc.) |

In a 3-qt. mixing bowl, soften gelatin in cold water. Then pour boiling water over gelatin, stirring until completely dissolved. Add cold water or fruit juice and frozen orange juice. As juice melts, gelatin will become thick. Add fruit. May be served in 20 minutes, or wait to serve until set to desired firmness. Note: This makes a large bowlful, depending on the amount of fruit you add.

*Mrs. Lloyd (Mary Etta) Miller*

---

*Even the smallest light can make a difference in the darkest night.*

# Pineapple Ring Dessert

1 box butterscotch sugar-free
    instant pudding mix
1 can unsweetened, sliced
    pineapple (drained)

2 c. milk
2 c. whipped topping
10 maraschino cherries with stems

Place pineapple slices on a tray. Mix milk and pudding and let set until thickened. Then spoon pudding onto each pineapple slice and top with a dab of whipped topping and a maraschino cherry.

*Mrs. Samuel (Viola) Miller*

# Orange Ice Cream

16 oz. orange juice concentrate
    (or 1 can & enough water
    to make 16 oz.)

2 tsp. vanilla
$1/2$ gal. milk or cream*
3 eggs

*Cream makes a smoother texture. Beat all ingredients together and freeze in ice cream freezer like any other ice cream. *It's simple but refreshing.* Almost tastes like sherbet. $1^1/2$–2 c. sugar may be added. Yield: Approx. 1 gallon.

*Mrs. Mervin (Emma) Yoder*

# Banana Orange Frozen Push-Ups

2 bananas
1 - 6 oz. can frozen orange
    juice (thawed)

$1/2$ c. instant nonfat dry milk
$1/2$ c. water
1 c. plain lowfat yogurt

Peel and mash bananas. Add remaining ingredients and whip together until foamy. Pour into small paper cups and freeze. To eat squeeze bottom of cup. *Very healthy and refreshing!*

*Mrs. Freeman (Mabel) Yoder*

---

*A day hemmed in prayer seldom unravels.*

# Banana Shake

| | |
|---|---|
| 2 bananas (mashed) | 1 c. pineapple juice |
| 2 c. skim milk | 1 Tbsp. honey |
| 2 c. nonfat vanilla yogurt | |

Process all ingredients in blender or Salsa Master until smooth. Serve immediately. Best when all ingredients are cold. Serves 4.

*Mrs. Freeman (Mabel) Yoder*

# Split Pea Chowder

| | |
|---|---|
| 6 c. boiling water | 1 c. diced carrots |
| $1/2$ c. brown rice | 1 c. diced celery |
| 1 c. split peas | 1 tsp. basil |
| 2 tsp. salt | $1/4$ tsp. pepper |
| 1 c. chopped onions | |

Add rice and peas to boiling water; lightly boil for $1^1/2$ hours. Add remaining ingredients and continue to cook until vegetables are soft (about 30–40 minutes). Lower heat so it won't stick to bottom of kettle.

*Mrs. Freeman (Mabel) Yoder*

# Tortilla Roll-Ups

| | |
|---|---|
| 8 oz. fat-free cream cheese | $1/2$ c. ham or lean meat |
| 8 oz. fat-free sour cream | $1/2$ c. carrots |
| 1 pkg. Hidden Valley Ranch dressing mix | $1/2$ c. broccoli |
| $1/2$ c. grated cheese | 6–8 tortillas |

Put ham, carrots and broccoli in food processor to process. Mix cream cheese, sour cream, dressing mix and grated cheese together. Add processed food. Spread over tortillas. Roll up and cover tightly with plastic wrap. Refrigerate for several hours. Slice and serve with salsa.

*Mrs. David (Mary Lou) Whetstone*

# Homemade Tacos or Tortillas

³/₄ c. cornmeal
1 c. wheat flour
1¹/₂ c. water

1 tsp. salt
3 Tbsp. oil
2 eggs

Fry like pancakes, only bigger. Tip the frying pan around so the batter spreads into a thin, round tortilla or spread thin with back of spoon. Top with mashed beans, browned hamburger, chopped lettuce, tomatoes and onions, grated cheese, sour cream and salsa. I like to mix the beans and meat with taco seasoning and tomato sauce. We let each person fix their own at the table. If you prefer tacos, drape the soft tortillas over oven rack in warm oven until crisp.

*Mrs. Lloyd (Marietta) Miller*

# Nacho Casserole

1 c. salsa
4 oz. green chilies
¹/₄ tsp. cumin
¹/₂ c. plain yogurt
¹/₄ c. water
1 lb. hamburger

¹/₂ c. onion (chopped)
1 c. fat-free refried beans
1 c. reduced fat shredded cheddar
    cheese
4 c. crushed corn flakes

Mix salsa and chilies; set aside. Brown hamburger and onions. Add cumin, beans, yogurt, half of cheese, salsa and water. Simmer. Spread 2 c. corn flakes in a greased 9" x 13" cake pan. Spoon meat mixture over the top. Cover with remaining corn flakes. Bake at 350° for 35 minutes. Sprinkle remaining cheese on top and bake for 5 minutes longer.

*Mrs. Freeman (Mabel) Yoder*

---

*Those who bring sunshine into the lives of others
cannot keep it from themselves.*

# Zucchini Cheese Casserole

3 medium zucchini
$1/2$ c. chopped onion
2 fresh tomatoes (sliced)
2 Tbsp. vegetable oil

1 lb. lowfat cottage cheese
1 tsp. basil
$1/2$ tsp. oregano
$1/3$ c. Parmesan cheese

Peel and cut seeds from zucchini and cut up fine. Sauté in oil with onions. Whip cottage cheese, basil and oregano. Place zucchini in a greased casserole dish, layer cottage cheese on top, then tomatoes and Parmesan cheese. Bake uncovered for 25–30 minutes.

*Mrs. Freeman (Mabel) Yoder*

# Low-Fat Italian Dressing

5 Tbsp. frozen apple juice
  (concentrated, thawed)
$1/4$ c. cider vinegar
$1/4$ c. lemon juice
1 garlic clove (minced)
$1/2$ tsp. onion powder

$1/8$ tsp. crushed dried rosemary
$1/2$ tsp. paprika
$1/2$ tsp. dried mustard
$1/2$ tsp. oregano
$1/4$ tsp. dried basil
$1/8$ tsp. dried thyme

In a jar with a tight-fitting lid, mix all ingredients. Chill for several hours or overnight. Shake well before using. Serve over your favorite lettuce salad.

*Mrs. Dean (Rebecca) Troyer*

# Salt Substitute

2 Tbsp. onion powder
1 Tbsp. garlic powder
1 Tbsp. paprika
1 Tbsp. dry mustard

1 tsp. thyme
$1/2$ tsp. pepper
$1/2$ tsp. celery seed

Mix well. Yield: $1/3$ c.

*Mrs. Freeman (Mabel) Yoder*

# Meats & Main Dishes

WHETHER THEREFORE YE EAT, OR DRINK, OR
WHATSOEVER YE DO, DO ALL TO THE GLORY OF GOD.
I CORINTHIANS 10:31

LET THE WORDS OF MY MOUTH AND THE MEDITATION
OF MY HEART BE ACCEPTABLE IN THY SIGHT,
O LORD, MY STRENGTH AND MY REDEEMER.
PSALM 19:14

# It's Always Darkest Before the Dawn

### 1.
Are you discouraged, and are you blue?
Are clouds obscuring the sun from view?
Keep trusting Jesus though storms assail,
You have His promise, He will not fail.

### Cho.
It's always darkest before the dawn,
Don't be discouraged, but carry on;
He'll not forsake you, the sun will break through,
It's always darkest before the dawn.

### 2.
He knows your heartaches, He understands,
Just put your problems in His great hands;
No trouble meets you but in His will,
He's not forgotten, He loves you still.

# A Quick Sunday Morning Special

4 c. water
1 tsp. salt
2 Tbsp. butter
1–1½ c. chopped apples

1 c. raisins
2 c. old-fashioned oats
1 tsp. cinnamon

Combine water, salt and butter in a saucepan; bring to a full boil. Stir in apples and raisins; let simmer for 10 minutes. Add oats and cinnamon. Cook for 5 minutes, stirring occasionally.

*Mrs. Floyd (Darlene) Yoder*

# BLT Egg Bake

¼ c. mayonnaise
5 slices bread (toasted)
5 slices American cheese
1 lb. bacon (cooked & crumbled)
4 eggs
1 medium tomato (cut into small pieces)

2 Tbsp. butter
2 Tbsp. flour
salt & pepper
1 c. milk
½ c. shredded cheese
½ c. green onions (cut up)
lettuce, *optional*

Spread mayonnaise on one side of each piece of bread. Cut into small pieces and spread in a greased baking dish. Top with cheese slices and crumbled bacon. In a skillet, fry eggs over medium heat and place over bacon. Top with tomatoes; set aside. Melt butter in skillet, stir in flour, salt and pepper until smooth. Gradually add milk. Bring to a boil until thickened. Pour over tomatoes. Sprinkle with cheese and onions. Bake uncovered at 325° for 10 minutes. Serve with lettuce.

*Mrs. Freeman (Mabel) Yoder*

---

*Family—a group of people, no two of whom*
*like their eggs cooked the same way!*

---

# Breakfast Burrito Casserole

16 oz. sour cream
3 cans cream of chicken soup
burrito shells
1 doz. scrambled eggs
1 1/2 c. cooked, shredded potatoes

1 pkg. smokey links
1 lb. seasoned sausage (fried with
   1 onion)
1 1/2 lb. shredded cheese

Mix sour cream and soup. Put a layer in bottom of baking dish. Cover with burrito shells. Put eggs, potatoes, meat and half of the cheese in layers on top. Add another layer of sour cream mixture and burrito shells. Put remaining sour cream mixture and remaining cheese on top. Bake at 350° for 40–60 minutes. May add peppers and mushrooms if desired.

*Mrs. Mervin (Ruth) Yoder*

# Breakfast Casserole

1 lb. bacon (cooked crisp
   & crumbled)
6 slices bread (buttered &
   cubed)
2 c. milk

6–12 eggs
1–1 1/2 c. grated cheese
2 tsp. salt
1/2 tsp. pepper

Butter a 9" x 13" pan. Spread thickly with grated cheese. Add bacon, eggs, milk and seasonings. Pour over bread. Refrigerate overnight. The next morning bake at 350° for 45–60 minutes.

*Mrs. Vernon (Nelda) Miller*

---

*The best angle to approach a problem is the try angle.*

# Breakfast Casserole

12 slices bread
any kind of meat
6 slices cheese
salt & pepper

6 large eggs
3 c. milk
1 c. crushed corn flakes
$^1/_4$ c. butter (melted)

Grease a 9" x 13" pan. Put 6 slices of bread in bottom of pan. Top with meat and cheese. Lay remaining 6 slices of bread on top, making a sandwich. Beat eggs and mix with milk. Pour over all. Mix corn flakes and melted butter and sprinkle on top. Refrigerate overnight or chill a few hours. Bake for 1 hour at 325°. This is good served with sausage or hamburger gravy.

*Mrs. David (Rachel) Plank*

# Breakfast Casserole

3 c. cubed bread
3 c. cubed ham or bacon
3 c. shredded cheese
1 Tbsp. flour

1 Tbsp. mustard
1 bag Tater Tots (small size)
7 eggs (beaten)
$3^1/_2$ c. milk

Place bread in bottom of a 9" x 13" pan and add remaining ingredients. Refrigerate overnight or put in oven right after mixing. Bake at 350° for 1 hour, uncovered.

*Mrs. John (Susie) Kuhns*

# Breakfast Pizza

$1^1/_2$ lb. sausage
$1^1/_2$ c. pizza sauce
12 slices bread
12 slices cheese

5 eggs
3 c. milk
1 tsp. salt

In a 9" x 13" pan layer 6 slices bread and 6 pieces cheese. Add pizza sauce, meat, cheese and the rest of bread. Beat eggs, milk and salt together. Pour over bread. Bake at 350° for 35–45 minutes.

*Mrs. David (Arlene) Chupp*

# Breakfast Pizza

| | |
|---|---|
| $^1/_4$ c. margarine | $^1/_4$ c. warm water |
| 2 Tbsp. sugar | 1 egg (beaten) |
| $^1/_4$ c. boiling water | $1^1/_2$ c. all-purpose flour |
| 1 Tbsp. yeast | 1 tsp. salt |

Combine margarine, sugar and boiling water in mixing bowl. Stir until margarine is melted. Dissolve yeast in warm water then add yeast and beaten egg to the butter mixture. Add flour and salt; mix well. Spread evenly on a well greased 10" x 15" pan (I prefer a 9" x 13" cake pan with better sides). Fingers need to be well greased to spread dough in pan. On top of the unbaked crust, top with the following in order given:

| | |
|---|---|
| American cheese slices | $^1/_4$ c. green pepper (chopped) |
| 2 c. sausage or ham | 4 eggs (beaten, with a dash salt & |
| 1 small can mushrooms | pepper) |
| $^1/_4$ c. chopped onion | 1 c. cheddar or Co-Jack cheese |

Bake at 325° for 30 minutes. *A delicious brunch dish!*

*Mrs. Dennis (Mary) Bontrager*

# Brunch Enchiladas

| | |
|---|---|
| 2 c. cubed & cooked ham | 1 c. cream |
| $^1/_2$ c. chopped green onions | 1 c. milk |
| 10 - 8" flour tortillas | 6 eggs (beaten) |
| 2 c. shredded cheddar cheese | dash of salt |
| 1 Tbsp. flour | |

Combine ham and onions. Place $^1/_3$ c. or so on each tortilla. Sprinkle 2 Tbsp. cheddar cheese on top. Roll up and place seam-side down on greased 9" x 13" pan. In a bowl, combine flour, cream, milk, eggs and salt until smooth. Pour over tortillas. Refrigerate, covered, for 8 hours or overnight. Remove 30 minutes before baking. Cover and bake at 350° for 25–30 minutes. Uncover and sprinkle with remaining cheese. Bake for 10 minutes longer. Let set for several minutes before serving.

*Mrs. Freeman (Mabel) Yoder*

# Butterscotch Oatmeal

| | |
|---|---|
| 12 eggs | 2 c. quick oats |
| 3¹/₂ c. milk | ¹/₄ c. butter |
| 1 c. brown sugar | maple flavoring, *optional* |
| ¹/₂ tsp. salt | |

Beat eggs, milk, sugar and salt. Heat until bubbly; add oatmeal and butter. Stir well, cover and let set for 15 minutes. Serve with milk and fruit if desired.

*Mrs. Mervin (Emma) Yoder*

# Fluffy Oven Egg 'n Bacon

| | |
|---|---|
| ¹/₂ lb. bacon or ham | 1¹/₄ c. milk |
| ¹/₂ c. chopped onions | ¹/₄ tsp. salt |
| ¹/₂ c. Bisquick | ¹/₈ tsp. pepper |
| 3 eggs | ¹/₂ c. cheese |

Heat oven to 375°. Fry bacon and onion and spread in bottom of casserole. Beat Bisquick, eggs, milk, salt and pepper until smooth. Pour over bacon and onions. Add cheese on top. Bake uncovered for approximately 35 minutes.

*Mrs. Reuben (Alma) Miller*

# Hidden Eggs

| | |
|---|---|
| 4 Tbsp. butter | salt |
| 6–7 eggs | pepper |
| sliced bread | cheese |

Melt butter in a foil pie pan. Reserve half of butter for top. Break up bread to cover bottom of pan. Drop eggs onto bread; add salt and pepper. Break up more bread and place on top of eggs. Drizzle with butter and dot with cheese. Bake for 15–20 minutes or until eggs are done. *Delicious!*

*Mrs. David (JoAnn) Mast*

# Sheepherder's Breakfast

1 lb. bacon (diced)
1 medium onion (chopped)
32 oz. hash brown potatoes
5 eggs

2 c. shredded cheddar cheese
salt & pepper to taste
chopped fresh parsley

In a large skillet, cook bacon and onion until bacon is crisp; drain all but $^1/_2$ c. drippings. Add hash brown potatoes to skillet mixture; mix well. Cook over medium heat for 10 minutes, turning when browned. Make 5 "wells" evenly spaced in the potatoes. Place 1 egg in each "well." Sprinkle with salt and pepper and cheese. Cover and cook over low heat for 10 minutes or until eggs are set. Garnish with parsley and serve immediately. Makes 5 servings.

*Mrs. Joe (Karen) Graber*

# Egg & Potato Dish

6 large potatoes
1 lb. hamburger
1 small onion
8 eggs (beaten)

$^1/_2$ c. milk
$^1/_4$ c. margarine
cheese slices (American or
  processed)

Peel and slice potatoes. Heat large skillet and melt margarine and spread sliced potatoes over the margarine. Add salt and pepper to taste; cover. In a small pan fry hamburger with onions. Combine eggs and milk; set aside. When potatoes are crisp tender, turn, then spread hamburger over potatoes. Pour eggs over all; season with Lawry's seasoning salt and pepper. Cook until eggs are set. Cover with cheese. *A quick supper dish.*

*Charlene Yoder (Daughter)*

---

*The light that shines the farthest, shines the brightest nearest home.*

# Farmer's Pride Loaf

| | |
|---|---|
| 3 large potatoes | $1/4$ c. evaporated milk |
| 1 green pepper | 2 eggs |
| 2 large onions | 2 tsp. salt |
| 1 lb. ground beef | $1/4$ c. crushed crackers |
| 1 lb. sausage | 8 oz. tomato sauce |

Clean vegetables and coarsely grind in a food grinder. Mix ground beef, sausage, evaporated milk, eggs, salt and crackers together. Mix vegetables and meat together. Put into a 9" x 5" loaf pan or 2 qt. baking dish. Cover with tomato sauce. Bake at 350° for $1 1/2$ hours. Let set for 10 minutes before serving. Serves 8 people.

*Mrs. Levi (Carolyn) Schrock*

# Golden Parmesan Potatoes

| | |
|---|---|
| 6 large potatoes (raw) | $1/8$ tsp. pepper |
| $1/4$ c. flour | $1/3$ c. butter |
| $1/4$ c. grated Parmesan cheese | parsley flakes |
| $3/4$ tsp. salt | |

Pare and put potatoes through a French fryer. Combine flour, cheese, salt and pepper in a bag. *Moisten potatoes with water and shake a few at time in the bag, coating potatoes well with dry mixture. Melt butter in a 9" x 13" pan. Place potatoes in pan. Bake at 375° for 1 hour, turning once during baking when they are golden brown. Sprinkle with parsley flakes. Note: *Waneta rolls her potatoes in butter, not water, to moisten.

*Mrs. Wilbur (Esther) Yoder, Mrs. Wilbur (Waneta) Nisley*

---

*Good habits are like muscles, the more you use them the stronger they get.*

---

# Oven-Fried Potatoes

6 large potatoes
1/4 c. oil
2 Tbsp. grated Parmesan
   cheese, *optional*
1 1/2 tsp. salt

1 tsp. seasoning salt
1/2 tsp. garlic powder
1 tsp. paprika
1/2 tsp. pepper

Scrub potatoes well and cut into 1/2" strips; set aside. Combine remaining ingredients in a plastic bag. Add potatoes and shake well to coat. Spread strips on two cookie sheets in single layer. Bake at 400° for 20–30 minutes or until golden and tender, stirring once. These resemble potato wedges that can be bought. *Very good!* Variation: Use 1/2 c. butter instead of oil, and 1/4 c. Parmesan cheese and add 1/2 c. flour to seasonings in bag. Serve with mayonnaise or ketchup.

      *Mrs. Dennis (Mary) Bontrager, Mrs. James (Sara Marie) Yoder*

# Carameled Sweet Potatoes

5 medium-sized sweet
   potatoes (cut in chunks
   & cooked)
1 tsp. salt
1 c. brown sugar

2 Tbsp. butter
3 Tbsp. flour
8 large marshmallows
1 c. cream

In a bowl, mix together the last 6 ingredients. Pour over potatoes and bake at 350° until hot (approx. 45 minutes).

      *Mrs. Allen (Elsie) Bontrager*

---

*Wishing to be friends is quick work, but friendship is a slow-ripening fruit!*

# Sausage and Wild Rice Casserole

| | |
|---|---|
| 6 oz. rice | $1/2$ c. green peppers (diced) |
| 1 lb. sausage | $1/2$ c. shredded cheese |
| $10^1/2$ oz. mushroom soup | $1/2$ c. chicken broth |
| 1 c. mushrooms | 1 tsp. parsley |
| $1/2$ c. onions (diced) | |

Cook rice according to directions on pkg. Brown sausage and drain fat. Combine rice, sausage and remaining ingredients in a greased 2-qt. casserole dish. Bake at 350° for 1 hour. Serves 6–8.

*Mrs. Joseph (Barbara) Bontreger*

# Hush Puppies

| | |
|---|---|
| 1 c. yellow cornmeal | 1 egg |
| 1 c. white all-purpose flour | approx. 1 c. water |
| 1 Tbsp. baking powder | 1 med. yellow onion (finely |
| $1^1/2$ tsp. salt | chopped) |
| $1/8$ tsp. black pepper | approx. $1/2$ c. vegetable oil |
| pinch of cayenne pepper | |

In a mixing bowl, combine first 6 ingredients. In a small bowl, beat egg with half of the water; stir into cornmeal mixture. Stir in the onion and just enough additional water to make a thick batter. Batter should drop, not pour from spoon. Pour enough oil into a heavy skillet to measure about $1/4$" deep. Heat oil until very hot. Drop batter by heaping tablespoonfuls into the oil and cook, uncovered, about 3 minutes per side. Drain on paper towel. Keep warm in oven while you cook remaining puppies. Yield: 24 puppies.

*Mrs. Lester (Verna) Bontrager*

---

*Life's most perplexing problems usually come in the form of people.*

# No-Cook Mush

1 c. cornmeal
2 Tbsp. flour (slightly rounded)

1 tsp. salt
2 c. boiling water (must be boiling)

Mix first 3 ingredients together, then add boiling water, all at once. Stir well and drop by tablespoonfuls into hot skillet with grease. When turning patties, flatten to desired thickness. Fries quicker and isn't such a greasy mess like the old-time cooked mush.

*Mom (Elsie) Yoder, Mrs. Vern (Irene) Schlabach*

# Oven-Baked Barbecue Chops or Roast

4 lb. meat (chops, roast
    or spareribs)
1 c. sliced onions
1 c. water
1 1/2 tsp. salt
1/2 tsp. pepper

1 c. ketchup
1 Tbsp. Worcestershire sauce
3/4 c. brown sugar
1 tsp. dry mustard
1/2 c. vinegar

Place meat in a large roaster. Slice onion over meat. Combine all other ingredients in a small bowl and mix well. Pour over onion and meat. Bake covered at 350° for 2–2 1/2 hours. Spoon sauce over meat occasionally. Remove cover and bake for 10 minutes more.

*Mrs. Freeman (Mabel) Yoder*

# Oven Beef Stew

2 lb. raw lean beef
    (cut for stew)
10 oz. pkg. frozen peas
1 c. chopped onions
2 c. 1" sliced carrots
2 c. diced potatoes

1 1/2 tsp. salt
1/4 tsp. pepper
1 tsp. chopped parsley
10 3/4 oz. can tomato soup
10 3/4 oz. can cream of mushroom
    soup

Put all ingredients except soups into covered baking dish in order given. No need to stir it at all. Pour soups over all. Bake at 275° for 5 hours. Variation: Use raw hamburger instead of stew chunks and bake for 1 1/2–2 hours. *We love it!* Yield: About 3 quarts.

*Mrs. David (JoAnn) Mast*

# Oven Barbecued Ribs

1 onion (chopped)
$^1/_4$ c. lemon juice

salt & pepper
ribs

BARBECUE SAUCE:
1 Tbsp. paprika
2 Tbsp. brown sugar
1 tsp. salt
1 tsp. dry mustard
$^1/_4$ tsp. chili powder

2 Tbsp. Worcestershire sauce
$^1/_4$ c. vinegar
1 c. tomato sauce
$^1/_4$ c. ketchup
$^1/_2$ c. water

Place ribs in shallow pan or roaster and top with chopped onion, lemon juice and salt and pepper. Bake uncovered at 450° for 45 minutes. For Barbecue Sauce: Mix all ingredients and simmer for 15 minutes until slightly thickened. Pour sauce over ribs and bake covered at 200° for $1^1/_2$ hours.

*Mrs. John (Lora) Bontrager*

# Salmon Patties

$15^1/_2$ oz. can salmon (flaked)
1 medium onion (chopped)
$^1/_2$ c. dry bread crumbs
2 eggs (beaten)

salt & pepper to taste
3 Tbsp. butter
3 Tbsp. vegetable oil

Combine all ingredients in a bowl, except butter and oil. Melt butter and oil in skillet. Form mixture into patties. Fry on both sides until golden brown, turning once. Serves 4–5.

*Mrs. Calvin (Martha) Lehman*

---

*A Bible that is falling apart probably belongs to someone who isn't.*

---

# Mary Lou's Special Coating

8 c. flour
8 Tbsp. salt
6 Tbsp. paprika
4 tsp. garlic salt
4 tsp. onion salt
2 - 3.2 oz. pkg. Hidden Valley
   Ranch salad dressing mix

$^1/_2$ c. vegetable oil
8 c. fine cracker crumbs
4 Tbsp. sugar
6 c. crushed Rice Krispies
2 - 8 oz. Parmesan cheese

Mix all dry ingredients together then add oil. Mix very well. Store in glass jars in a cool place. Use for chicken or fish. Roll meat in oleo then in crumbs. Bake uncovered at 350° for 1 hour, then cover loosely with tinfoil for another hour at 300°. *Very good!*

*Mrs. David (Mary Lou) Whetstone*

# Bar B-Q Sauce

2 c. vinegar
2 c. water
1 c. oleo
$^1/_2$ c. salt
1 Tbsp. onion salt

5 Tbsp. Worcestershire sauce
$^1/_2$ tsp. garlic salt
$^1/_2$ c. brown sugar
1 Tbsp. black pepper

Combine all ingredients. Heat in saucepan and brush over chicken while grilling.

*Mrs. Chris (Esther) Bontrager*

# Chicken Bar-B-Q Sauce

$^1/_2$ lb. butter
26 oz. bottle ketchup
1 Tbsp. mustard
2 tsp. vinegar

$^1/_2$ tsp. Worcestershire sauce
salt & pepper to taste
$^1/_2$ c. brown sugar

Melt butter in a saucepan and add the remaining ingredients. Cook for several minutes. This is very good when cooked, deboned chicken is added, then simmered for several minutes.

*Mrs. John (Christina) Yoder*

# Fish Batter Seasoning

4 Tbsp. seasoning salt
2 Tbsp. paprika
$3/4$ tsp. salt
1 tsp. sage

1 tsp. cayenne red pepper
3 c. flour
1 egg (beaten)
1 c. milk

Mix first 6 ingredients well, then combine egg and milk. Dip fish into the egg and milk mixture then in the dry mixture. Deep fat fry until golden brown. This recipe may also be used for onion rings.

*Mrs. Wilbur (Esther) Yoder*

# French Fry Batter

1 c. flour
1 tsp. baking powder
1 tsp. salt
2 eggs*

1 tsp. paprika
1 Tbsp. sugar
$2/3$–1 c. milk

Beat all ingredients well. For chicken nuggets, cut a chicken breast into 1" cubes, dip in batter and deep fat fry until golden brown. For onion rings, separate an onion into rings and do them the same way. *Christina uses 2 eggs and 2 tsp. baking powder instead of 1 tsp. Rhoda does not.

*Mrs. John (Christina) Yoder, Mrs. Paul (Rhoda) Yoder*

# Hot Dog Sauce

$1^1/3$ lb. hamburger
$3/4$ lb. sausage (unseasoned)
2 c. water
1 Tbsp. salt

$1^1/2$ Tbsp. chili powder
1 c. chopped onion
1 qt. ketchup

Fry sausage and hamburger with water in a large saucepan. Add salt, chili powder and chopped onion. Simmer for 30 minutes. Add ketchup and cook for 10–15 minutes. Use on hot dogs or chili dogs.

*Mrs. Lavern (Martha) Yoder*

# To Fix Chicken

approx. 1 - 6 lb. fryer
1 c. flour
5–6 tsp. salt

4 tsp. paprika
1 tsp. dry mustard
1 tsp. black pepper

Mix all together and roll chicken pieces in it. Put in roaster and pour 1 c. milk over this and bake at 350° until tender. Use less salt if you soak the chicken in Tender Quik first. Cover with foil while baking.

*Mrs. Perry (Rosemary) Miller, Mrs. Harley (Martha) Raber*

# Shake & Bake for Chicken Breasts

6 c. Rice Krispies (crushed)
1 Tbsp. chicken seasoning

1 lb. butter (melted)
1 c. milk

Mix Rice Krispies and chicken seasoning. Mix melted butter and milk. Dip chicken breasts in butter mixture, then roll in crumbs. Put in a roaster. Bake for 1 hour at 325°–350°.

*Mom (Elsie) Yoder*

# Port-A-Pit Chicken

6 c. water
2$^{1}/_{2}$ Tbsp. Worcestershire
   sauce
2 tsp. garlic powder
$^{1}/_{4}$ c. salt

$^{1}/_{2}$ c. brown sugar
$^{1}/_{2}$ tsp. pepper
6 Tbsp. margarine
1$^{1}/_{2}$ c. cider vinegar

Mix together and boil 15 minutes. Add chicken of your choice and simmer for 20–30 minutes. Then grill chicken until done.

*Mrs. Larry (Rose) Mullett*

---

*Just when you're successful enough to sleep late,*
*you're so old you always wake up early.*

---

# Italian Chicken Breasts

$1/2$ c. Tender Quik
6 c. water

Italian dressing
$1/2$ tsp. Worcestershire sauce

Mix Tender Quik and water and soak chicken breasts in this for 12 hours. Drain; soak for 12 hours in Italian dressing mixed with Worcestershire sauce. Drain, but reserve. Grill chicken breasts. Put into roaster with reserved Italian dressing mixture. Bake at 350° for 1–1$1/2$ hours.

*Mrs. Glen (Ruby) Yoder*

# Oven Barbequed Chicken

cooking oil
3–4 lb. chicken pieces
$1/3$ c. chopped onion
3 Tbsp. butter or margarine
$3/4$ c. ketchup
$1/3$ c. vinegar

3 Tbsp. brown sugar
$1/2$ c. water
2 tsp. mustard
1 Tbsp. Worcestershire sauce
$1/4$ tsp. salt
$1/8$ tsp. black pepper

Heat a small amount of oil in a large skillet; fry chicken until browned. Drain, place chicken in a 9" x 13" baking dish. Sauté onion in butter until tender; stir in remaining ingredients. Simmer for 15 minutes. Pour over chicken. Bake at 350° for 1 hour or until chicken is done, basting occasionally.

*Mrs. David (Arlene) Chupp*

---

*Happiness is the art of making a lovely bouquet
of the flowers that are within our reach.*

---

# Chicken Breast Strips

| | |
|---|---|
| $1/2$ c. flour | $1/4$ tsp. salt |
| $1/8$ tsp. garlic powder | egg |
| $1/4$ tsp. chicken base | milk |
| $1/8$ tsp. paprika | chicken strips (white meat only) |
| $1/8$ tsp. black pepper | |

Combine dry ingredients. Combine milk and egg. Dip chicken strips in milk/egg mixture, then roll in flour mixture. Fry in a $1/2$" layer of vegetable oil. *Delicious!*

*Mrs. Eli (Pollyanna) Miller*

# Chicken Casserole

| | |
|---|---|
| 4 c. soft bread crumbs | $1/2$ tsp. celery salt |
| $1/4$ tsp. pepper | 2 Tbsp. minced onion |
| $1/4$ tsp. sage | $1/4$ c. butter (melted) |

Stir all ingredients together and press into bottom of a greased 9" x 13" pan. Bake at 375° for 15 minutes.

| | |
|---|---|
| 6 Tbsp. butter | 2 c. milk |
| 6 Tbsp. flour | 2 c. cooked chicken (chopped) |
| $1/4$ tsp. celery salt | 1 c. potatoes (cooked) |
| $1/8$ tsp. pepper | $1/2$ c. peas (cooked) |
| $1/2$ tsp. salt | $1/2$ c. carrots (cooked) |
| 2 c. Rice Krispies | 1 Tbsp. butter |

Melt 6 Tbsp. butter in a 3-qt. kettle. Add flour, celery salt, salt and pepper and mix well. Add milk gradually. Stir in meat and vegetables and pour over baked crumb crust. Slightly crush Rice Krispies and mix with 1 Tbsp. butter. Sprinkle over filling and bake at 350° for 1 hour.

*Mrs. Ferman (LuEtta) Miller*

---

*Faults are like headlights on a car; those of others always seem more glaring than our own.*

---

# Chicken Casserole

9 slices bread (crumbled)
4 c. cooked chicken (cut up)
1 c. oleo (melted)
1/2 c. salad dressing
1 tsp. salt

4 eggs (beaten)
1 c. milk
1 c. chicken broth
9 slices cheese (your choice)
2 cans cream of celery soup

Put crumbled bread slices in bottom of a 9" x 13" cake pan or small roaster. Top with 4 c. cut-up cooked chicken. Mix melted oleo, salad dressing, salt, eggs, milk and chicken broth and pour over chicken. Top with cheese and celery soup. Top with buttered bread crumbs. Cover and refrigerate overnight. Bake at 350° for 1 1/2 hours.

*Mrs. Harry (Edna Mae) Bontrager*

# Chicken Casserole

2 qt. chicken broth
5 eggs
1/2 pkg. noodles
2 small onions

12 slices toast
1 pt. corn
1 can mushroom soup
1 1/2 c. milk

Beat eggs. Cook noodles until halfway done. Cut up toast. Mix all together and bake at 350° for 45 minutes.

*Mrs. Chris (Esther) Bontrager*

# Chicken Divan

2 c. chicken (cooked)
1 pkg. mixed vegetables
   (cooked)
1 c. Miracle Whip

1 c. Velveeta cheese
2 cans cream of chicken soup
1 tsp. curry powder
1 tsp. lemon juice

Mix everything together. Bake at 350° for 45 minutes. Serve over cooked rice.

*Mrs. Dan (Esther) Miller*

# Chicken Dressing

$2^1/2$ loaves bread (toasted)
2 –$2^1/2$ qt. chicken broth
   with meat
$^1/4$ c. chicken soup base
$2^1/2$ Tbsp. seasoning salt
$1^1/2$ tsp. black pepper
16 eggs

1 c. onions
$^1/4$ c. parsley flakes
1 qt. carrots
1 qt. celery
6 c. potatoes
2 c. milk (add more if too dry)

Cook vegetables until soft. Pour over bread and mix everything together.
Bake at 350° for $1^1/2$ hours.

*Mrs. Eugene (Ruth) Yoder*

# Chicken-Fried Steaks

1 lb. ground beef
$^1/2$ c. flour

soda cracker crumbs
2 eggs

Mix meat and flour so that it sticks together and can be rolled out into
$^1/4$" steaks. Dip into beaten eggs then into crushed cracker crumbs. These
may be fried immediately or frozen for later use. It takes approximately
7 minutes to fry them.

*Mrs. Joe (Karen) Graber*

# Chicken Garden Bake

3 Tbsp. butter
$1^1/2$ c. chicken broth
8 oz. can peas (drained)
2 medium carrots
   (cooked & sliced)
2 Tbsp. chopped pimentos,
   *optional*

3 Tbsp. flour
3 c. diced, cooked chicken
3 oz. can sliced mushrooms
$^1/4$ c. chopped onion
$^3/4$ tsp. salt
about 6 biscuits

Melt butter; blend in flour. Add chicken broth and cook until mixture
thickens. Add chicken, vegetables and salt. Heat until bubbly, then pour
into a $1^1/2$-qt. casserole dish. Add about 6 biscuits on top. Bake at 425°
for 8–10 minutes or until biscuits are done. Yield: 5 servings.

*Mrs. Willis (Mary) Bontrager*

# Chicken in a Crumb Basket

6 c. bread crumbs
1 tsp. celery salt
$1/2$ tsp. poultry seasoning

$1/4$ c. chopped onions
$1/2$ c. melted butter

Mix together and line a 2-qt. baking dish. Bake uncovered for 15 minutes at 350°. Make a white sauce of the following:

$1/2$ c. butter
$1/2$ c. milk
$1/4$ c. flour

$1^1/2$ c. chicken broth
$1/2$ tsp. salt
dash pepper

Add the following. Heat thoroughly and pour over crumbs.

3 c. cooked chicken

1 c. peas or corn

*Mrs. Wilbur (Alta) Beechy*

# Chicken Nuggets

1 lg. chicken breast (cut
   in bite-sized pieces)
$1/2$ c. fine bread crumbs
$1/8$ c. Parmesan cheese
$1/4$ c. shredded cheddar cheese

$1/4$ tsp. basil
$1/2$ tsp. salt
$1/4$ tsp. pepper
several shakes seasoning salt
melted butter

Mix dry ingredients and cheddar cheese. Dip chicken breast pieces in melted butter and then in first mixture. Preheat oven at 400° and bake for 10 minutes.

*Mrs. Joe (Karen) Graber*

*To Jesus all thy wants confide; He will protect thee and provide.*

# Chicken & Rice Casserole

4 c. cooked rice
$1/4$ c. melted butter
2 c. milk
1 tsp. seasoned salt
$1/4$ tsp. pepper
$1/4$ c. flour
2 tsp. chicken bouillon

$1/2$ tsp. garlic powder
4–5 c. cooked boneless chicken
12 oz. Velveeta cheese
2 c. sour cream
$1/4$ c. melted butter
1 pkg. Ritz crackers (crushed)

Put cooked rice into a 9" x 13" greased pan. Mix next 7 ingredients and cook until thickened. Pour over rice. Put cooked chicken on top of sauce. Melt Velveeta a little and stir in sour cream and put on top of chicken. Top with melted butter and Ritz crackers. Bake until heated through.

*Mrs. Reuben (Alma) Miller*

# Chicken Souffle

4–5 c. cooked chicken
(chopped)
$2/3$ c. chopped celery
$1/3$ c. chopped onion
$3/4$ c. Miracle Whip or
mayonnaise

$1/2$ tsp. salt
12–16 slices bread
5 eggs
3 c. milk
1 can golden mushroom soup
shredded cheese

Combine chicken, celery, onion, salad dressing and salt. Line a 9" x 13" cake pan with 6–8 slices bread. Spread chicken mixture on top of the bread. Top with another layer of bread slices. Beat together eggs and milk and pour over bread. Refrigerate for 6–8 hours or overnight. Bring souffle to room temperature before baking. Bake at 350° for 15 minutes. Spread with mushroom soup and top with shredded cheese. Bake for 1 hour. Serve plain or with chicken gravy.

*Mrs. Ervin (Anna Mary) Miller*

---

*To wait on God is no time lost.*

---

# Chicken Spaghetti

$1^1/_2$–2 c. chicken broth
3 lb. chicken (cooked &
    cut up)
12 oz. linguine spaghetti
    noodles
$^1/_2$ green pepper

1 small onion
1 can cream of mushroom soup
1 can cream of chicken soup
salt & pepper to taste
Velveeta cheese

Cook noodles; add chicken and other ingredients. Put into a 9" x 13" pan. Put cheese on top. Bake at 350° for 45 minutes.

*Mrs. Marvin (Katie) Miller*

# Spaghetti & Chicken Casserole

1 - 16 oz. pkg. spaghetti
1 can cream of mushroom
    soup
1 medium onion

$^1/_4$ lb. butter (melted)
1 qt. chicken (cooked & deboned)
1 lb. Velveeta cheese

Cook spaghetti in chicken broth. Dice onion and brown in butter. Add cheese and stir until melted. Remove from heat and fold in soup and chicken pieces. Put cooked spaghetti in a 9" x 12" baking dish. Pour soup and cheese mixture over all. Bake at 350° for 25–30 minutes.

*Mrs. Orva (Marietta) Yoder*

# Crispy Chicken Roll-Ups

3 whole boneless chicken
    breasts (halved & pounded)
    (about $1^1/_2$ lb.)
6 slices cooked ham
    (about 6 oz.)

6 slices Swiss cheese (about 6 oz.)
2 eggs (beaten)
2 Tbsp. margarine
Mary Lou's Special Coating or
    Team Flakes crumbs

Top each chicken breast with 1 slice of ham and cheese. Roll up, secure with toothpick. Dip in beaten eggs and coat with Mary Lou's Special Coating or Team Flakes crumbs. Place chicken rolls in a greased baking dish. Drizzle with margarine. Bake at 350° for 40 minutes or until done.

*Mrs. David (Mary Lou) Whetstone*

# Delicious Kentucky-Fried Chicken

| | |
|---|---|
| 1 whole chicken | 2 tsp. salt |
| 1 egg | 1 tsp. paprika |
| 2/3 c. water | dash of red or black pepper |
| 1/4 c. cooking oil | 3/4 c. flour |

Beat egg, water and cooking oil together. Add salt, paprika, pepper and flour; mix until smooth. Dip cut-up chicken pieces into batter and roll in flour. Fry in enough hot oil to cover. Turn chicken often while frying. Fry for 30–45 minutes until golden brown and crisp. *Delicious!*

*Mrs. Joe (Karen) Graber*

# Potluck Potatoes

| | |
|---|---|
| 2 lb. boiled potatoes | 1 tsp. salt |
| 4 Tbsp. melted butter | 1 pt. sour cream |
| 1/2 c. chopped onion | 2 c. grated sharp cheddar cheese |
| 1 can cream of chicken soup | 2 c. crushed corn flakes |
| 1/4 tsp. pepper | 4 Tbsp. melted butter |

In a large bowl, combine potatoes with 4 Tbsp. melted butter. Add salt, pepper, onions, soup, sour cream and cheese; blend thoroughly. Add milk if this is too dry. Pour into a greased casserole dish. Combine corn flakes and 4 Tbsp. melted butter and put on top. Bake at 350° until golden brown. This may be made the day before serving. Do not put crushed corn flakes on top until ready to bake.

*Mrs. John (Elsie) Yoder, Mrs. Reuben (Martha) Yoder*

---

*Jumping to conclusions is not nearly as good exercise as digging for facts.*

# Sweet Potato Casserole

3 c. sweet potatoes (mashed)          $^1/_4$ c. melted butter
$^1/_2$ c. brown sugar                       $^1/_2$ c. milk
$^1/_2$ tsp. salt

TOPPING:
1 c. brown sugar                        6 Tbsp. melted butter
$^2/_3$ c. flour

Combine sweet potatoes, brown sugar, salt, butter and milk. Pour into a greased $1^1/_2$-qt. casserole dish and top with topping. Bake at 325° until bubbly.

*Mrs. Dan (Esther) Miller*

# Baked Potato Stacks

6–8 lb. potatoes* (with skins)       1 tsp. salt
2–3 lb. hamburger                      $^1/_2$ tsp. pepper
1 medium onion (chopped)           1 large pkg. California Blend
3 Tbsp. taco seasoning                   vegetables
1 c. butter or margarine              16 oz. sour cream
$1^1/_2$ c. flour                            hot pepper rings or chopped bell
6–7 c. milk                                  peppers, *optional*
$1^1/_2$ lb. Velveeta cheese

*New potatoes work well (use small ones). Place potatoes in a large baking dish and cover. Bake at 350° for $1^1/_2$ hours or until tender. Fry hamburger in skillet over medium heat; add onion and taco seasoning. In the meantime make a cheese sauce. Melt butter or margarine; add flour, blend well, gradually add milk, salt and pepper, stirring constantly. Blend in cheese. Fix vegetables according to directions on pkg. Drain and add to cheese sauce. Serve in the following order: potatoes, meat, cheese sauce and vegetable blend, sour cream and pepper rings or chopped peppers if desired. *Delicious!*

*Mrs. Samuel (Viola) Miller*

# Stuffed Baked Potatoes

3 large baking potatoes
   (1 lb. each)
1½ tsp. vegetable oil, *optional*
½ c. onions
½ c. margarine (divided)
½ c. light cream

½ c. sour cream
1 tsp. salt
½ tsp. pepper
1 c. shredded cheese
paprika

Rub potatoes with oil if desired. Pierce with a fork. Bake at 400° for 1 hour and 20 minutes or until tender. Allow potatoes to cool to the touch. Cut potatoes in half lengthwise. Carefully scoop out pulp, leaving a thin shell. Place pulp in a large bowl. Sauté onions in ¼ c. butter until tender. Add to potato pulp along with cream, sour cream, salt and pepper. Beat until smooth. Fold in cheese. Stuff potato shells and place in a 9" x 13" pan. Melt remaining butter and drizzle over the potatoes. Sprinkle with paprika. Bake at 350° for 20–30 minutes or until heated through. *Delicious!*

*Mrs. Mervin (Ruth) Yoder*

# Twice-Baked Potatoes

4 large baking potatoes
2 Tbsp. butter
½ c. milk (hot)
½ tsp. salt
⅛ tsp. pepper

4 slices bacon (fried & crumbled)
2 Tbsp. Parmesan cheese
4 Tbsp. grated cheddar cheese
3 green onions (chopped fine)

Prick each potato with a fork several times. Bake on a rack at 400° for approx. 1 hour or until tender. Cut a thin slice from the top of each potato and scoop out pulp into a bowl. Beat in milk, butter, salt, pepper and green onions. Mix in bacon. Spoon potatoes into shells. Sprinkle with cheeses. Place potatoes on a baking sheet and return to oven for 10 minutes or until heated through and cheeses are melted.

*Amy Yoder (Daughter)*

# Crunchy Potato Balls

2 c. mashed potatoes (very stiff)
2 c. finely chopped fully
   cooked ham
1 c. shredded cheddar or
   Swiss cheese
$1/3$ c. mayonnaise

1 egg (beaten)
1 tsp. prepared mustard
$1/2$ tsp. pepper
2–4 Tbsp. flour
$1^3/4$ c. crushed corn flakes

In a bowl, combine the potatoes, ham, cheese, mayonnaise, egg, mustard and pepper; mix well. Add enough of the flour to make a stiff mixture. Chill. Shape into 1" balls and roll in corn flakes. Place on a greased baking sheet. Bake at 350° for 25–30 minutes. Yield: About 6 dozen.

*Mrs. Orva (Marietta) Yoder, Mrs. Floyd (Marietta) Troyer*

# Scalloped Cheesy Potatoes

1 - $10^3/4$ oz. can condensed
   cream of mushroom soup
8 oz. shredded cheddar cheese
2 lb. potatoes (peeled & sliced)

1 medium onion (sliced thin)
$3/4$ c. crushed Ritz crackers
   (about 18 crackers)

In a large bowl, stir together the soup and cheese. With a rubber spatula, fold in onion and potatoes until thoroughly coated. Scrape into a greased 9" x 13" x 2" baking dish. Cover with tinfoil. Bake for 1 hour or until potatoes are tender. Sprinkle top with cracker crumbs. Bake until top is golden brown (about 5–10 minutes). Let set for 10 minutes before serving. Yield: 8 servings.

*Mrs. Freeman (Mabel) Yoder*

---

*God doesn't comfort us to make us comfortable,*
*but to make us comforters.*

---

# Haystack Supper

2 lb. hamburger
$1/2$ c. chopped onion
1 Tbsp. prepared mustard
1 Tbsp. taco seasoning
2 Tbsp. brown sugar
$1/2$ c. ketchup
1 tsp. salt

3 qt. mashed potatoes (without milk)
4 tomatoes (cut up)
1 pepper (cut up), *optional*
1 small head lettuce (cut up)
1 - 15 oz. bag Doritos (crushed)
cheese sauce (recipe below)

**CHEESE SAUCE:**
$1/2$ c. margarine
$3/4$ c. flour
4–6 c. milk
1 - $10^{1}/_2$ oz. can cream of mushroom soup

1 lb. Velveeta cheese
2 tsp. taco seasoning
salt & pepper to taste

Combine first 7 ingredients in a frying pan and brown. For Cheese Sauce: Melt margarine and add flour; blend well. Gradually add milk and mushroom soup, stirring constantly. Add Velveeta cheese and more milk if mixture is too thick. Add taco seasoning and salt and pepper to taste. Serve with meat on plate first, then in order given, each forming his own "haystack." *Delicious and always a specialty at our house!*

*Mrs. Freeman (Mabel) Yoder*

# Runza Casserole

2 tubes crescent rolls
1 lb. hamburger
2 c. chopped cabbage
$1/4$ c. chopped onions

1 - $10^{3}/_4$ oz. can cream of mushroom soup
$3/4$ c. cheddar cheese (shredded)
$3/4$ c. mozzarella cheese

Brown hamburger; drain and add cabbage and onions. Simmer for 10 minutes. Add mushroom soup. Press 1 tube crescent rolls into a 9" x 13" pan. Put hamburger mixture on top of this. Sprinkle cheeses over meat. Place remaining tube of crescent rolls over the top. Bake at 350° for about 20 minutes (until browned).

*Mrs. Wayne (Marilyn) Yoder*

# Easy Burrito Casserole

2 lb. hamburger (browned)
1 can refried beans
1 pkg. taco seasoning
2 cans cream of mushroom soup

2 c. sour cream
8–10 soft tortillas
$2^{1}/_{2}$ c. shredded cheddar cheese

Combine browned hamburger, refried beans and taco seasoning. Mix mushroom soup and sour cream; set aside. Put half of soup mixture in the bottom of a 9" x 13" x 2" baking dish. Layer half of the tortillas on top of the soup mixture. Use all the hamburger on the layer of tortillas. Put the remaining tortillas on top. Spread the remaining soup over that. Bake for 1 hour at 325°. Top with cheddar cheese. Return to oven until cheese is melted. Serve with lettuce, tomatoes, sour cream and taco sauce or salsa.

*Mrs. Darrel (Erma) Yoder*

# Taco Bake

$1^{1}/_{2}$ c. Bisquick mix
$^{1}/_{2}$ c. cold water
1 egg
$1^{1}/_{2}$ c. sour cream
1 c. cheddar cheese
$^{1}/_{2}$ c. mayonnaise

2 lb. ground beef (browned)
1 pkg. taco seasoning
1 pt. pizza sauce
1 can pork & beans

**SALAD DRESSING:**

2 c. Miracle Whip
$1^{1}/_{2}$ c. sugar
$^{1}/_{3}$ c. vinegar
$2^{1}/_{2}$ Tbsp. mustard

6 Tbsp. ketchup
1 tsp. garlic salt
$2^{1}/_{2}$ Tbsp. lemon juice
1 Tbsp. salad oil

Combine Bisquick, cold water and egg. Press into a 9" x 13" pan. Bake at 350° for 10 minutes. Mix sour cream, cheddar cheese and mayonnaise and spoon over crust. Brown ground beef and add taco seasoning, pizza sauce and pork & beans. Put on top of sour cream mixture. Bake uncovered at 350° for 30 minutes. Serve with diced tomatoes, lettuce and salad dressing (recipe above). Mix all salad dressing ingredients well.

*Mrs. Dan (Esther) Miller*

# Taco Casserole

1 pizza crust
8 oz. sour cream
1 can cream of chicken soup
1 can cheddar cheese soup,
  *optional*

hamburger (fried)
taco seasoning
ham or sausage, *optional*
Dorito chips
pizza cheese

Mix sour cream and soups together. Put on crust. Fry hamburger and add taco seasoning. Add ham or sausage if desired. Bake (as you would pizza). When it's about halfway through baking, put Dorito chips and pizza cheese on top. Finish baking. Serve with lettuce and tomatoes.

*Mrs. Ervin (Edna) Bontrager*

# Taco Pizza

1½ lb. hamburger
1 - 16 oz. can refried beans
1 Tbsp. taco seasoning

⅔ c. cream of mushroom soup
⅔ c. sour cream
2 c. shredded cheddar cheese

CRUST:
2 c. flour
2 tsp. baking powder
1 tsp. salt

¼ c. oil
⅔ c. milk

For Crust: Combine dry ingredients; add oil and milk. Stir together to form dough. Roll out on a 14" pizza pan. Bake at 350° for 25 minutes. While crust is baking, brown hamburger, then add beans and taco seasoning. Mix mushroom soup and sour cream. Spread this on baked crust. Put hamburger mixture on top of sour cream mixture, then top with cheddar cheese. Return to oven until cheese is melted. Serve with salsa, lettuce, tomatoes and onions.

*Mrs. Wilbur (Alta) Beechy*

*Experience tells you what to do; confidence allows you to do it.*

# Taco Potato Shells

3 large baking potatoes
1 Tbsp. butter or margarine
(melted)
1 lb. ground beef
1 - 14$^1/_2$ oz. can diced
tomatoes (undrained)

1 env. taco seasoning
$^1/_2$ c. shredded cheddar cheese
$^1/_3$ c. sour cream
2 green onions (sliced)

Scrub and pierce potatoes. Bake at 375° for 1 hour or until tender. Cut in half lengthwise. Carefully scoop out pulp, leaving a thin shell (refrigerate pulp for another use). Brush inside and outside of potato shells with butter. Bake, uncovered, at 375° for 20 minutes. Meanwhile, in a skillet, cook beef over medium heat until no longer pink; drain. Add tomatoes and taco seasoning. Bring to a boil. Reduce heat; simmer, uncovered, for 20 minutes. Spoon into potato shells; sprinkle with cheese. Bake, uncovered, for 5–10 minutes longer or until cheese is melted. Top with sour cream and onions. Yield: 6 servings.

*Mrs. Lester (Verna) Bontrager*

# Taco Skillet

1 lb. ground beef
1 pkg. (6 Tbsp.) taco seasoning
1 pt. tomato juice
$^3/_4$ c. water
1 c. rice (uncooked)
2 Tbsp. brown sugar

1 c. shredded cheddar cheese
shredded lettuce
chopped onions
sour cream
salsa or taco sauce

Brown beef in a large skillet with lid. Add seasoning, tomato juice, water, rice and brown sugar. Simmer for 20 minutes or until rice is tender, stirring several times. Top with cheese and let melt. Serve with lettuce, onions, sour cream and salsa or taco sauce. Green peppers are also good!

*Mrs. David (JoAnn) Bontrager*

*Only speak when your words are an improvement over silence.*

# Upside Down Pizza

1 lb. meat (browned)
1 medium onion
$^1/_4$ c. chopped green pepper
1 pt. pizza sauce
2 c. shredded cheese

1 c. flour
2 eggs
1 c. milk
1 Tbsp. vegetable oil
$^1/_2$ tsp. salt

Brown meat with onion and green pepper. Add pizza sauce. Put in a 9" x 13" baking dish. Sprinkle shredded cheese on top. Mix flour, eggs, milk, oil and salt. Pour over cheese and bake, uncovered, at 425° for 25–30 minutes until browned.

*Mrs. Lester (LaVerda) Yoder*

# Tater Tot Stack

6 c. frozen Tater Tots
$^1/_2$ c. chopped onions
2 lb. hamburger
3 Tbsp. taco seasoning
2 c. shredded cheddar cheese

2 whole tomatoes (cut up)
$^3/_4$ c. sliced olives (green or black)
4 c. shredded lettuce
8 Tbsp. taco sauce
1 c. sour cream, *optional*

Bake Tater Tots until crisp and browned. Meanwhile, fry hamburger, onions and taco seasoning together. Divide Tater Tots on 6–8 serving plates. Spoon hamburger over each plate of Tater Tots. Divide cheese on top of hamburger, continue with tomatoes, olives, lettuce, taco sauce and sour cream.

*Mrs. Freeman (Mabel) Yoder*

*Oh Lord, help my words to be tender and gracious today for tomorrow I may have to eat them.*

# Texas Hash

| | |
|---|---|
| 2 large onions | $^1/_2$ c. uncooked rice |
| 3 Tbsp. butter | 1 tsp. chili powder |
| 2 green peppers (chopped) | $1^1/_2$ tsp. salt |
| 1 lb. hamburger | $^1/_4$ tsp. pepper |
| 2 c. canned tomatoes | |

Fry minced onions and green peppers in butter until onions are brown. Add hamburger and fry for several minutes. Then add tomatoes, rice, and seasonings. Pour into a large casserole dish. Cover and bake at 375° for about 50 minutes.

*Mrs. Eli (Pollyanna) Miller*

# Toastada (Mexican Haystack)

| | |
|---|---|
| 2 lb. hamburger (browned) | 1 pkg. taco seasoning |
| 1 can refried beans | $^3/_4$ c. water |

Mix the above ingredients; bring to a boil and simmer for 10 minutes. Place small amount of each on a stack on plate, in order given below. Garnish with sour cream and salsa.

| | |
|---|---|
| 1 bag tortilla chips (crushed) | 4 tomatoes (diced) |
| hot hamburger mixture | 1 lb. shredded Colby cheese |
| 1 head lettuce (shredded) | 2 qt. cheese sauce (heated) |

*Mrs. Ray (Irene) Mullett*

---

*What we desire our children to become we must endeavor to be before them.*

---

*When looking for faults, use a mirror, not a telescope.*

# Tomato Gravy

2 c. tomato juice
1/4 c. water
1/2 tsp. salt

1 c. milk
1 tsp. sugar
3 Tbsp. flour

Place juice and water in a saucepan and bring to a boil. Meanwhile, blend the flour, salt and sugar with the milk. Pour into the hot juice, stirring constantly until it boils and is thickened and smooth.

*Mrs. Ervin Lee (Lydia) Yoder*

# Underground Ham Casserole

**BOTTOM PART:**
4 c. cooked & chunked ham*
4 Tbsp. oleo

1/2 c. chopped onion
1 Tbsp. Worcestershire sauce

Combine all ingredients and boil until onions are tender. Place in bottom of a medium-sized roaster. *This is delicious using crumbled, browned hamburger instead of ham.

**MIDDLE PART:**
2 cans cream of mushroom soup
1 c. milk

2 c. Velveeta cheese or American cheese slices

In a saucepan, heat together soup, milk and cheese until cheese melts. Pour over ham and onions.

**TOP PART:**
4 qt. mashed potatoes
1 tsp. salt
1 pt. sour cream

1 c. milk
browned & crumbled bacon, *optional*

Mash potatoes, add salt, sour cream and milk. You may substitute more milk for the sour cream. Spread over top of cheese mixture and sprinkle with bacon. Bake at 350° for 20 minutes. The cheese mixture comes to the top when done. *A favorite!*

*Mrs. Allen (Elsie) Bontrager, Mrs. Perry (Lena) Lehman*

# Stove Top Cabbage Casserole

1 lb. ground beef
1 small onion
$^1/_3$ c. rice
1 tsp. salt

4 c. coarsely chopped cabbage
1 can tomato soup
1 c. water
4 slices American cheese

In a 3-qt. saucepan, brown hamburger with onion. Add rice, soup, salt, cabbage and water. Simmer over low heat for 30 minutes or until rice is tender. Remove from heat. Put cheese slices on top and let set for 5 minutes to melt cheese. Stir in cheese and serve.

*Mrs. Ervin Lee (Lydia) Yoder*

# Western Beef Casserole

1 lb. ground beef
1 tsp. salt
1 - 16 oz. can pork & beans
$^1/_4$ c. barbecue sauce
$^1/_2$ c. ketchup

1 Tbsp. minced onion
2 Tbsp. brown sugar
1 c. shredded cheddar cheese
1 can flaky biscuits

Brown ground beef and season with salt. Add pork & beans, barbecue sauce, ketchup, onion and brown sugar. Heat until bubbly. Place in a medium-sized roaster. Sprinkle shredded cheese on top and place biscuits on top of that. Bake at 375° for 25–30 minutes or until biscuits are golden brown.

*Mrs. David (JoAnn) Bontrager*

---

*Happiness is a perfume you cannot pour on others
without getting a few drops on yourself.*

---

# White Sauce

1¹/₂ c. butter
3 c. flour
12 c. milk

1¹/₂ lb. Velveeta cheese
2 tsp. salt (regular or Lawry's)
1 tsp. pepper

Melt butter and stir in flour; add milk, 3 c. at a time, allowing to thicken after each addition. Stir constantly over low heat. Slice in cheese and turn off heat. Allow cheese to melt, then add salt and pepper and stir thoroughly. For added flavors add 2 pt. sour cream or 2 - 16 oz. jars Ranch dressing. This is enough for a roaster full of potatoes, hamburger, etc. Yield: 6 quarts. *The best!*

*Mrs. Eli (Martha) Mullet*

# Zucchini Fritters

6 c. grated zucchini
3 c. flour
1 medium-sized onion

2 eggs
1¹/₂ tsp. salt

Mix all ingredients together and stir well. It will seem sticky for awhile, but will get thinner as you stir. Drop batter by spoonfuls into hot skillet and brown on both sides. Drain on paper towels. *This is an all-time favorite for our family during the summer!*

*Mrs. Orva (Marietta) Yoder, Mrs. Floyd (Marietta) Troyer*

# Zucchini Patties

²/₃ c. Bisquick baking mix
¹/₄ c. Parmesan cheese
2 eggs (beaten)

2 c. grated zucchini
1 small onion (chopped)
salt & pepper

Combine all ingredients and drop by spoonfuls into heavy skillet containing a thin layer of hot margarine. Spread out and flatten as you turn them with a spatula. Fry until golden brown on both sides.

*Mrs. Harry (Edna Mae) Bontrager*

# Zucchini Pizza

1 medium zucchini
1 c. flour
1 tsp. baking powder
1/2 tsp. black pepper
1 tsp. Italian seasoning or
  oregano

2 eggs
2/3 c. milk
1 1/2 c. pizza sauce
1/4 c. chopped onion
1 c. browned hamburger
grated cheese

Lightly oil a 9" x 13" pan. Peel and slice zucchini into 1/2" rounds, enough to cover bottom of pan. Put in oven at 400° until heated through and is starting to bake. Meanwhile, mix flour, baking powder, black pepper, Italian seasoning or oregano, eggs and milk. Pour over and between hot zucchini. Return to oven and bake for 25–30 minutes longer. Top with pizza sauce, onion, hamburger and cheese. Return to oven for 10–15 minutes.

*Mrs. Glenn (Polly) Yoder*

# Squash Casserole

2 c. cooked squash
1/4 c. melted butter
1 medium onion (chopped)

2 c. crumbled corn bread
1 c. cream of chicken soup
salt & pepper to taste

Combine all ingredients and place in casserole dish. Bake at 350° for 30–40 minutes.

*Mrs. Allen (Elsie) Bontrager*

---

*Peace in the world begins with us.*

---

*To be thankful with much is good; to be thankful with little is better.*

# Bar-B-Q Green Beans

$1/2$ lb. bacon
1 medium onion (chopped)
2 qt. green beans (drained)
$3/4$ c. brown sugar

$1/2$ c. ketchup
$1/3$ c. corn syrup
1 tsp. liquid smoke
$1/2$ tsp. salt

Fry bacon and onion together. Drain grease then add to green beans. Mix the remaining ingredients in a small saucepan. Heat until sugar is dissolved. Pour over green beans. Bake at 325° fo 1 hour.

*Mrs. Lavern (Martha) Yoder*

# Summer Vegetable Casserole

2 c. grated zucchini
$1^1/2$ c. diced celery
1 medium onion (chopped)
$1/2$ c. green pepper (diced)

1 Tbsp. cooking oil
1 tomato (cut in eighths)
$3/4$ c. grated cheddar or longhorn
 cheese

Toss zucchini, celery, onion and green pepper in a 2-qt. casserole. Add salt and pepper to taste. Sprinkle with oil. Arrange tomato on top and sprinkle with cheese. Bake, covered, at 350° until vegetables are tender. Yield: 4–6 Servings.

*Mrs. Glenn (Polly) Yoder*

---

*Progress has little to do with speed, but much to do with direction.*

---

*He who is afraid of doing too much always does too little.*

# Green Bean Corn Casserole

| | |
|---|---|
| 2 cans green beans (drained) | 8 oz. sour cream |
| 2 cans corn (drained) | 1 c. grated cheese |
| 1 medium chopped onion | $1/2$ tsp. salt |
| 1 c. chopped celery | 1 pkg. Ritz crackers (crushed) |
| 1 can cream of celery soup | $1/2$ c. melted butter |

Mix all but last 2 ingredients together. Mix Ritz crackers and butter. Put on top. Bake at 350° until bubbly and browned.

*Mrs. Samuel (Viola) Miller*

# Cheese Zucchini Casserole

| | |
|---|---|
| 3 eggs | $1/2$ tsp. salt |
| $1/2$ c. milk | $1/4$–$1/2$ tsp. cayenne pepper |
| $1/2$ c. Bisquick (or homemade baking mix) | $1/2$ tsp. pepper |

Mix top ingredients together. Layer the following in a 9" x 13" glass baking dish.

| | |
|---|---|
| 3 c. chopped zucchini | $1/2$ c. chopped onion |
| 2 c. chopped tomatoes | 8 oz. shredded cheddar cheese |

At this point the two mixtures may be refrigerated separately until ready to use. Pour egg mixture over vegetables. Bake, uncovered, at 350° for 45–50 minutes or until golden brown. Let set for 10 minutes before serving.

*Mrs. Lloyd (Mary Etta) Miller*

---

*He who has no money is poor, but he who has nothing but money is even poorer.*

---

# Broccoli Casserole

| | |
|---|---|
| 2 Tbsp. butter | 1 c. milk |
| 2 Tbsp. flour | 2 - 10 oz. pkg. frozen broccoli |
| 3 oz. cream cheese (softened) | (cooked & drained) |
| 1/4 c. Velveeta cheese | 1/3 c. Ritz crackers (crushed) |

In saucepan melt butter. Blend in flour and cheeses; add milk. Cook and stir until mixture boils. Stir in broccoli. Place in a greased casserole dish. Top with cracker crumbs. Bake at 350° for 30 minutes. Yield: 8–10 servings.

*Mrs. Wayne (Marilyn) Yoder*

# Venison Balls in Sour Cream Sauce

| | |
|---|---|
| 1/2 lb. ground venison | 1 egg |
| 1 large onion (chopped) | 1/2 tsp. salt |
| 1 small garlic clove (minced) | 1/4 tsp. pepper |
| 1/4 c. whole grain bread (dried & crushed) | 1/4 tsp. parsley flakes |
| | 2 Tbsp. butter |

SAUCE:

| | |
|---|---|
| 3/4 c. sour cream | 1 Tbsp. lemon juice |
| 1 egg yolk | 1/8 tsp. nutmeg |

Mix all top ingredients thoroughly except butter and form into 1" balls. Brown well (about 10 minutes) in butter. Mix sauce ingredients together and pour over venison balls. Cover and heat for 2–3 minutes (do not boil). Garnish with fresh chopped parsley. Serve with buttered egg noodles.

*Mrs. Lester (Verna) Bontrager*

---

*A chain is as strong as its weakest link.*
*A brain is as strong as its weakest think.*

# Brown Gravy

<sup></sup>1/2 c. oleo or butter
1/2 c. flour
2 c. hot water
2 c. milk
1 pkg. brown gravy mix
   (2 1/2 Tbsp.)

1/2 can cream of mushroom soup
1/2 tsp. pepper
dash of salt
1 Tbsp. Kitchen Banquet
   seasoning salt

Melt butter in a saucepan and add flour. Mix well. Add remaining ingredients and stir well. Keep stirring until it boils.

*Mrs. Devon (Marietta) Troyer, Mom (Elsie) Yoder*

# Simple Pan Gravy

1/2 c. margarine, lard or
   pre-creamed shortening
1 c. flour

1 qt. cold water
2 c. hot water
salt & pepper to taste

Melt shortening in a large skillet; add flour and stir with spatula over medium high heat until well browned. Gradually add cold water, stirring with a potato masher to avoid lumps. Add hot water and salt and pepper to taste. Some milk may be used instead of all water.

*LuAnn Yoder (Daughter)*

# Stroganoff

2 lb. hamburger
1 lb. bulk sausage
3 slices bacon
1/2 c. chopped onion
1 1/2 Tbsp. flour
3/4 tsp. salt

1/4 tsp. paprika
dash of pepper
1 can cream of mushroom soup
1 c. sour cream
Velveeta cheese, *optional*

Brown beef, sausage and bacon. Add onion and cook until tender but not brown. Drain. Blend flour and seasonings into meat mixture. Stir in soup and cook slowly for 20 minutes. Stir in sour cream and heat through. May be served on buns, rice or noodles.

*Mrs. Joseph (Barbara) Bontrager*

# Noodle Crispy

Velveeta cheese
1 can cream of mushroom soup
$^1/_2$ c. milk
2 c. noodles (cooked & drained)

1 qt. hamburger or any kind of
   meat
$^1/_2$ c. cracker crumbs
2 Tbsp. oleo (melted)

Heat cheese (amount desired), mushroom soup and milk over low heat. Stir until sauce is smooth. Add cooked noodles and meat. Pour into a 2-qt. casserole dish. Toss crackers with oleo and put on top. Bake at 325° for 20 minutes.

*Mrs. Perry (Rosemary) Miller*

# Easy Baked Macaroni with Cheese

3 Tbsp. melted butter
$2^1/_2$ c. macaroni
1 tsp. salt

$^1/_4$ tsp. pepper
$^1/_2$ lb. cheese (cubed)
1 qt. milk

Stir melted butter and macaroni together. Then add salt, pepper, cubed cheese and milk. Bake uncovered at 325° for $1^1/_2$ hours.

*Mrs. Ervin Lee (Lydia) Yoder*

# Macaroni Casserole

1 c. macaroni (uncooked)
1 can cream of mushroom soup
$1^1/_4$ c. milk

1 c. Velveeta cheese (cut up)
2 c. meat of your choice
$^1/_4$ c. chopped onions

Mix all together and let set in cool place overnight. Put in a baking dish and bake at 350° for 1 hour.

*Mrs. Delmar (Pauline) Weaver*

---

*When angry count to ten before you speak. When very angry count to 100.*

# Crafty Crescent Lasagna

**MEAT FILLING:**

1 lb. hamburger
$^3/_4$ c. chopped onion
1 Tbsp. parsley flakes
$^1/_2$ tsp. basil

$^1/_2$ tsp. oregano
6 oz. tomato paste
$^1/_2$ tsp. salt

Brown meat; drain well and add remaining ingredients and simmer for 5 minutes.

**CHEESE FILLING:**

1 can creamed small curd
   cottage cheese

$^1/_4$ c. Parmesan cheese
1 egg

**CRUST:**

2 cans crescent dinner rolls
2 - 4" x 7" slices mozzarella
   cheese

1 Tbsp. milk
1 Tbsp. sesame seeds, *optional*

Unroll crescent rolls and separate into 8 rectangles. Place side by side on an ungreased cookie sheet, overlapping edges slightly to form a 15" x 13" rectangle. Spread half of meat mixture lengthwise down center of dough. Top meat mixture with cheese filling. Spoon remaining meat mixture on top, forming 3 layers. Place cheese slices over meat mixture. Pull sides of dough over meat and cheese, overlapping $^1/_4$". Pinch seams and ends together. Brush with milk, sprinkle with sesame seeds. Bake at 375° for 30 minutes or until golden brown.

*Mrs. Eli (Martha) Mullet*

---

*Never look down on someone unless you're helping them up.*

---

# Potato & Hamburger Casserole

2 lb. hamburger
1 pkg. or 1 Tbsp. taco
  seasoning
8 potatoes (cooked &
  shredded)
16 oz. sour cream

$^1/_2$ c. milk
$^1/_2$ c. butter (divided)
1 tsp. salt
1 can cream of mushroom soup
1 lb. cheese (melted)
$3^1/_2$ c. corn flakes (crushed)

Cook potatoes. Brown hamburger; drain and mix with taco seasoning.
Shred cooked potatoes and mix with sour cream, milk, $^1/_4$ c. butter, salt,
cream of mushroom soup and cheese. Put hamburger in roaster and put
potatoes on top. Mix $^1/_4$ c. butter and corn flake crumbs and put on
top. Bake at 350° for 1 hour.

*Mrs. Orva (Marietta) Yoder, Mrs. John (Susie) Kuhns*


# Hamburger & Cheese Casserole

1 lb. hamburger
$^1/_2$ c. onion
16 oz. tomato sauce
1 tsp. sugar
$^3/_4$ tsp. salt
$^1/_4$ tsp. garlic salt
$^1/_4$ tsp. pepper

4 c. noodles (uncooked)
8 oz. cheese
1 c. cottage cheese
$^1/_4$ c. sour cream
$^1/_4$ c. green peppers
$^1/_4$ c. Parmesan cheese

Combine onion and meat until brown. Stir in tomato sauce, sugar, salt,
garlic salt and pepper. Remove from heat. Meanwhile, cook noodles
and drain. Combine cheeses, sour cream and peppers. Spread half of
noodles in an 11" x 17" pan. Top with some of meat sauce and then top
with all of cheese mixture. Add remaining noodles and meat sauce. Last,
top with Parmesan cheese. Bake at 350° for 30 minutes.

*Mrs. Raymond (LeEtta) Yoder*

# Potato Haystack

| | |
|---|---|
| 8-10 medium potatoes | 3 lb. hamburger (browned) |
| 2 pkg. buttermilk Hidden Valley Ranch dressing mix | onions |
| | 1 pkg. taco seasoning |
| 1 c. sour cream | 1 bag nacho or Dorito chips |
| 1 c. milk | |

Cook potatoes in skins, peel and shred. Layer in bottom of a casserole dish. Mix next 3 ingredients and spread over potatoes. Brown hamburger with onions and add taco seasoning. Layer over sour cream mixture. Pour cheese sauce over all (recipe below). Bake at 325° until hot. Just before serving, spread crushed nacho chips over the top. More or less cheese sauce may be used.

**CHEESE SAUCE:**

| | |
|---|---|
| $1/4$–$1/2$ c. butter | $2^1/2$–3 c. shredded cheese |
| $1/2$ c. flour | $1/2$ tsp. salt |
| 3 c. milk | 1 Tbsp. taco seasoning |

Melt butter in medium saucepan. Add flour. Gradually add milk. Then add shredded cheese. Stir until smooth and add salt and taco seasoning.

*Mrs. David (Rachel) Plank*

# Hamburger Casserole

| | |
|---|---|
| $1/2$ lb. (or more) hamburger | 1 can mushroom soup |
| 1 pt. green beans | mashed potatoes |
| small onion (chopped) | cubed cheese |

Brown hamburger and put in bottom of casserole dish. Mix green beans with onion and put on top of hamburger. Spread mushroom soup over green beans. Spread mashed potatoes 3" thick over top. Dot top of potatoes with cubes of cheese. Bake at 350° for 30–35 minutes. Bake, covered, and let cool slightly before serving.

*Mrs. Menno (Ruby) Mullet*

# Hamburger Hot Dish

1 lb. hamburger
2 c. cooked macaroni*
1 onion (chopped)
1 can peas

1 can mushroom soup
2 c. diced cheese
1 c. tomato juice

*Take 4 c. water and 1 c. uncooked macaroni to make 2 c. cooked macaroni. More macaroni may be added. Fry hamburger and onion together until slightly browned. Add remaining ingredients, adding tomato juice until desired thickness. Put in a casserole dish. Bake at 350° until bubbling hot. Crumbs or chips may be put on top. Serves 10.

*Mrs. Vernon (Nelda) Miller*

# Cheeseburger 'n Fries Casserole

2 lb. lean ground beef
1 onion (chopped)
1 can condensed cream
   of mushroom soup

1 can condensed cheddar cheese
   soup
1 - 20 oz. pkg. frozen crinkle-cut
   French fries

In a skillet, brown beef and onion; drain. Stir in soups. Pour into a 9" x 13" x 2" baking dish. Arrange fries on top. Bake, uncovered, at 350° for 50 minutes or until fries are golden brown.

*Mrs. Daniel (LeAnn) Yoder*

# One-Pot Dinner

1 lb. cooked hamburger
$3/4$ lb. cooked bacon
1 c. chopped onion (sautéd)
2 - 15 oz. cans pork & beans
1 - 15 oz. can kidney beans
1 - 15 oz. can lima beans
   (drained)

1 c. ketchup
1 Tbsp. liquid smoke
3 Tbsp. vinegar
1 tsp. salt
$1/4$ c. brown sugar
$1/4$ tsp. black pepper

Cover and simmer over low heat for 1–2 hours. Serve on corn bread. I use 2 lb. dry beans, cooked soft, instead of tin can beans.

*Mrs. Ervin (Anna Mary) Miller*

# Skillet Supper

1 lb. fresh (or canned) sausage
1 onion (chopped)
1 pt. tomato juice (or may use
  half pizza sauce)
1 pt. pizza sauce
2 c. uncooked macaroni

2 Tbsp. sugar
1 green pepper (chopped), *optional*
$1/2$ c. water
1 tsp. salt
2 tsp. chili powder

Brown sausage, onion and pepper together; drain. Stir in remaining ingredients. Bring to a boil, cover, and simmer, stirring often until macaroni is tender. 2 c. sour cream or cheese may be added before serving. May use hamburger instead of sausage. May also bake in a casserole dish for 1 hour.

*Mrs. Harry (Edna Mae) Bontrager, Mrs. Gerald (Darla) Yoder*

# Sloppy Joe

4 lb. ground beef
2 c. diced celery
2 c. diced onion
$1/4$ c. brown sugar
$1/2$ c. vinegar

3 c. catsup
2 tsp. dry mustard
$1/2$ c. flour
1 Tbsp. Worcestershire sauce

Brown beef with onions and celery. Mix in remaining ingredients and bring to a boil. Serve on buns.

*Mrs. Christy (Anna) Bontrager*

# Sloppy Joe

$2^1/2$ lb. hamburger
$1/2$ c. chopped onions
$1/2$ c. ketchup
$1/3$ c. brown sugar

$2^1/2$ Tbsp. Worcestershire sauce
1 Tbsp. prepared mustard
1 can cream of mushroom soup
$1/2$ tsp. salt

The soup takes out the greasiness. This may be doubled, put in jars, and pressure canned at 10 lb. for 30 minutes.

*Mom (Elsie) Yoder*

# Meatballs with Cream Sauce

1 egg (slightly beaten)
$1/4$ c. milk
2 Tbsp. ketchup
1 tsp. Worcestershire sauce
$3/4$ c. quick oats
$1/4$ c. finely chopped onion

$1/4$ c. fresh parsley
1 tsp. salt
$1/4$ Tbsp. pepper
$1^1/2$ lb. ground beef
3 Tbsp. flour

CREAM SAUCE:
2 Tbsp. butter or oleo
2 Tbsp. flour
$1/4$ tsp. thyme
salt & pepper to taste

$1^1/2$ c. chicken broth
$2/3$ c. cream or whole milk
2 Tbsp. parsley

In a bowl, combine the first 9 ingredients. Add beef and mix well. Shape into balls, roll in flour, shaking off excess. Place on greased baking pan. Bake, uncovered, at 400° for 10 minutes. Turn meatballs and bake for 15 minutes longer or until meat is no longer pink. Meanwhile, for Cream Sauce: Melt butter in a saucepan over medium heat. Stir in flour, thyme, salt and pepper until smooth. Gradually add broth and cream; bring to a boil. Cook and stir until thickened. Drain meatballs and transfer to a serving dish. Top with sauce and sprinkle with parsley. *Very good!*

*Mrs. Leland (Orpha) Yoder*

# For Grilled Hamburgers

5 lb. hamburger
$1/3$ c. chopped onions
2 tsp. salt
$1/2$ tsp. pepper

2 slices bread crumbled in 1 c.
  milk or water
1 Tbsp. soy sauce

Mix, shape into patties and grill.

*Mrs. Daryl (Marsha) Miller*

# Meat Loaf Superb

| | |
|---|---|
| 1 lb. ground ham | $^3/_4$ c. tomato juice |
| $^1/_2$ lb. ground beef | $^1/_4$ c. finely chopped onion |
| $^1/_2$ lb. ground lean pork | $^1/_4$ tsp. pepper |
| 2 eggs (beaten) | 4 slices mozzarella, processed, |
| 1 c. quick-cooking oats | American or Swiss cheese |

Heat oven to 350°. Mix all ingredients except cheese. Put in ungreased loaf pan. Bake uncovered for 1–1$^1/_4$ hours or until done. Remove from oven. Put cheese on top. Put in oven for 3–4 minutes or until cheese is slightly melted.

*Mrs. David (JoAnn) Bontrager*

# Burritos

| | |
|---|---|
| 2 c. hamburger (browned) | 1 can cream of mushroom soup |
| 8 oz. refried beans | 1 c. sour cream |
| 1$^1/_2$ Tbsp. taco seasoning | grated cheese |
| 1 c. pizza sauce | taco shells |

Brown hamburger, add refried beans, taco seasoning and pizza sauce. Fill taco shells. Mix soup and sour cream and put a layer in bottom of pan. Then add shells and remaining soup mixture. Add cheese. Bake at 300° for 30 minutes. Serve with lettuce and tomatoes if you wish.

*Mrs. Calvin (Martha Sue) Lehman*

---

*A whispered lie is just as wrong as one that is thundered loud and long.*

# Cheesy Enchiladas

2 lb. hamburger (fried)
1 medium onion (minced)
1 pkg. taco seasoning

salt to taste
12 flour tortilla shells

**CHEESE SAUCE:**
$^1/_2$ c. oleo
4 Tbsp. flour
3 c. milk

8 oz. Velveeta cheese
8 oz. sour cream

Fry hamburger with onion. Add seasoning and place in tortilla shells; roll up, and place in a greased casserole dish. Make cheese sauce and pour over top. Bake at 350° until cheese sauce starts to bubble and turn brown. Remove from oven and top with shredded lettuce and chopped tomatoes.

*Mrs. Ervin (Edna) Bontrager*

# Mexican Casserole

2 lb. ground beef
2 Tbsp. taco seasoning
2 cans chili or pork & beans
1 qt. pizza sauce
2 c. cheese sauce (recipe below)

2 c. rice (cooked)
1 pt. sour cream
lettuce
tortilla chips
tomatoes

**CHEESE SAUCE:**
4 Tbsp. melted butter
3 Tbsp. flour
4 c. milk

1 tsp. salt
$^1/_4$ tsp. pepper, *optional*
2 c. diced cheese

When rice is cooked, add 2 c. cheese sauce and put in bottom of casserole dish. Fry ground beef then add seasoning, beans and pizza sauce. Put on top of rice. Bake at 350° until hot (15–30 minutes). When ready to serve spread sour cream on top. Top with lettuce, tortilla chips, tomatoes or whatever you desire. Put cheese sauce on top of each serving. To make Cheese Sauce: Melt butter in saucepan. Stir in flour, then add half of the milk. Stir rapidly to remove all lumps, then add remaining milk, salt and pepper. Cook for 1 minute, stirring constantly. Add cheese and stir until melted.

*Mrs. Ervin Lee (Lydia) Yoder*

# Mexican Corn Bread

2 eggs (slightly beaten)
1 c. self-rising cornmeal
1 - 17 oz. can cream-style corn
1 c. milk
$^1/_4$ c. vegetable oil

1 lb. ground beef
2 c. shredded cheddar cheese
1 large onion (chopped)
2–4 jalepeño peppers (finely chopped)

Combine first 5 ingredients in a bowl; set aside. Cook ground beef until browned. Drain well and set aside. Pour half of cornmeal mixture into a greased 2-qt. casserole dish. Sprinkle evenly with beef; top with cheese, onion and peppers. Pour remaining batter over top. Bake at 350° for 45–50 minutes. Let set 5 minutes before serving.

*Mrs. Allen (Elsie) Bontrager*

# Mock Turkey

2 lb. hamburger (browned)
2 cans cream of chicken soup
1 can cream of celery soup

4 c. milk
1 loaf bread (cut in squares)

Mix all together and put in a 9" x 13" baking pan. Bake at 350° for 45 minutes. May use cream of mushroom soup instead of chicken.

*Mrs. Delmar (Pauline) Weaver*

# Meatza

3 lb. hamburger
4 slices bread (crumbled)
$^1/_2$ c. milk
1 c. pizza sauce

ketchup
oregano
Velveeta cheese slices

Mix hamburger, salt and pepper with bread that has been soaked in milk. Add pizza sauce. Press into a 9" x 13" baking pan. Top with ketchup and sprinkle oregano on top. Bake at 325° for 30 minutes. Then add Velveeta cheese slices on top and return to oven for 6 minutes or until cheese is melted.

*Mrs. Harry (Edna Mae) Bontrager*

# Pepperoni Macaroni

2¹/₂ c. uncooked elbow
   macaroni
1 lb. bulk Italian sausage
1 large onion (chopped)
1 - 15 oz. can pizza sauce
1 - 8 oz. can tomato sauce
¹/₃ c. milk

1 - 4¹/₂ oz. jar sliced
   mushrooms (drained)
1 - 3¹/₂ oz. pkg. sliced pepperoni
   (halved)
1 - 2¹/₄ oz. can sliced ripe olives
   (drained)
4 oz. shredded mozzarella cheese

Cook macaroni according to pkg. directions. Meanwhile, in a skillet over medium heat, cook sausage and onion until browned; drain. Drain macaroni. In a large bowl, combine pizza sauce, tomato sauce and milk. Stir in sausage mixture, macaroni, pepperoni, mushrooms and olives. Transfer to a greased 13" x 9" x 2" baking dish. Cover and bake at 350° for 30 minutes. Uncover; sprinkle with cheese. Bake 10–15 minutes longer or until bubbly and cheese is melted. Yield: 8–10 servings.

*Mrs. Freeman (Mabel) Yoder*

# German Pizza

1 lb. hamburger
¹/₂ medium onion (chopped)
¹/₂ green pepper (diced)
salt & pepper to taste
2 Tbsp. butter or margarine

6 medium potatoes (finely shredded)
3 eggs (beaten)
¹/₃ c. milk
2 c. shredded cheese

Brown hamburger in skillet with onion, green pepper and salt and pepper to taste. Remove meat from skillet. Melt butter and spread potatoes over butter; add salt. Top with beef mixture. Combine eggs and milk; pour over all. Cook, covered, until potatoes are tender (about 30 minutes). Top with cheese. Cover and heat until cheese is melted.

*Mrs. David (Arlene) Chupp*

---

*The smallest deed is better than the greatest invention.*

# Deep Dish Pizza

1 loaf frozen bread dough
   or biscuit dough
1 lb. ground beef (browned)
2 c. spaghetti sauce
$^1/_2$ c. onion
1 tsp. garlic salt

8 oz. shredded cheese
1 can mushrooms
$^1/_2$ c. green peppers
1 tsp. oregano
$^1/_4$ c. Parmesan cheese
salt & pepper to taste

Thaw bread dough and spread in a 9" x 13" greased pan. Spread beef over dough. Mix oregano, salt, pepper and garlic salt with spaghetti sauce. Spread over dough. Top with remaining ingredients. Bake at 400° for 10–15 minutes.

*Mrs. Wilmer (Marilyn) Schmucker*

# Pizza

**CRUST:**
3 c. flour
$4^1/_2$ tsp. baking powder
$1^1/_2$ tsp. salt

1 c. milk
$^1/_2$ c. cooking oil

Mix crust ingredients well. Roll out on pizza pan. Bake for 45 minutes at 350°. Top with the following ingredients in order given. Return to oven until the cheese is melted.

1 qt. sausage (browned)
1 qt. green beans (chopped)
3 c. pizza sauce

1 c. chopped peppers
bacon bits or sliced wieners
shredded cheese

*Mrs. Fred (LeEtta) Yoder*

---

*He who keeps his face toward the sun finds that
the shadows fall behind him.*

---

# Pizza Burgers

| | |
|---|---|
| 2 tsp. oregano leaves | 1 tsp. salt |
| 2 lb. ground turkey or | $1/4$ c. brown sugar |
| hamburger | 1–2 c. pizza sauce |
| 1 can refried beans | $1/4$ tsp. liquid smoke |
| 2 Tbsp. mustard | 9 slices bread |
| $1/2$ c. chopped onion | cheese slices |

In a skillet, brown meat and onions. Add oregano leaves, refried beans, mustard, salt, brown sugar, pizza sauce and liquid smoke. Simmer. Meanwhile, butter bread on both sides and toast until golden. Place on a greased 10" x 15" x 2" cookie sheet. Spread meat mixture on toast and place a cheese slice over each one. Heat at 350° for 10–15 minutes or until cheese is melted. A good way to use up that less-than-fresh bread.

*Mrs. Freeman (Mabel) Yoder*

# Pizza Cups

| | |
|---|---|
| biscuit or pizza dough | 1 c. pizza sauce |
| 1 lb. seasoned pork sausage | 1 c. shredded mozzarella cheese or |
| (browned & drained) | American cheese slices |

Make your favorite biscuit or pizza dough and line a 12 c. muffin pan with dough divided evenly. Press over bottom and up the sides. Fill each cup half full of sausage, spoon 1 Tbsp. pizza sauce over sausage and sprinkle cheese over each cup. If using American cheese slices, cut 1 slice in fourths and put 2 squares on each cup. Bake at 375° for approximately 20 minutes or until cups are golden brown on the bottom. *This is great for lunches. Children love them when heated for a quick filling meal.* Variation: Beef may be used and meat and pizza sauce mixed together, then spooned into cups.

*Mrs. Freeman (Mabel) Yoder, Mrs. Harley (Martha) Raber*

---

*No one ever hurt his eyesight by looking on the bright side of life.*

# Pizza Burgers

2 lb. hamburger
2 tsp. salt
1 Tbsp. oregano
$^1/_2$ tsp. black pepper

$^1/_2$ c. pizza sauce
6 Tbsp. oatmeal
1 small onion

Mix all together, shape into patties and fry. Put in layers in roaster with pizza sauce (1 Tbsp. or more on top of each patty). Bake at 350° until done.

*Mrs. Allen (Rosemary) Bontrager*

# Pizza Potatoes

6 lb. potatoes (cooked & sliced)
SAUCE:
$^1/_4$ c. oleo
$^1/_4$ c. flour
$1^1/_2$ Tbsp. salt
$^1/_2$ tsp. pepper

$2^2/_3$ lb. hamburger
salt & pepper

2 Tbsp. oregano
2 small onions
4 Tbsp. brown sugar
2 qt. pizza sauce

Melt oleo. Add flour and stir well. Add remaining ingredients. Then add potatoes and hamburger. Put slices of Velveeta cheese on top and bake at 275° for 2 hours. Yield: 25 servings.

*Mrs. Delmar (Pauline) Weaver*

# Pop-Over Pizza

1 lb. sausage
1 small onion (chopped)
1 pt. pizza sauce
1 small can mushrooms
1 small pkg. pepperoni
2 eggs

$^1/_3$ c. milk
$^1/_4$ tsp. salt
1 c. flour
1 Tbsp. vegetable oil
mozzarella cheese

Brown sausage and onion together; drain. Add pizza sauce, mushrooms and pepperoni. Pour into an 8" x 8" cake pan. Then mix eggs, milk, salt, flour and vegetable oil. Mix well. Pour on top of meat mixture. Bake, uncovered, at 350° for 40 minutes. Top with mozzarella cheese.

*Mrs. Larry (Mary) Troyer*

# Simple Pizza Dough

2 c. flour
1 Tbsp. baking powder
1 tsp. salt

²/₃ c. milk
¹/₃ c. vegetable oil

Sift flour, baking powder and salt. Add milk and vegetable oil. Pat dough on bottom of a 12" pizza pan. Top with your favorite toppings. Bake at 375° for 25–30 minutes. *Easy and fast!*

*Amy Yoder (Daughter)*

# Ranch Cheeseburgers

1 pkg. Hidden Valley Ranch
  dressing mix
¹/₂ tsp. salt
2 lb. ground beef

1 c. shredded cheddar cheese
1 c. shredded mozzarella cheese
large hamburger buns

Combine all ingredients except hamburger buns. Shape into patties, flatten and fry in a greased skillet over medium heat until browned and no longer pink. Serve on hamburger buns with pickles, lettuce and to-matoes. Yield: 8 burgers.

*Mrs. Freeman (Mabel) Yoder*

# Stromboli

1 Tbsp. yeast
1 c. warm water
1 tsp. sugar
1 tsp. salt

2 Tbsp. vegetable oil
2¹/₂ c. flour
seasoned salt

FILLING:
shaved ham
salami
sausage

cheese
onions
peppers or whatever you desire

Dissolve yeast in warm water. Mix all together except seasoned salt, add-ing flour last, and let rise for 5 minutes. Divide dough into 2 parts and roll out in a rectangle (quite thin). Sprinkle with seasoned salt. Add fill-ing in layers through the middle and fold on either side (seal ends). Bake at 350° for 20 minutes.

*Mrs. Wilbur (Waneta) Nisley*

# Pancakes, French Toast, Syrups & Cereals

*The only food that doesn't get expensive is food for thought.*

THAT YE MAY APPROVE THINGS THAT ARE EXCELLENT;
THAT YE MAY BE SINCERE AND WITHOUT OFFENSE TILL
THE DAY OF CHRIST; BEING FILLED WITH THE FRUITS OF
RIGHTEOUSNESS, WHICH ARE BY JESUS CHRIST, UNTO
THE GLORY AND PRAISE OF GOD.
PHILIPPIANS 1:10–11

# Notes

Charlene Yoder

*I*nstant coffee, instant tea,
Life is lived so instantly.
What I need for my noisy brood
Is more than just instant food.
What is it I am shortest of?
Instant patience, instant love.
Instants I need for myself
Are not found on the grocery shelf.

# Apple Nut Hotcakes

1 c. flour
3 Tbsp. sugar
2 tsp. baking powder
1/2 tsp. salt
1 tsp. cinnamon
3/4 c. milk

3 Tbsp. butter
2 tsp. vanilla
2 egg whites
1/2 c. chopped, peeled apples
1/2 c. chopped walnuts

**APPLE SYRUP:**
1/4 c. sugar
4 tsp. cornstarch

1/4 tsp. allspice
1 1/2 c. apple juice

Combine first 5 ingredients in a bowl. In another bowl, combine milk, butter and vanilla. Mix well and stir into dry ingredients. Beat egg whites and fold into batter along with apples and nuts. Fry like pancakes. Serve with apple syrup. For Apple Syrup: Combine sugar, cornstarch and allspice; stir in apple juice. Cook in a saucepan until thickened. Maple syrup is also good served with this.

*Mrs. Jonathan (Lou Ida) Miller*

# Golden Pancakes

1 1/2 c. flour
3/4 tsp. salt
3 tsp. baking powder
4 Tbsp. sugar

1/4 tsp. soda
2 eggs
1 c. milk
4 Tbsp. oil

Mix dry ingredients together; set aside. In another bowl beat eggs; add milk and oil. Mix slowly into dry ingredients. Bake on a hot griddle. Serve with hot syrup. May use a little less salt and baking powder.

*Mrs. Freeman (Mabel) Yoder, Mrs. Allen (Rosemary) Bontrager*

---

*We are never more discontented with others than
when we are discontented with ourselves.*

---

# One of Everything Pancakes

1 c. flour
1 tsp. baking powder
1 tsp. soda
1 Tbsp. sugar

1 pinch of salt
1 egg
1 c. milk
1 tsp. vegetable oil

Combine all ingredients and mix well. Fry on hot griddle.

*Mrs. Wilbur (Alta) Beechy*

# Pancake Mix

6 c. white flour
6 c. whole wheat flour
6 c. oatmeal

3 Tbsp. soda
6 Tbsp. baking powder
$^1/_2$ c. sugar

Combine all ingredients. When ready to make: Combine 1 c. mix, 1 egg, 1 c. milk and 2 Tbsp. melted butter. *Yummy!*

*Mrs. Joe (Karen) Graber*

# Pancakes

$2^1/_4$ c. flour
$^1/_2$ c. sugar
1 tsp. salt
1 Tbsp. baking powder

2 eggs
5 Tbsp. vegetable oil
2 c. milk

Mix flour, sugar, salt and baking powder. Add remaining ingredients. Mix well. Fry on ungreased hot griddle.

*Mrs. Glen (Ruby) Yoder*

---

*A thankful heart is not only the greatest virtue,*
*but the parent of all other virtues.*

---

# Pancakes

| | |
|---|---|
| 4¹/₂ c. flour | 7¹/₂ tsp. baking powder |
| 1¹/₂ c. wheat flour | 4 eggs (well beaten) |
| ¹/₂ c. sugar | 10¹/₂ Tbsp. salad oil |
| 1¹/₂ tsp. salt | 4¹/₂ c. milk |
| 1 c. oatmeal | 2 tsp. cream of tartar |

Stir dry ingredients together. Add beaten eggs, salad oil and milk. Fry on hot griddle. It is good to separate the eggs and beat the whites. *Our favorite pancakes!*

*Mrs. Calvin (Erma) Schmucker*

# Blueberry-Stuffed French Toast

| | |
|---|---|
| 4 large eggs | 8 oz. cream cheese |
| 1 c. milk | 2 c. blueberry pie filling |
| 2 tsp. vanilla | 8–12 pieces white bread (sliced |
| ¹/₄ c. white sugar | ³/₄" thick) |
| ¹/₂ tsp. salt | powdered sugar, *optional* |

Let bread slices dry for 5 hours or overnight. When you're ready to assemble toast, whisk first 5 ingredients together and set aside. Spread *each* slice of bread with a thick layer of cream cheese and spoon 2–3 Tbsp. pie filling on half of the bread. Then press slices together to form a sandwich (with cream cheese and filling in the middle). Drag sandwiches through egg mixture until lightly saturated. Fry on medium-hot, lightly sprayed griddle until golden brown on both sides. Dust with powdered sugar if desired. Serve immediately with warm maple or pancake syrup. *This is not as complicated as it sounds and the results are absolutely scrumptious!* Yield: 4–6 servings.

*Mrs. Lester (Verna) Bontrager*

---

*The man that removes mountains begins by carrying away small stones.*

# Crunchy Crust French Toast

1 egg
$^1/_3$ c. milk
2 tsp. sugar
$^1/_8$ tsp. cinnamon

$^1/_2$ c. flaked coconut
$^1/_3$ c. crushed corn flakes
3 Tbsp. butter or margarine
4 slices bread

Blend egg, milk, sugar and cinnamon. Mix coconut and corn flakes (if you don't use coconut you will need more corn flakes). Dip bread into egg mixture, then in corn flakes. Heat margarine in skillet. Brown bread slices on both sides. Serve hot with your favorite pancake syrup.

*Mrs. David (JoAnn) Mast*

# Oven French Toast (with Nut Topping)

1 - 12 oz. loaf French bread
  (cut in 1" slices)
8 large eggs
2 c. milk
2 c. half & half or evaporated milk

2 tsp. vanilla
$^1/_2$ tsp. nutmeg
$^1/_2$ tsp. cinnamon
$^1/_2$ tsp. mace

**TOPPING:**
$^3/_4$ c. butter (softened)
$1^1/_3$ c. brown sugar

3 Tbsp. corn syrup
$1^1/_3$ c. pecans (chopped)

Combine all the topping ingredients; set aside until time to bake. Heavily butter a 13" x 9" x 2" pan. Fill pan with bread slices to within $^1/_2$" of the top; set aside. Then mix the remaining ingredients. Pour this mixture over bread slices in pan. Cover and refrigerate overnight. Put the topping on just before you bake it. Bake at 350° for 50 minutes or until puffed and golden. Note: Cover with tinfoil if top browns too quickly.

*Mrs. Darrel (Erma) Yoder*

---

*Where there is room in the heart, there is room in the house.*

# Sour Cream Waffles

| | |
|---|---|
| 3 c. flour | 4 eggs (separated) |
| 1$^{1}/_{2}$ tsp. baking powder | 2 c. sour cream |
| 1 tsp. soda | 3 Tbsp. melted butter or |
| 1 tsp. salt |    shortening |
| 1 Tbsp. sugar | 1$^{1}/_{2}$ c. milk |

Sift dry ingredients together. Drop in egg yolks; add sour cream and shortening. Stir until smooth. Add milk and mix well. Fold in stiffly beaten egg whites. Bake on a hot waffle iron. Butter waffle iron between each waffle (this makes them nice and golden). Serve immediately. Yield: 12 waffles.

*Mrs. Freeman (Mabel) Yoder, Mrs. Harley (Martha) Raber*

# Western Flapjacks

| | |
|---|---|
| 5 Tbsp. buttermilk powder | $^{1}/_{2}$ tsp. soda |
| 1$^{1}/_{4}$ c. flour | 1 Tbsp. shortening (softened) |
| 1 tsp. sugar | 1 egg (separated) |
| 1 tsp. baking powder | 1 c. water |
| $^{1}/_{2}$ tsp. salt | |

In a medium-sized bowl, mix all ingredients in the order given, except egg white. Last, beat egg white until stiff and add to remaining ingredients. *These are the only pancakes we make; our favorite!*

*Mrs. Dennis (Mary) Bontrager, Mrs. Lester (Verna) Bontrager*

# Caramel Pancake Syrup

| | |
|---|---|
| 1$^{1}/_{2}$ c. brown sugar | $^{1}/_{3}$ c. light corn syrup |
| 1 - 12 oz. can evaporated milk | 1 Tbsp. butter or margarine |

Mix all ingredients in a small saucepan, stirring constantly over low heat until butter and sugar are melted. It will curdle if allowed to boil.

*Mrs. Lester (Verna) Bontrager*

# Cinnamon Sauce

1 c. sugar
$^1/_2$ tsp. salt
3 Tbsp. flour
2 c. boiling water

3 Tbsp. brown sugar
4 Tbsp. butter
1 tsp. cinnamon

Blend first 3 ingredients in saucepan. Stir boiling water in gradually to keep it smooth. Cook until clear (4–5 minutes). Remove from heat and stir in brown sugar, butter and cinnamon. *Delicious on pancakes!*

*Mrs. Eli (Pollyanna) Miller*

# Quick Pancake Syrup

1 c. brown sugar
$1^1/_2$ c. water

1 Tbsp. cornstarch
1 tsp. maple flavoring

Combine sugar, water and cornstarch in saucepan. Cook until slightly thickened, stirring constantly. Remove from heat. Add maple flavoring. Serve on pancakes, waffles, etc.

*Mrs. Floyd (Marietta) Troyer*

# Pancake Syrup

1 c. sugar
6 Tbsp. flour
$^1/_4$ tsp. salt
4 c. water

4 Tbsp. butter
6 Tbsp. brown sugar
maple flavoring, *optional*

Combine first 3 ingredients in a saucepan. Gradually stir in water and cook until clear (4–5 minutes). Remove from heat and add butter, brown sugar and maple flavoring if desired.

*Mrs. Calvin (Erma) Schmucker*

# Cereal Cake

| | |
|---|---|
| 4 c. oatmeal | 2 tsp. soda |
| 2 c. whole wheat flour | 1/2 tsp. salt |
| 3/4 c. honey or 1 c. molasses (sorghum) | 1 1/2–2 c. milk or buttermilk |
| 1/2 c. oil | 2 tsp. vanilla |

Mix all together and put in a 9" x 13" cake pan. Bake at 350° for 35–45 minutes or until the middle of cake springs up. A good breakfast cereal in cake form or crumbled and toasted like granola. 1 1/2 c. sugar may be used instead of honey. Variations: Add coconut, raisins, dates or maple flavoring if desired.

*Mrs. David (Arlene) Chupp, Mrs. Wilma (Marilyn) Schmucker*

# Granola

| | |
|---|---|
| 15 c. oatmeal | 1 1/2 tsp. salt |
| 3 c. whole wheat flour | 3 tsp. soda |
| 1 box graham crackers (coarsely crushed) | 2 c. butter (melted) |
| 2 c. brown sugar | 2–3 c. peanut butter |
| 3 c. coconut | 2–3 c. butterscotch or chocolate chips |

Combine first 7 ingredients. Add butter and mix well. Bake at 300° for 40 minutes, stirring every 10 minutes. When still warm add peanut butter and butterscotch or chocolate chips.

*Mrs. Devon (Marietta) Troyer*

# Granola

| | |
|---|---|
| 20 c. oatmeal | 4 c. brown sugar |
| 4 c. wheat germ | 2 pkg. graham crackers (crushed) |
| 4 c. coconut | 2 1/2 c. butter (melted) |
| 4 c. sunflower seeds, *optional* | 1/2 c. honey (melted in butter) |
| 4 c. flax seed (should be ground) | 1 box corn flakes (crushed) |
| | 2 Tbsp. salt |

Mix all ingredients together, then toast in oven at 350° for 20 minutes, stirring several times to toast evenly. Cool. Store in airtight container.

*Mrs. Willis (Mary) Bontrager*

# Granola

| | |
|---|---|
| 22 c. oatmeal | 1 c. water |
| 4 c. coconut | 1 Tbsp. vanilla |
| 3 c. brown sugar | 1 Tbsp. maple flavoring |
| 2 c. oil | 1 c. peanut butter |

Mix first 2 ingredients together. In another bowl mix peanut butter and sugar together. Gradually add the remaining ingredients. When well mixed, add to the first mixture and mix well with hands. Toast on cookie sheets at 300° until golden.

*Mrs. Fred (LeEtta) Yoder*

# Granola

| | |
|---|---|
| 10 c. oatmeal | $^1/_2$ c. vegetable oil |
| 2 c. wheat germ | 2 tsp. vanilla |
| 2 c. coconut | 1 tsp. salt |
| $1^1/_2$ c. brown sugar | 3 tsp. cinnamon |
| 1 small pkg. almonds | |

Mix all together and put on cookie sheets. Toast at 270° until golden brown, stirring occasionally. *My favorite granola recipe!*

*Mrs. Allen (Elsie) Bontrager*

# Granola Cereal

| | |
|---|---|
| $12^1/_2$ lb. quick oats | 4 c. brown sugar |
| 5 lb. regular oats | $^1/_3$ c. vanilla |
| 3 lb. sunflower seeds | $1^1/_2$ qt. canola oil |
| $2^1/_2$ lb. coconut flakes | |

Mix and toast in oven.

*Mrs. John (Elsie) Yoder*

---

*Prayer is the key to the day and the lock to the night.*

# Pies

*Directions to heaven?*
*Turn right and go straight.*

FOR GOD SO LOVED THE
WORLD THAT HE GAVE HIS
ONLY BEGOTTEN SON, THAT
WHOSOEVER BELIEVETH IN HIM
SHOULD NOT PERISH BUT HAVE
EVERLASTING LIFE.
JOHN 3:16

Charlene Yoder

# A Songbird

*I* like to be a songbird;
God likes to hear me sing;
I like to sing His praises while
I do most anything!
I sing when I do dishes;
I sing when I do chores;
I sing when I'm at work outside
Or when I play indoors!
It makes me very happy
And helps me laugh and smile,
The next time you feel grouchy
Just stop and sing awhile!


*T* he Bible has the answer,
It's the compass and the chart;
You'll have the right directions,
When God's Word is in your heart.


*Pessimist* — someone who looks at the land of milk and honey and sees only cholesterol and calories!


*E* verything gets easier with practice except getting up in the morning!


*A* cupful of sunshine, a bowl full of smiles,
Makes a good frosting, that spreads for many miles!

# Impossible French Apple Pie

| | |
|---|---|
| 6 c. sliced, pared tart apples | 2 eggs |
| 1¼ tsp. ground cinnamon | 1 c. sugar |
| ¼ tsp. ground nutmeg | ½ c. Bisquick baking mix |
| ¾ c. milk | |
| 2 Tbsp. margarine or butter (softened) | |

**NUT STREUSEL:**

| | |
|---|---|
| 3 Tbsp. margarine or butter (firm) | ½ c. chopped nuts |
| | ⅓ c. firmly packed brown sugar |
| 1 c. Bisquick baking mix | |

Heat oven to 325°. Grease pie plates. Mix apples, cinnamon and nutmeg. Turn into pie plates. Beat remaining ingredients in blender on high speed for 15 seconds or with wire whisk or hand beater for 1 minute until smooth. Pour into pie plates. Sprinkle with Nut Streusel. Bake for 55–65 minutes or until a knife inserted in center comes out clean.

*Mrs. David (JoAnn) Bontrager*

# Pumpkin Apple Pie

| | |
|---|---|
| 1 - 9" unbaked pie shell (deep dish) | ½ c. brown sugar |
| | 1 Tbsp. cornstarch |
| 1 c. apple butter | 1½ tsp. cinnamon |
| 16 oz. pumpkin | ½ tsp. ginger |
| 12 oz. evaporated milk | ¼ tsp. cloves |
| 2 large eggs | ½ tsp. nutmeg |

**CRUNCHY NUT TOPPING:**

| | |
|---|---|
| 1¼ c. walnuts or pecans (coarsely chopped) | ¾ c. brown sugar |
| | 2 Tbsp. butter (melted) |

Preheat oven to 400°. Spread apple butter in bottom of pie crust. Combine remaining ingredients and carefully pour on top of apple butter. Bake pie for 55 minutes or until knife inserted 1" from edge comes out clean. Cool. Combine nut topping ingredients and spoon over pie. Place pie on broiler rack about 7" from source of heat, and broil for 2–3 minutes until topping is golden.

*Mrs. Floyd (Darlene) Yoder*

# Shoestring Apple Pie

| | |
|---|---|
| 2$^1/_2$ c. (scant) sugar | $^1/_2$ tsp. salt |
| 2 Tbsp. flour | 4 c. shoestring apples |
| 3 eggs (well beaten) | 2 unbaked pie shells |
| 4 Tbsp. water | cinnamon |

Put apples in pie shells. Mix first 5 ingredients together and pour over apples. Sprinkle cinnamon on top. Bake at 325° for 30–40 minutes or until firm. Yield: 2 pies.

*Mrs. Harry (Edna Mae) Bontrager*

# Sour Cream Apple Pie

**FILLING:**

| | |
|---|---|
| 2 Tbsp. flour | 1 c. sour cream |
| $^1/_8$ tsp. salt | 1 tsp. vanilla |
| $^3/_4$ c. sugar | $^1/_4$ tsp. nutmeg |
| 1 egg | 2 c. diced apples |

**TOPPING:**

| | |
|---|---|
| $^1/_3$ c. brown sugar | 1 tsp. cinnamon |
| $^1/_3$ c. flour | $^1/_4$ c. cold butter |

Combine all filling ingredients and pour into an unbaked pie shell. Bake at 400° for 12 minutes. Reduce heat to 350° for 15 minutes. Meanwhile, with pastry blender, cut butter into topping ingredients until size of large peas. When pie has been baked for 15 minutes at 350°, remove from oven and sprinkle topping evenly over top and bake for 10 minutes longer. Yield: 1 pie.

*Mrs. Allen (Elsie) Bontrager*

---

*Nothing lies beyond the reach of prayer except
that which lies outside the will of God.*

# Banana Breeze Pie

**NO-BAKE CRUST:**

$^1/_3$ c. margarine or butter

$^1/_4$ c. sugar

$^1/_2$ tsp. cinnamon

1 c. corn flake crumbs

**NO-COOK FILLING:**

8 oz. cream cheese (softened)

1 can sweetened condensed milk

$^1/_3$ c. lemon juice

1 tsp. vanilla

4 medium ripe bananas

Melt margarine or butter, sugar and cinnamon in a saucepan. Place over low heat, stirring constantly until bubbles form around edges of pan. Remove from heat. Add corn flakes; mix well. Press mixture evenly into a 9" pie pan to form crust. Chill. For Filling: Beat cream cheese until light and fluffy. Add condensed milk and blend thoroughly. Add lemon juice and vanilla; stir until thickened. Slice 3 bananas and mix. Pour filling into crust. Refrigerate for 2–3 hours or until firm. Do not freeze. Garnish with banana slices.

*Mrs. Lonnie (Norma) Bontrager*

# Butterscotch Pie

3 c. brown sugar

3 Tbsp. butter

10 Tbsp. cream

4 c. milk

4 Tbsp. flour

2 Tbsp. cornstarch*

3 eggs (beaten)

$^1/_2$ tsp. butterscotch flavoring

whipped topping

3 baked pie shells

Boil first 3 ingredients together for 5 minutes. Combine milk, flour, cornstarch* and eggs. Cook until thickened. Add butterscotch flavoring. Pour into baked pie shells. Top with whipped topping. *Marilyn uses 6 Tbsp. cornstarch and white sugar instead of brown. Yield: 3 pies.

*Mrs. Raymond (LeEtta) Yoder, Mrs. Wilmer (Marilyn) Schmucker*

---

*If you don't fall now and again it's a sign you're playing it safe.*

# Chocolate Mandarin Pie

8 oz. cream cheese (softened)
14 oz. sweetened condensed
  milk
$^1/_2$ c. orange juice concentrate
$^1/_2$ c. sour cream
8 oz. frozen Cool Whip
  (slightly thawed)

1 can mandarin oranges (drained)
approx. 15 chocolate cookies
  (crushed fine)
2 Tbsp. melted butter

In a mixing bowl, beat cream cheese; add milk, orange juice and sour cream. Beat until smooth. Fold in Cool Whip. Crush chocolate cookies very fine; add butter and press into a 9" or 10" pie plate and up the sides. Spoon half of filling into crust. Arrange oranges over filling, then spoon remaining filling on top. Reserve 8 oranges for garnish and arrange on top. Swirl with chocolate ice cream syrup.

*Mrs. Freeman (Mabel) Yoder*

# Frozen Peanut Butter Pie

**GRAHAM CRACKER CRUST:**
$^3/_4$ c. *plus* 2 Tbsp. butter
$1^1/_2$ Tbsp. sugar

2 pkg. graham crackers (crushed)

**FILLING:**
8 oz. cream cheese
2 c. powdered sugar
$^2/_3$ c. peanut butter

1 c. milk
9 oz. Cool Whip

Mix crust ingredients together and press into 2 pie tins. For Filling: Beat cream cheese and powdered sugar together until smooth. Add peanut butter, milk and Cool Whip. Pour into crusts and freeze. Keep frozen until ready to serve. *Enjoy!*

*Mrs. Gerald (Darla) Yoder*

---

*Where God guides, He provides.*

# Peanut Butter Pie

| | |
|---|---|
| $^1/_2$ c. peanut butter | baked 9" pie shell |
| $^3/_4$ c. powdered sugar | Cool Whip |

Mix peanut butter and powdered sugar together to make crumbs.

**FILLING:**

| | |
|---|---|
| $^1/_3$ c. flour or cornstarch | 1 tsp. vanilla |
| $^1/_2$ c. sugar | $^1/_8$ tsp. salt |
| 2 c. milk (divided) | 3 egg yolks (slightly beaten) |

Mix all filling ingredients together except 1 c. milk. Put 1 c. milk in a saucepan until it reaches boiling point. Quickly pour filling into saucepan and stir with wire whisk until thickened. Cool. Put half of crumbs into bottom of baked pie shell. Add filling. Top with Cool Whip. Put remaining crumbs on top of Cool Whip.

*Mrs. Larry (Rose) Mullett, Mrs. Fred (LeEtta) Yoder*

# Chocolate Peanut Butter Pie

3 baked pie shells

**FILLING:**

| | |
|---|---|
| $2^1/_2$ c. milk (divided) | 2 Tbsp. flour |
| 3 egg yolks | 1 tsp. salt |
| $^1/_2$ c. brown sugar | 1 Tbsp. vanilla |
| $^1/_2$ c. sugar | 2 Tbsp. butter |
| 2 Tbsp. cornstarch | $^1/_2$ c. chocolate chips |

**BOTTOM PART:**

| | |
|---|---|
| $^1/_2$ c. peanut butter | 1 c. whipping cream (whipped) |
| $^1/_2$ c. powdered sugar | 8 oz. cream cheese |

For Filling: Heat 2 c. milk. Mix egg yolks, sugars, $^1/_2$ c. milk, cornstarch, flour and salt together. Add to heated milk and cook until it thickens. Remove from heat. Add vanilla, butter and chocolate chips. Cool. For Bottom Part: Mix all ingredients together until creamy. Then pour into pie shells. Pour filling over this. Top with **whipped cream.** Mix $^1/_2$ **c. peanut butter** and $^3/_4$ **c. powdered sugar** together and sprinkle over top.

*Mrs. Willis (Mary) Bontrager*

# Chocolate Pie

| | |
|---|---|
| 2 baked pie shells | whipped topping |

FILLING:

| | |
|---|---|
| 4 egg yolks | 3 Tbsp. cocoa |
| 1¼ c. sugar | 5 c. milk (divided) |
| 8 Tbsp. cornstarch | 2 Tbsp. margarine |
| ½ tsp. salt | 1 tsp. vanilla |

Beat egg yolks; add sugar, cornstarch, salt, cocoa and 1 c. milk. Heat rest of milk to boiling, then stir into above mixture. Continue stirring until thickened, then add margarine and vanilla. Pour into baked pie shells. Cool and garnish with whipped topping. For a different taste I sometimes put pieces of a Hershey bar on top. Or, for a peanut butter taste on chocolate, mix ½ c. peanut butter and ¾ c. powdered sugar until it forms crumbs. Sprinkle over whipped topping. *Enjoy! A family favorite!*

*Mrs. Larry (Rose) Mullett*

# Fudge Sundae Pie

| | |
|---|---|
| 1 c. evaporated milk | ¼ tsp. salt |
| 6 oz. chocolate chips | 1 qt. vanilla ice cream (softened) |
| 1 c. miniature marshmallows | vanilla wafers |

Line bottom and sides of a 9" pie pan with wafers. Combine evaporated milk, chocolate chips, marshmallows and salt. Stir over medium heat until marshmallows and chocolate chips melt and mixture thickens. Cool. Spread half of ice cream over cookies. Spread with half of the chocolate sauce. Spread remaining ice cream over chocolate sauce. Freeze again. When hard, spread with remaining chocolate sauce. Garnish with pecans or walnut halves. Wrap well and freeze until ready to serve. Serves 6–7.

*Mrs. Lonnie (Norma) Bontrager*

# Fudgy Mocha Nut Pie

6 Tbsp. butter or margarine
$^1/_3$ c. cocoa
1 - 14 oz. can sweetened
   condensed milk
$^1/_3$ c. water
2 eggs (beaten)

2 Tbsp. instant coffee
1 c. semisweet chocolate chips
1 tsp. vanilla
1 c. pecans or walnuts (chopped)
1 unbaked pie shell
whipped topping, *optional*

Preheat oven to 350°. Melt butter or margarine and cocoa in saucepan over low heat. Stir until smooth. Then stir in condensed milk, water, eggs, coffee and chocolate chips. Whisk until well blended. Remove from heat and stir in vanilla and nuts. Pour into pie shell and bake for 50 minutes. Cool completely before serving. Serve with a dollop of whipped topping if desired.

*Mrs. Freeman (Mabel) Yoder*

# Cream Cheese Pastry

3 oz. cream cheese
$^2/_3$ c. butter or oleo

$1^2/_3$ c. flour
$^1/_2$ tsp. salt

Mix cream cheese with butter or oleo. Sift flour and salt. Blend cream cheese mixture into dry ingredients. Roll into ball. Chill. Roll $^1/_8$" thick; fit to pan. This is rich and browns quickly (watch closely). Use in recipes that ask for baked pie shells.

*Mrs. Lonnie (Norma) Bontrager*

# Easy Pecan Pie

1 c. pecans
3 eggs (slightly beaten)
1 Tbsp. butter (melted)
$^1/_4$ c. milk
$^1/_4$ tsp. salt

1 c. Karo
$^1/_2$ tsp. vanilla
$^3/_4$ c. sugar
1 unbaked pie shell

Arrange pecans in bottom of pie shell. Mix remaining ingredients well and pour over pecans. Let set until pecans rise to top. Bake at 350° for 50 minutes.

*Mrs. Levi (Carolyn) Schrock*

# Pecan Cream Cheese Pie

9" pie shell
1 c. powdered sugar
8 oz. cream cheese
$^1/_4$ c. melted margarine

8 oz. Cool Whip
$^1/_2$ c. coconut
1 c. pecans
1 jar caramel ice cream topping

Bake pie shell and let cool. Mix powdered sugar, cream cheese and melted margarine. Then fold in Cool Whip. Put in pie shell. Mix coconut and pecans and toast in oven at 350° for 10–15 minutes (do not burn). Let cool and put on top of pie. Pour the amount of caramel topping you want on top of pie. Refrigerate.

*Mrs. Nelson (Irene) Miller*

# Fresh Blueberry Pie

baked pie shell or graham
   cracker crust
1 c. water
3 Tbsp. cornstarch
1 Tbsp. corn syrup
pinch of salt

1 c. sugar
1 Tbsp. lemon juice
3 Tbsp. lemon Jell-O
$2^1/_2$ c. blueberries
Cool Whip

Cook water, cornstarch, corn syrup, salt, sugar and lemon juice together until thick. Add lemon Jell-O. Cool. Add blueberries. Pour into pie shell or graham cracker crust. Top with Cool Whip.

*Mrs. Daniel (LeAnn) Yoder*

---

*Christians should erase from their memory the sins
God has erased from the record.*

---

# Fresh Fruit Custard Pie

1 egg yolk
$^1/_2$ c. milk
$^3/_4$ c. sugar
$^1/_4$ c. flour

butter
fresh fruit pie filling
baked pie shell

Beat egg yolk and add milk. Add sugar and flour and cook until boiling. Remove from heat and stir in a chunk of butter until dissolved. Put in bottom of baked pie shell. Top with pie filling.

*Mrs. Daryl (Marsha) Miller*

# Mom's Coconut Custard Pie

2 eggs (slightly beaten)
1 c. milk (heated)
$^1/_4$ c. butter (melted)
1 Tbsp. flour
$^3/_4$ c. sugar

1 tsp. vanilla
$^3/_4$ c. moist coconut
$^1/_3$ tsp. salt
unbaked pie shell

Mix first 8 ingredients together and pour into unbaked pie shell. Bake at 350° for 50–55 minutes or until golden and set. Yield: 1 pie.

*Mrs. Allen (Elsie) Bontrager*

# Fresh Fruit Pie Filling

$^2/_3$ c. sugar
3 Tbsp. clear jel (rounded)
$^1/_2$ tsp. salt

$^1/_2$ c. Jell-O
3 c. water
2 c. fresh fruit

Boil first 5 ingredients together for 1 minute. Cool. Add fresh fruit. Use Jell-O flavors according to fruit.

*Mrs. Ray (Irene) Mullett*

---

*The only place you'll find success before work, is in the dictionary.*

---

# Fried Pies

**DOUGH:**

4 c. sifted flour

8 Tbsp. butter

4 egg yolks

$^2/_3$ c. HOT milk (important)

$^1/_2$ tsp. salt

your favorite pie filling

Put vegetable oil into a deep fat fry pan to heat (while mixing dough). Cut butter into flour. Combine beaten egg yolks, salt and HOT milk. Pour onto flour and butter mixture. Knead to make a smooth dough. Divide dough into 4 parts. Roll out, 1 part at a time. Cut into approx. 6" circles, using an upside-down bowl, and cut around the edge with a table knife. Once the frying oil is hot, spoon pie filling onto the center of crust (only 1 pie at a time), using approx. 2–3 Tbsp. filling per pie. (Too much filling tends to push out the edges and makes it difficult to seal properly.) Wet the edge around circle with water. Fold pie in half and press edges together firmly. Flute edges if you like. Drop into hot oil and fry both sides to a golden brown. Remove and drain on paper towels. Roll each warm pie into dry powdered sugar. *Delicious!*

*Mrs. Ervin (Anna Mary) Miller*

# Lemon Cream Cheese Pie

1 large box lemon pudding
  (not instant)

8 oz. cream cheese

$2^1/_4$ c. whipped topping

2 c. powdered sugar

$1^1/_2$ c. whipped topping (divided)

lemon slices

3 baked pie shells

Cook lemon pudding as directed on box, using $^1/_2$ c. less water. Put waxed paper over pie filling to cool. Once cooled, add cream cheese, $2^1/_4$ c. whipped topping and powdered sugar. Put $^1/_2$ c. whipped topping on each pie and several lemon slices. Yield: 3 pies.

*Mrs. Devon (Marietta) Troyer*

---

*A true leader walks his talk.*

---

# Lemon Blossom Pie

3 baked pie shells

**FILLING:**

3 c. water

$^1/_2$ tsp. salt

2 c. sugar

8 Tbsp. (level) cornstarch

6 egg yolks (beaten)

4 Tbsp. butter

$^1/_2$ c. lemon juice

**MERINGUE:**

egg whites (stiffly beaten)     $^1/_2$ c. sugar

For Filling: Boil water and salt together. Mix remaining ingredients until smooth and slowly add to boiling water. Cook until thick. Pour hot filling into baked pie shells. For Meringue: Beat egg whites until stiff peaks form. Add sugar and beat well. Spread over filling to the edge to seal. Brown meringue in oven at 350° until golden (10–15 minutes). Variation: $^1/_2$ tsp. cream of tartar may be added and beaten into meringue and $^3/_4$ tsp. lemon flavoring may be added to filling. Yield: 3 pies.

*Mrs. Freeman (Mabel) Yoder, Mrs. Vernon (Nelda) Miller*

# Lemon Sponge Pie

9 eggs (separated)

$3^1/_2$ c. sugar

9 Tbsp. flour

pinch of salt

rind and juice of 3 lemons*

4 Tbsp. butter

6 c. milk (scalded)

4 unbaked pie shells

Beat egg yolks; add sugar, flour and salt. Mix well. Add lemon rind and juice, butter and milk. Fold in stiffly beaten egg whites last. Pour into unbaked pie shells. Bake at 425° for 15 minutes, then reduce heat to 325° until done. May use 2 tsp. lemon extract and 1 c. water to substitute lemons. Adjust to suit taste. Yield: 4 large pies.

*Mrs. Reuben (Martha) Yoder*

# Peach Crumb Pie

1 9" unbaked pie shell

**FILLING:**

| | |
|---|---|
| 2$^1$/$_2$ Tbsp. minute tapioca | $^1$/$_4$ tsp. salt |
| $^3$/$_4$ c. sugar | 4 c. sliced peaches |

**CRUMB TOPPING:**

| | |
|---|---|
| $^1$/$_3$ c. brown sugar | $^1$/$_2$ tsp. cinnamon |
| $^1$/$_4$ c. flour | 2 tsp. butter (softened) |

Mix filling ingredients and pour into unbaked pie shell. Top with crumb mixture and bake at 425° for 45–50 minutes. Other fruit may be used, especially apples.

*Mom (Rosa) Bontrager*

# Pudding for Wedding Cream Pies

| | |
|---|---|
| 18 c. milk (divided) | 1 c. flour |
| $^1$/$_2$ c. margarine | 1 c. clear jel |
| 8 eggs | 1 tsp. salt |
| 1 c. brown sugar | 2 Tbsp. vanilla |
| 2 c. sugar | |

Heat 16 c. milk and margarine to boiling (just till it barely bubbles). In the meantime, mix remaining ingredients, gradually adding the 2 c. milk last. Stir well with wire whisk to avoid lumps. Stir into heated milk, stirring constantly. Remove from heat at the first sign of a boiling bubble. Cool. Pour into baked pie shells and top with whipped cream.

*Mrs. Paul (Rhoda) Yoder*

---

*The more good we find to say about a person,*
*the more good that person will become.*

---

# Raisin Custard Pie

| | |
|---|---|
| 2 c. raisins | 4 Tbsp. butter |
| 2 c. water | 1 Tbsp. vinegar |
| 1/2 c. sugar | 1/8 tsp. salt |
| 2 eggs | 1 - 9" baked pie shell |
| 2 Tbsp. flour | whipped topping or egg white |
| 2 Tbsp. cornstarch | meringue |

Cook raisins with water. Add sugar, eggs, flour, cornstarch, butter, vinegar and salt; cook until thickened. Cool. Pour into pie shell and top with whipped topping or egg white meringue. If using meringue, put in oven until light brown.

*Mrs. Noah (Verena) Schwartz*

# Strawberry Cream Cheese Pie

| | |
|---|---|
| 8 oz. cream cheese | 1 c. whipping cream |
| 1/4 c. sugar | 1/4 c. powdered sugar |
| 1/2 tsp. vanilla | 9" ready-crust graham cracker |
| 1 1/2 c. strawberries | pie crust |

Combine softened cream cheese, sugar and vanilla, mixing until well blended. Mash 3/4 c. strawberries and stir into cream cheese mixture. Whip cream with powdered sugar until soft peaks form and stir into cream cheese mixture. Fold remaining 3/4 c. strawberries into cream cheese mixture. Spoon into crust. Chill several hours or overnight. Garnish the top with strawberries.

*Mrs. Lonnie (Norma) Bontrager*

*Pray not for lighter burdens . . . but for stronger backs.*

# Strawberry Fresh Fruit Pie

3 oz. strawberry Jell-O
$3^1/_2$ oz. vanilla pudding
  (not instant)
2 c. water

1 tsp. lemon juice
1 c. sliced strawberries
baked pie shell
Cool Whip

Combine first 4 ingredients and bring to a boil. Cool. Add sliced strawberries and pour into baked pie shell. Garnish with Cool Whip and strawberries. This is very much like Danish dessert!

*Mrs. Lester (LaVerda) Yoder*

# Strawberry Pie

$1^1/_4$ c. water
$^3/_4$ c. sugar
2 Tbsp. clear jel
3 oz. strawberry Jell-O

1 c. mashed strawberries
1 - 9" baked pie shell
whipped topping, *optional*

Cook water, sugar and clear jel together until thick. Remove from heat and stir in Jell-O. Cool. Add strawberries. Pour into baked pie shell. Serve with whipped topping if desired.

*Mrs. Dan (Esther) Miller*

# Sunrise Cherry Pie

8 oz. cream cheese
2 Tbsp. pineapple juice
$^1/_2$ tsp. vanilla
$^1/_2$ c. cherry pie filling

$^1/_4$ c. crushed pineapple (drained)
1 c. cream (whipped) or 8 oz.
  Cool Whip
$^1/_3$ c. powdered sugar

Cream first 3 ingredients together. Add cherry pie filling and crushed pineapple. Fold in whipped cream or Cool Whip and powdered sugar. Spoon into cooled pie crust and decorate with rest of drained pineapple and cherry pie filling. Spoon the pineapple in middle and cherry pie filling around outer edge. *This makes it look nice and is delicious!*

*Mrs. Gerald (Darla) Yoder*

# Sweet Cherry Blueberry Pie

9" pastry for double crust pie
2½ c. pitted sweet cherries
(Bing)
1½ c. fresh blueberries

1 c. sugar (scant)
¼ c. all-purpose flour
⅛ tsp. ground nutmeg
1 Tbsp. butter or margarine

Line a 9" pie plate with bottom crust; set aside. In a bowl, combine sugar, flour and nutmeg. Stir in fruit. Let this set for 15–20 minutes. Stir well. Pour into crust, dot with butter, put remaining crust on top. (Optional: Beat 1 egg yolk with ¼ c. milk. Brush over crust. Sprinkle with sugar. This makes a nice brown crust. Bake at 425° for 15 minutes. Reduce heat to 375° and bake for 30 minutes or until pastry is golden brown and filling is bubbly. A nice way to use fresh Bing cherries in the summer.

*Mrs. Freeman (Mabel) Yoder*

# Toll House Pie

2 eggs
½ c. sugar
1 c. butter
½ c. flour
½ c. brown sugar

1 c. chopped nuts
½ c. milk
1 c. chocolate chips
pinch of salt

Melt chocolate chips and cool slightly. In a large bowl combine sugars and eggs; beat until fluffy. Blend in butter, flour and salt. Add melted chips and nuts. Add milk last. Pour into a 9" unbaked pie shell and bake at 350° for approx. 1 hour or until firm. *Great served with ice cream!*

*Mrs. Noah (Verena) Schwartz*

*A man who can't forget is worse off than one who can't remember.*

# Turtle Pie

1 9" baked pie crust

1 - 14 oz. can sweetened condensed milk (caramelized*)

1 - 3.4 oz. box instant chocolate pie filling (or cook your own chocolate filling)

$^1/_2$ c. coarsely chopped pecans or walnuts

2 c. whipped cream

Cover pie crust with pecans. Slice *caramelized milk over pecans. Fix instant pie filling according to directions on package. Pour over *caramelized milk. Spread whipped cream over the top. *To caramelize sweetened condensed milk, cook sealed cans in boiling water for $2^1/_2$–3 hours, covered; (don't let water get low because cans will explode if there is no water left) or pressure cook at 10 lb. pressure for 45 minutes. I usually do 6 cans at one time. This is nice for desserts. Open both ends of can to push caramel through.

*Mrs. Freeman (Mabel) Yoder*

---

*Reputation is what others think you are;*
*character is what God knows you are.*

---

# Vanilla Crumb Pie

**3 - 9" unbaked pie shells**

**CRUMBS:**

2 c. flour
1/2 c. sugar
1 tsp. cream of tartar

1/2 c. lard
1 tsp. soda

Mix together until crumbly. Divide into 3 equal amounts. Set aside.

**FILLING:**

4 c. milk
4 Tbsp. flour
2 c. brown sugar

1 1/2 c. Karo
2 eggs (beaten)
1 tsp. vanilla

Boil milk, flour, brown sugar, Karo and eggs together. Add vanilla. Divide filling into unbaked pie shells. Top with crumbs, 1 part for 1 pie. Bake at 400° for 10 minutes. Reduce heat to 350° for approx. 30 minutes.

*Mrs. Reuben (Martha) Yoder*

# Pie Crust

4 c. flour
1 1/2 tsp. salt
1 Tbsp. baking powder
1 3/4 c. lard

1 egg (beaten)
1 Tbsp. vinegar
1/2 c. cold water

Mix flour, salt, baking powder and lard with a pastry cutter until crumbly. If you are using a home-rendered lard, use as directed. If using store-bought lard or pre-creamed shortening, use 2 cups. Beat egg, vinegar and cold water together. Then add, all at once, to flour mixture. Fold together gently. Handle as little as possible. Pie dough will stay flakier the less it is handled after liquid has been added. A good glaze for your pie tops: Beat 1 egg and 1/4 c. milk together and brush or spoon over the top and sprinkle with sugar. Makes them golden and they do not get soggy. Makes 3 double 8" crusts.

*Mrs. Freeman (Mabel) Yoder*

# Pie Crust

1 c. flour
1/4 c. Crisco

1/4 c. oleo (softened)
2 Tbsp. powdered sugar

Mix with hands and press into pie pan. Bake at 350° for about 10 minutes or until lightly browned. Yield: 1 pie crust.

*Mrs. Lester (LaVerda) Yoder*

# Pie Dough Mix

5 lb. Gold Medal flour
3 lb. butter-flavored Crisco
1/2 c. sugar

2 Tbsp. salt
1 Tbsp. baking powder

Mix all together thoroughly and store in a tight container in a cool place. 1 c. mix and 2 Tbsp. water will make 1 crust.

*Mrs. Ray (Irene) Mullett, Mrs. Ferman (LuEtta) Miller*

---

*The aged women likewise, that they be in behavior as becometh holiness,
not false accusers, not given to much wine, teachers of good things;
That they may teach the young women to be sober,
to love their husbands, to love their children, To be discreet, chaste,
keepers at home, good, obedient to their own husbands,
that the Word of God be not blasphemed.*

*Titus 2:3–5*

---

# Soups & salads

WHERE TO LOOK FOR HELP:

When you are discontent—Philippians 4:4–13

When you are afraid—Psalm 46

When you are lonely—Psalm 23

When you are sick—Psalm 121

When you are discouraged—Isaiah 40:28–31

When you are in sorrow—Psalm 34

When you are in danger—Psalm 91

When friends fail you—Psalm 27

When you need an ideal—I Corinthians 13

When you want peace—John 14

When God seems far away—Psalm 130

When you have sinned—Psalm 51

When you forget your blessings—Psalm 103

When your faith seems failing—Hebrews 11

When the world seems too big—Psalm 90

When you want Christian assurance—Romans 8

When you want to pray—Psalm 86

When you seek happiness—Colossians 3

When you feel misused—Matthew 5:3–10

When you are tempted—James 4

When you are thankful—Psalm 95

# Mother's Recipes

Most women have a pantry filled
With spices, herbs and stuff
Salt and pepper, yeast and flour,
But that's not quite enough.

My mom's the finest cook around,
And she told me long ago
That bread's no good unless you add
Some loving to the dough.

And when you're baking pies she says
A pinch of faith and trust
If added to the shortening—
Makes a tender, flaky crust.

You must add a cup of patience
When making cookie dough,
With temperance as your partner
Place them in a neat row.

Add some kindness to your yeast
And when the doughnuts rise,
They'll sweeter be (though made in grease),
You'll meet a glad surprise!

Now these things can't be purchased
In the store across the way!
But Mother keeps them in her heart
And uses them each day!

*Submitted by Mrs. Joe (Karen) Graber*

# Bean with Bacon Soup

2 c. navy beans
1 c. chopped onions
2 tsp. salt

1 lb. bacon (cut up fine)
7 c. water

Cook for 2 hours or until beans are tender. Eat with crackers.

*Mrs. Perry (Lena) Lehman*

# Senate Restaurant Bean Soup

1 lb. dry navy beans (soaked overnight)
1 c. chopped onion
1 c. chopped ham
1 c. chopped celery

3 c. chopped raw potatoes
2 qt. ham stock
chopped parsley to taste
salt & pepper to taste

Soak beans overnight. Mix all ingredients together and simmer for $2^1/_2$ hours. Makes 1 gallon.

*Mrs. Christy (Anna) Bontrager*

# Beef Vegetable Soup

1–2 lb. cooked beef & broth
1 pt. cubed potatoes
1 pt. green beans
1 c. chopped onions
1 pt. spaghetti, *optional*
1 pt. carrots

1 pt. peas or corn
1 pt. celery (soaked)
salt to taste
3 pt. tomato juice
$^1/_4$ c. brown sugar
1 Tbsp. chili powder

Cook beef and strain broth. Cook vegetables slightly and add salt to taste. Mix all together, adding brown sugar and chili powder last. This recipe may be doubled. Put in quart jars and pressure cook at 10 lb. for 30–45 minutes.

*Mrs. Mervin (Ruth) Yoder*

# Cheesy Vegetable Soup

1 bag California Blend
    vegetables
2–3 potatoes (peeled & diced)
1 c. celery (diced)
2 qt. chicken broth or add
    water to make 2 qt.

16 oz. cheese spread
1 can cream of mushroom soup
1 can cream of chicken soup
salt to taste

Mix first 4 ingredients and simmer until vegetables are soft. Add remaining ingredients.

*Mrs. Daryl (Marsha) Miller*

# Chicken Soup or Stew

5 medium carrots (sliced)
3 celery stalks (sliced)
1 qt. water
$1/4$ c. soup base (chicken)
$2^1/2$ lb. chicken (cut up &
    cooked)

1 tsp. minced garlic
2 c. egg noodles
1 tsp. salt
$1/2$ tsp. pepper

Cook all together until vegetables and noodles are soft. Very good. Note: LeEtta uses potatoes instead of noodles. She also crumbles 4 pieces bread and toasts it in skillet with butter. She serves it with stew.

*Mrs. David (Mary Lou) Whetstone, Mrs. Fred (LeEtta) Yoder*

# Chili Soup

5 lb. hamburger (browned)
4 qt. tomato juice
2 qt. pizza sauce
1 c. brown sugar
1 pkg. taco seasoning

1 pepper, *optional*
1 onion
2 pt. kidney beans
1 tsp. chili powder

Heat till boiling.

*Mrs. Fred (LeEtta) Yoder*

# Pepperoni Pizza Chili

1 lb. ground beef
16 oz. kidney beans (rinsed & drained)
15 oz. pizza sauce
14 1/2 oz. Italian stewed tomatoes
8 oz. tomato sauce
1 1/2 c. water
3 1/2 oz. sliced pepperoni
1/2 c. chopped green pepper
1 tsp. pizza seasoning or Italian seasoning
1 tsp. salt
shredded mozzarella cheese, *optional*

In a large saucepan cook beef over medium heat until no longer pink; drain. Stir in the next 9 ingredients. Bring to a boil. Reduce heat. Simmer, uncovered, for 30 minutes or until chili reaches desired thickness. Garnish with cheese if desired.

*Mrs. Lester (Verna) Bontrager*

# Schoolhouse Chili

1/2 c. onion
1/4 c. green pepper
16 oz. kidney beans
1 qt. tomato juice
1 lb. hamburger
1 1/2 tsp. chili powder
1 1/2 tsp. salt
1/2 tsp. pepper

In a large saucepan or Dutch oven, brown hamburger. Chop onion, green pepper and kidney beans in Salsa Master. Add seasonings and vegetables to meat. Add tomato juice and simmer over low heat for 1 hour.

*Mrs. Ferman (LuEtta) Miller*

*Life is fragile, handle with prayer.*

# Cold Bread Soup

2 qt. milk (cold)
6–8 pieces homemade bread
3/4 c. sugar

1–2 qt. fresh fruit (peaches,
   blueberries or strawberries)

Break bread into bite-sized pieces in a large mixing bowl. Sprinkle sugar over bread. Just before serving add milk and stir well. Spoon fresh fruit over soup. Use whatever fruit is in season. *This is an old favorite in Amish homes during the summer. Bananas may also be sliced and used with strawberries and/or blueberries. More or less milk may be used. We like ours with plenty of milk.*

*Mrs. Freeman (Mabel) Yoder*

# Cream of Broccoli Soup

2 1/2 lb. broccoli
6–8 Tbsp. butter
1/2 c. chopped mushrooms
2 Tbsp. chopped onions
1 c. chicken broth

5–8 Tbsp. flour
7 c. milk
2 lb. cheddar cheese
2 tsp. salt

Cook broccoli, chop and set aside. Melt butter in a large heavy pan. Add mushrooms and onion. Sauté until tender. Add flour and stir until bubbly. Gradually add 3 c. milk, stirring constantly to prevent lumps. Add cheese and stir until smooth. Add chicken broth and remaining milk. Add broccoli and heat thoroughly. Note: Loretta does not use mushrooms, and uses less milk. Karen does not use chicken broth.

*Mrs. Joe (Karen) Graber, Mrs. Marlin (Loretta) Bontrager*

*The fruit of our lives reveals its roots.*

# Cream of Tomato Soup

2 c. tomato juice
2 Tbsp. oleo
2 Tbsp. onions (chopped)
3 Tbsp. flour
2 tsp. sugar

1 tsp. salt
$^1/_8$ tsp. pepper
dash of oregano
dash of basil
2 c. cold milk

Sauté onion in oleo. Blend in sugar, flour, salt, pepper and seasonings. Remove from heat, gradually stir in tomato juice. Boil for 1 minute. Stir hot soup into cold milk. Heat almost to boil and serve. *A family favorite!*

*Mrs. Joe (Karen) Graber*

# Old-Fashioned Cream of Tomato Soup

1 qt. canned tomato chunks
   or juice
$^1/_4$ c. butter
2 Tbsp. sugar
1 c. chicken broth or cream
   of chicken

$^1/_2$ c. chopped onion
$^1/_8$ tsp. soda
$^3/_4$ c. flour
$1^1/_2$ c. heavy cream

In a saucepan combine the first 5 ingredients. Cover and let simmer; add baking soda. Blend cream and flour and pour into boiling mixture. Thickness may vary depending if you use cream of chicken or broth. *This is one of our favorites!*

*Mrs. Mervin (Emma) Yoder*

---

*Life will be poorer or richer by how you use today.*

# Duchess Soup

1 c. finely diced carrots
1 c. finely diced celery
$^1/_4$ c. butter
1 Tbsp. chopped onion
$^1/_2$–$^3/_4$ c. flour

2 c. chicken broth
2 c. milk
1 c. diced American cheese
seasoning to taste
parsley flakes, *optional*

Cook carrots and celery until tender. Melt butter in a large saucepan. Add chopped onion and cook until soft. Stir in flour and cook for 1 minute. Do not brown. Add chicken broth and then milk. Cook and stir until thickened. Add American cheese and stir until melted. Stir in cooked vegetables and season to taste. Garnish with parsley flakes if desired. May add other vegetables like potatoes, cauliflower, or broccoli. Serve with muffins.

*Mrs. Floyd (Darlene) Yoder*

# Egg Soup

8 hard-boiled eggs
2 qt. milk
4 green onions
1 c. chicken bologna (chopped)

$^1/_8$ tsp. black pepper
$^1/_2$ tsp. salt
3 Tbsp. margarine

In a medium saucepan, boil eggs for 8–10 minutes (covered with water). Meanwhile, cut up green onions and sauté in the margarine until almost tender. Add milk, bologna, salt and pepper. Peel, then chop hard-boiled eggs. Add to milk and heat through. Serve with crackers. We don't always use bologna, sometimes browned hamburger or other home-canned meat.

*Mrs. Freeman (Mabel) Yoder*

---

*No problem is too big for God's power; no person too small for God's love.*

# Quick Golden Stew

4 carrots (cut into 1" pieces)
1 1/2 c. diced potatoes
2 medium onions (cut into
   chunks)

1 pkg. frozen peas
2 c. cubed fully cooked ham
1 can cream of celery soup
8 oz. cheese spread

Place carrots, potatoes and onions in a large saucepan. Add just enough water to cover. Cook, covered, until the vegetables are tender. Add peas and ham. Cook for 5 more minutes. Drain. Stir in soup and cheese; heat through. Serves 4–6.

*Mrs. Glenn (Polly) Yoder*

# Tasty Potato Soup

2 c. hamburger
4 medium potatoes
1/2 c. chopped onions
2 Tbsp. butter
1 tsp. salt

1/4 tsp. pepper
1 can cream of mushroom soup
3 c. milk
7 slices Velveeta cheese

Brown hamburger with 1/4 c. onions and salt and pepper to taste. Cover diced potatoes with water (level with potatoes) and cook with 1/4 c. onions, salt and butter. When potatoes are tender, add remaining ingredients, leaving water on potatoes. Add milk and cheese.

*Mrs. Perry (Lena) Lehman*

---

*The happiest people don't necessarily have the best of everything;*
*they just make the best of everything.*

---

# Zucchini Soup

3 c. diced zucchini
$^1/_2$ c. chopped onion
1 tsp. salt

$^1/_2$ c. water
2 tsp. chicken base

Cook until tender then put through blender or Salsa Master. To can use
10 lb. pressure for 25 minutes. To 1 pt. of this concentrate add the
following:

2 Tbsp. butter
2 Tbsp. flour

2 c. milk

Cook until thick, then add the concentrate.

*Mrs. David (Arlene) Chupp*

# 24-Hour Salad

2 heads lettuce
2 heads cauliflower
2 pkg. frozen peas
1 qt. mayonnaise
2 Tbsp. sugar

2 pkg. Hidden Valley Ranch
    dressing mix
16 oz. shredded cheese
2 lb. bacon (cooked & crumbled)

Cut up lettuce and put into a 13-qt. bowl. Next cut up cauliflower fine
and put on top of lettuce. Put frozen peas on top of cauliflower. Do not
mix! Spread mayonnaise over peas, sealing edges well. Sprinkle dry dressing mix on top of that, then sugar; sprinkle with cheese, then bacon.
Cover tightly with plastic wrap and keep cold until ready to serve. May
set in refrigerator for 24 hours. Stir well just before serving.

*Mrs. Eli (Pollyanna) Miller*

---

*To learn and never be filled is wisdom;*
*to teach and never be weary is love.*

---

# Bacon/Chicken Salad

$^1/_2$ c. mayonnaise
5 Tbsp. barbecue sauce
3 Tbsp. chopped onions
$^1/_2$ tsp. salt
1 Tbsp. lemon juice
3 Tbsp. sugar
$^1/_4$ tsp. pepper
$^1/_4$ tsp. hickory liquid smoke, *optional*

4 c. lettuce (torn)
4 c. spinach (torn)
2 large tomatoes (cut up)
$1^1/_2$ lb. boneless, skinless chicken breasts (cooked & cubed)
10 bacon strips (cooked & crumbled)
2 hard-boiled eggs (sliced)
shredded cheese, *optional*

Combine the first 8 ingredients; mix well, then chill until ready to serve. Place greens on a large platter; spread tomatoes, chicken, bacon and eggs over greens. Drizzle dressing over all.

*Mrs. Freeman (Mabel) Yoder*

# Bacon, Lettuce & Tomato Salad

$^1/_2$ lb. bacon (cut into pieces)
1 head lettuce

16 cherry tomatoes (halved)

**DRESSING:**
$^1/_2$ c. mayonnaise
2 Tbsp. vegetable oil
1 Tbsp. lemon juice

$^1/_4$ tsp. pepper
$^1/_4$ c. plain yogurt

Fry bacon and drain; cut up lettuce and tomatoes and mix. For Dressing: Combine all ingredients and mix well. Add to lettuce mixture just before serving.

*Mrs. Joseph (Barbara) Bontreger*

---

*The best vitamin for making friends is B-1.*

---

269

# Cabbage Salad

8 c. cabbage
2 c. broccoli
2 c. cauliflower

1 c. fried bacon
8 oz. cheddar cheese
onions (if desired)

DRESSING:
2 c. salad dressing
1 c. sugar

$1^1/_2$ Tbsp. Ranch dressing mix

Shred cabbage, broccoli and cauliflower; mix together. Add crumbled bacon, cheese and onions.

*Mom (Elsie) Yoder, Mrs. Wilbur (Esther) Yoder*

# Cottage Cheese Salad

12 oz. cottage cheese
1 small box orange Jell-O
   (omit water)
1 small can crushed pineapple
   (drained)

1 small can mandarin oranges
8 oz. Cool Whip

Sprinkle Jell-O over cottage cheese. Add drained pineapple and oranges. Last of all, fold in Cool Whip. *One of our favorite desserts!*

*Mrs. Calvin (Erma) Schmucker*

# Cranberry Fruit Salad

1 c. fresh cranberries (cut
   in half)
$^3/_4$ c. sugar
$^1/_2$ c. green grapes (cut in half)
$^1/_2$ c. red grapes (cut in half)

1 apple (cut up)
1 small can pineapple tidbits
3 c. mini marshmallows
12 oz. Cool Whip

Cut fresh cranberries in half and cover with sugar and let set for 1 hour. Add remaining ingredients and mix together in a large bowl. Then transfer to a glass serving bowl. Chill well. *Delicious and refreshing!*

*Mrs. Freeman (Mabel) Yoder*

# Frozen Party Salad

1 c. Miracle Whip salad
 dressing
8 oz. cream cheese
1 c. pineapple chunks

1 can fruit cocktail
$^1/_2$ c. maraschino cherries
2 c. miniature marshmallows
1 c. whipping cream

Blend cream cheese with salad dressing. Add pineapple, fruit cocktail, maraschino cherries and marshmallows. Whip the cream and fold into the fruit mixture. Place paper baking cups into muffin tin. Fill cups with salad and put into freezer. Let set at room temperature for several minutes before serving.

*Mrs. Ervin (Anna Mary) Miller*

# Fruit Salad

3 egg yolks
2 Tbsp. sugar
dash of salt
2 Tbsp. pineapple juice
2 Tbsp. vinegar
1 Tbsp. butter

1 c. whipping cream (whipped)
2 c. fresh green or red grapes
2 c. pineapple tidbits
2 c. oranges
$^1/_2$ c. sugar
24 miniature marshmallows

Cover oranges with $^1/_2$ c. sugar. Let set for 30 minutes before adding to other ingredients. Cook first 6 ingredients until thick. Then add fruits and marshmallows and chill for 24 hours. When ready to serve add whipped cream.

*Mrs. Glenn (Polly) Yoder*

# Grape Salad

4 lb. seedless grapes
8 oz. cream cheese
8 oz. sour cream

8 oz. Cool Whip
$1^1/_2$ c. powdered sugar
1 tsp. lemon juice

Wash grapes and drain well. Mix remaining ingredients well. Add grapes and mix thoroughly. *Very refreshing!*

*Mrs. Wilbur (Alta) Beechy, Mrs. Marlin (Loretta) Bontrager*

# Jell-O Salad

| | |
|---|---|
| 6 oz. Jell-O (desired flavor) | $^1/_2$ c. sugar |
| 2 c. hot water | 3 oz. cream cheese |
| 1 c. sour cream | 8 oz. Cool Whip |

Mix Jell-O and hot water. Let set just a little. Mix sour cream, sugar and cream cheese. Fold together Jell-O and cream cheese mixture. Add Cool Whip. Refrigerate.

*Mrs. Ray (Irene) Mullett*

# Layered Lettuce Salad

| | |
|---|---|
| 1 head lettuce | 1 sweet onion |
| 1 c. celery | 8 slices bacon (fried & crumbled) |
| 4 hard-boiled eggs | 2 c. mayonnaise ($^1/_2$ Miracle Whip) |
| 1 pkg. frozen peas | 2 Tbsp. sugar |
| $^1/_2$ c. green pepper | 4 oz. shredded cheddar cheese |

Chop first 7 ingredients and layer into a 9" x 13" pan. Mix mayonnaise, Miracle Whip and sugar together. Spread over vegetables and sprinkle with cheese. Cover and refrigerate for 8–12 hours.

*Mrs. Ferman (LuEtta) Miller*

# Overnight Potato Salad

| | |
|---|---|
| 18 cooked potatoes (shredded) | 2 c. celery (diced) |
| 18 hard-boiled eggs (shredded) | onions to taste |

DRESSING:

| | |
|---|---|
| 1 qt. salad dressing | 6 Tbsp. mustard |
| $2^1/_2$ c. sugar | $^1/_2$ c. milk |
| $^1/_4$ c. vinegar | |

This fills a Fix 'n Mix bowl. Works great to mix together the day before serving.

*Mrs. Perry (Lena) Lehman*

# Red Hot Salad

$1^1/_4$ c. water
$^1/_2$ c. red hots
3 oz. pkg. lemon Jell-O
8 oz. cream cheese
1 c. pineapple tidbits (drained)

$^1/_2$ c. chopped nuts
1 c. whipping cream (whipped)
$1^1/_4$ c. water
$^1/_2$ c. red hots
3 oz. pkg. cherry Jell-O

In a small saucepan, combine $1^1/_4$ c. water with $^1/_2$ c. red hots. Simmer until dissolved, stirring often. Remove from heat and add lemon Jell-O. Stir and pour into a glass bowl. Refrigerate. Combine the next 4 ingredients and layer over set Jell-O. In the meantime, combine $1^1/_4$ c. water and $^1/_2$ c. red hots. Simmer until dissolved. Add and stir cherry Jell-O until well mixed. Cool completely. When partially set, pour over cream cheese mixture. Let set completely before serving.

*Mrs. Freeman (Mabel) Yoder*

# Rotini Broccoli Salad

1 head broccoli (cut up)
1 c. Rotini Pasta* (cooked & drained)
$^1/_2$ lb. shredded cheese

1 lb. bacon (fried & crumbled)
1 c. peas (frozen)
$^1/_4$ c. diced sweet onion

DRESSING:
$1^1/_4$ c. Miracle Whip
$^1/_2$ c. sugar

1 Tbsp. vinegar

Mix broccoli, pasta, cheese, bacon, peas and onion together. Mix dressing ingredients well. Just before serving add dresssing. *Other macaroni may be used but rotini makes a prettier presentation.

*Mrs. Ervin Lee (Lydia) Yoder*

---

*An empty barrel makes the most noise.*

# Russian Creme

| | |
|---|---|
| 2 pkg. Knox gelatin | 2 tsp. vanilla |
| 1 1/2 c. sugar | 2 c. cottage cheese |
| 2 1/4 c. boiling water | 3 c. Cool Whip |
| 1 1/2 c. sour cream | |

In a large bowl mix Knox gelatin and 1/2 c. sugar. Pour boiling water over this and stir until dissolved. Add 1 more cup sugar and stir well. Cool until slightly thickened. Mix sour cream and vanilla together. Add to gelatin mixture and add cottage cheese; stir well. Cool again until slightly jelled. Add Cool Whip and stir until well mixed. Pour into Jell-O mold if you wish. This may be served just like this or with Danish dessert poured over the top.

*Mrs. Eugene (Ruth) Yoder*

# Summer Cool Salad

| | |
|---|---|
| 18 large marshmallows | 1 c. milk |
| 6 oz. lime gelatin | 1/2 c. salad dressing |
| 1 - #2 can crushed pineapple | 1 c. cream (whipped) |
| 1 c. shredded carrots | 1/2 c. chopped nuts |
| 1 c. finely chopped celery | 1 c. small curd cottage cheese |

Melt marshmallows and milk in top of double boiler over boiling water. Pour over gelatin and stir until gelatin is dissolved. Cool. Add pineapple, carrots, celery, cottage cheese and salad dressing. Chill until mixture starts to jell. Fold in whipped cream and nuts. Pour into a bowl and chill.

*Mrs. Willis (Mary) Bontrager*

---

*To do what you like, is to like what you do.*

# Sunny Vegetable Salad

5 c. broccoli florets
5 c. cauliflower florets
2 c. shredded cheddar cheese
$^2/_3$ c. chopped onions
$^1/_2$ c. raisins

1 c. mayonnaise
$^1/_2$ c. sugar
2 Tbsp. cider or red wine vinegar
6 bacon strips (cooked & crumbled)
$^1/_4$ c. sunflower seeds

In a large bowl toss broccoli, cauliflower, cheese, onions and raisins. In a small bowl combine mayonnaise, sugar and vinegar. Pour over salad; toss to coat. Cover and refrigerate for 1 hour. Sprinkle with bacon and sunflower kernels.

*Mrs. Eugene (Ruth) Yoder*

# Taffy Apple Salad

20 oz. crushed pineapple
2 c. mini marshmallows
2 Tbsp. flour
1 Tbsp. vinegar

$^1/_2$ c. sugar
3 c. diced apples
$1^1/_2$ c. Spanish peanuts
8 oz. Cool Whip

Drain pineapple and set juice aside. Mix pineapple and marshmallows. Refrigerate overnight. In a saucepan, mix juice, flour, vinegar and sugar. Cook over low heat until thickened. Cool and refrigerate overnight. In the morning, mix pineapple mixture and sauce. Fold in Cool Whip, apples and peanuts.

*Mrs. Daniel (LeAnn) Yoder*

# Tossed Broccoli Salad

2 lb. fresh broccoli (cut into
    1" pieces)
$^1/_2$ lb. bacon (cooked & crumbled)

8 c. shredded mozzarella cheese
$^1/_2$ red onion (sliced)

**DRESSING:**
1 c. mayonnaise
$^1/_2$ c. sugar

2 Tbsp. vinegar

In a large bowl combine broccoli, bacon, cheese and onion. In a small bowl combine dressing ingredients. Pour over salad and toss well to coat. Refrigerate. Serves 8–10.

*Mrs. Glenn (Polly) Yoder*

# Vegetable Pizza

## CRUST:

$^1/_4$ c. margarine

2 Tbsp. sugar

$^1/_4$ c. boiling water

1 Tbsp. active dry yeast

$^1/_4$ c. warm water

1 egg (beaten)

$1^1/_2$ c. all-purpose flour

1 tsp. salt

## DRESSING:

8 oz. cream cheese

1 pkg. Hidden Valley Ranch
   dressing mix

8 oz. sour cream

1 Tbsp. sugar

## TOPPINGS:

chopped broccoli

cauliflower

onion

green pepper

tomato

shredded cheese

The crust is a homemade crescent roll recipe. For Crust: Combine margarine, sugar and boiling water in a mixing bowl. Stir until the margarine is melted. Dissolve yeast in warm water, then add yeast and beaten egg to butter mixture. Add flour and salt; mix well. Spread evenly on a well-greased 10" x 15" pan (fingers need to be well greased). Bake at 325° just until golden brown. Cool. For Dressing: Soften cream cheese to room temperature. Mix all ingredients and spread on cooled crust. Top with toppings in order given. Cut into squares and serve. It is good to cut it into squares before adding vegetable layer. *Delicious!*

*Mrs. Dennis (Mary) Bontrager*

*Even if you are on the right track, you might get
run over if you just sit there.*

# Vegetable Pizza Bars

**CRUST:**
2 - 8 oz. pkg. crescent rolls

**DRESSING:**
2 - 8 oz. cream cheese
1 pkg. Ranch dressing mix

1 c. salad dressing

**TOPPINGS:**
broccoli
cauliflower
peppers

tomatoes
1 pkg. shredded cheddar cheese

Spread crescent rolls onto a large cookie sheet. Bake at 350° for 7–8 minutes. Let cool. Mix dressing and spread on crust. Then top with vegetable toppings. Gently press vegetables into dressing and top with cheddar cheese. Refrigerate. Cut into bars. It is good to cut bars before putting topping on.

*Mrs. John (Lora) Bontrager*

# Warm Taco Salad

2 lb. ground beef (browned)
taco seasoning to taste
$1/2$ head lettuce (chopped)
1 pt. corn (heated)
1 onion (chopped)
2 green peppers (chopped)

4 c. shredded cheese
4 tomatoes (chopped)
taco dressing (recipe below)
sour cream, *optional*
salsa, *optional*

**TACO DRESSING:**
2 c. mayonnaise
$1/3$ c. ketchup
1 c. sugar
$1/3$ c. vinegar

$3/4$ tsp. each: garlic powder, salt, pepper, paprika, dry mustard, Worcestershire sauce

Brown beef and add taco seasoning to taste. For Taco Dressing: Blend all ingredients until smooth. Allow each person to spoon ingredients on plate in order given. Garnish with sour cream and salsa if desired. This may be served as a main dish as well as a salad. *Enjoy!*

*Mrs. Lester (Verna) Bontrager*

# Salad Dressing

1½ c. mayonnaise
1 c. sour cream
1 c. salad dressing (Miracle Whip)
1 c. brown sugar
½ c. milk
½ tsp. liquid hickory smoke
¾ tsp. salt
2 Tbsp. prepared mustard
dash of pepper
2 Tbsp. red wine vinegar

Mix all together with a wire whisk until smooth. This dressing is enough for a Fix 'n Mix bowlful of salad greens, such as lettuce, broccoli, radishes, spinach, onions and carrots. I like to add crumbled bacon, 2 c. cooked spiral macaroni and shredded cheese. This is also good to use for individual servings of salad.

*Mrs. Freeman (Mabel) Yoder*

# French Dressing (for tossed salads)

2 c. sugar
2 c. Wesson oil
¾ c. ketchup
⅓ c. vinegar
2 tsp. Worcestershire sauce
½ c. chopped onions
1 c. salad dressing
pinch of salt

*Mrs. Larry (Rose) Mullett*

---

*Does destiny really shape our ends?*
*It's really one of life's profoundest riddles.*
*But there's certainly no question, friends,*
*That bread and potatoes shape our middles.*

---

# Cooking & Miscellaneous Hints

- Cut liver into strips like French fries. Coat liver strips in a bag of seasoned cornmeal and cracker crumbs. Then fry them in deep fat. Only takes a minute or two for frying. *They are very tender!*

- Instead of using powdered sugar in icings, try non-instant powdered milk.

- If you have a recipe asking for white flour and you wish to substitute whole grains, use this table:
  1 c. white flour =
  - $3/4$ c. whole wheat flour
  - $7/8$ c. rice flour
  - $1/4$ c. rye flour
  - $7/8$ c. cornmeal
  - $3/4$ c. buckwheat flour
  - $1^1/2$ c. oatmeal

- If your recipe asks for sugar and you wish to substitute maple syrup, honey or sorghum, use one-half the amount; i.e. 1 c. sugar equals $1/2$ c. maple syrup or honey.

- You can successfully use honey or maple syrup in cooked puddings if you add it (sweetener) before the thickener, or it will turn thin.

- To keep boiled syrup from crystalizing, add a pinch of soda.

- An apple cut in half and placed in a cookie jar, cake box or bread box will keep your baked goods fresh and moist.

- To keep bread crusts from getting hard, set a pan of water in the oven while it is baking. It also works to store bread in plastic bags before it is completely cooled.

- A stale loaf of bread tastes almost fresh if you wrap it in a wet towel, set on a pan and bake in slow oven until towel is dry.

- Old-timers felt honey was Nature's way to easy weight loss. Mix 2 tsp. honey into a glass of water and drink it 30 minutes before each meal.

- To clean oven racks, soak them in the tub with detergent and white vinegar in hot water.

- To clean oven grills, soak in liquid Cascade water for an hour or so. *Cleans really easy.*

- To clean the oven, sponge on a generous amount of household ammonia before you go to bed and close the oven door. The next morning, let the oven air out and then wipe it clean.

- To remove "burnt on" food from cookware, put in a liberal amount of soda, add a little water, let it boil several minutes, remove from heat and let set with lid on for several hours. *This will usually loosen the most stubborn burnt pan bottoms.*

- To clean your porcelain sinks and toilet bowl or bathtub stains, soak paper towels in bleach and plaster on. Let soak awhile, then scrub clean.

- Soda takes black marks off linoleum.

- To remove candle wax from cloth: Use paper towels as a blotter and run hot iron over it which will absorb the wax. To take the color out of a white tablecloth or doily, scrub with Orange Miracle from Stanley Products.

### Mustard Salve for Pneumonia

2 Tbsp. flour
2 Tbsp. lard
1 tsp. black pepper
1 tsp. dry mustard
1 tsp. soda

Put on a cloth and cover with cheesecloth or thin cloth, then put on chest. It will get very crumbly when dry, but will not blister! *Is very good and healing!*

# Index

## CAKES & FROSTINGS

## CANDIES, SNACKS, JAMS, JELLIES & MISCELLANEOUS

## CANNING & FREEZING

## COOKIES & BARS

## DESSERTS

## HEALTH SECTION

# MEATS & MAIN DISHES

## PANCAKES, FRENCH TOAST, SYRUPS & CEREALS

## PIES

## SOUPS & SALADS